MILITARY MIGRATION
AND STATE FORMATION

MILITARY MIGRATION AND STATE FORMATION

The British Military Community in
Seventeenth-Century Sweden

Mary Elizabeth Ailes

UNIVERSITY OF NEBRASKA PRESS

LINCOLN AND LONDON

© 2002 by the University of Nebraska Press
Manufactured in the United States of America

⊗

Library of Congress Cataloging-in-Publication Data

Ailes, Mary Elizabeth, 1966–
Military migration and state formation : the British military
community in seventeenth-century Sweden / Mary Elizabeth Ailes.
p. cm.—(Studies in war, society, and the military)
Includes bibliographical references and index.
ISBN 0-8032-1060-4 (cloth : alk. paper)
1. Sociology, Military—Sweden—History—17th century.   2. Sweden—Emigration
and immigration—History—17th century.   3. Great Britain—Emigration
and immigration—History—17th century.   4. Great Britain—Emigration
and immigration—History—17th century.—Sweden—History—17th
century.   5. British—Sweden—History—17th century.   I. Title.   II. Series.
UA790 .A673 2002
306.2'7'0948509032—dc21   2001027959

CONTENTS

ILLUSTRATIONS

Figures

Tables

PREFACE

Before I begin the discussion of military migration between the British Isles and Sweden, I would like to make a few clarifications and justifications. First I should establish criteria for defining an immigrant. When the Swedish crown hired mercenaries in the British Isles, the soldiers usually were shipped directly to the battlefields and did not spend time in Sweden before starting a campaign. As was the case in all contemporary European armies, a majority of the mercenaries either died during their military service or returned to their native countries when released from military duty. Most of them never traveled to Sweden or formed permanent ties to the Swedish kingdom. Thus, not every foreign mercenary who failed to return to the British Isles can be considered an immigrant. To avoid the pitfall of considering mercenaries who did not form permanent connections to Sweden as immigrants, this study focuses only upon those men for whom there is evidence that they settled in Sweden. To be considered an immigrant from the British Isles, a man had to be born in the British Isles, to enter Sweden through Swedish military service, to receive land in Swedish territory from the Swedish crown, and either he or a member of his family had to maintain a physical tie to the Swedish realm.

Along with these guidelines for defining an immigrant, an additional criterion for inclusion is that the immigrants had to be officers in the Swedish military because few substantial sources exist that deal with rank-and-file soldiers in Swedish service. The main sources for studying soldiers during the seventeenth century are the military rolls (*rullor*), which contain lists of names of every member of a given company for the purposes of paying the soldiers their salaries. More personal information is usually not recorded. In comparison, the officers left behind a more varied and substantial paper trail. The easiest group of people to distinguish are the officers who belonged to families that the Swedish crown ennobled as a reward for their service to the state. The main sources for studying this group are the genealogies of families introduced into the Swedish House of the Nobility (*Riddarhus*) compiled by Gustaf Elgenstierna.[1] Two supplemental works are the genealogies of noble families in Finland compiled by Jully Ramsay and the genealogies of noble Swedish families not introduced into the House of the Nobility by Bernhard Schlegel and Carl Arvid Klingspor.[2] Both of these collections provide information on families whom the Swedish crown ennobled but that do not appear in Elgenstierna's work. All of these genealogies give such information as the dates of birth and death of the officers, the names of their spouses, the careers of the officers, the date each family was ennobled, and the names and sometimes the careers of the officers' children.

Finding information on the nonnoble officers in Swedish service presents more problems than does building information on the noble families. Because few published genealogies of nonnoble families exist, researchers have only been able to piece together information about them from various archival sources, including family histories, information on landholding, and family papers.[3] Given the scattered nature of these sources, the information on nonnoble families is not as complete as it is for the noble families.[4]

The previously mentioned genealogies and family papers indicate that 119 officers, representing 86 families from throughout the British Isles, immigrated to Sweden during this period. Of the total number of officers, about 90 percent came from Scotland, while about 10 percent came from England and Ireland. Although most of the immigrants came from Scotland, I use the term "British" throughout this work to describe this group of Scottish, English, and Irish officers. Even though it is anachronistic to describe the inhabitants of the British Isles during the seventeenth century as British, I employ this term in order to be as concise as possible.

Second, in regard to the spelling of the immigrants' names, I chose to preserve the spellings as they were found in the documents. Because most of the primary source material is written in Swedish or German, the names of individuals from the British Isles were often given a Swedish or German form. For example, the name Malcolm is spelled Malkolm, Hugh becomes Hugo, and James is Jakob. The reason for this decision to preserve original spellings is that for members of the second generation it is impossible to know if an individual was given an

English name that was recorded in the Swedish form in the documents or if the person had a Swedish name. To avoid confusion with the proper names of members of the second generation, the spelling and forms of all the immigrants' names have been preserved as they were found in the documents. The only exceptions are very famous individuals, such as James Spens, who was known by the anglicized version of his name. For monarchs, I anglicized the Scandinavian names since English speakers are more familiar with the English version of their names. Thus, I use Gustavus Adolphus instead of the Swedish Gustav II Adolf, Charles X Gustavus instead of Karl X Gustav, and so forth. Modern English place names have been used where they are available.

Third, the Julian calendar was in use in both the British Isles and Sweden during the seventeenth century, so throughout the text, I left the dates in Old Style as they were recorded in the documents.[5]

Finally, there were three main types of currency in circulation in seventeenth-century Sweden: the *riksdaler,* which was roughly equivalent in value to the *thaler* that was the common currency of the Holy Roman Empire; the *daler silvermynt;* and the *daler kopparmynt,* the latter two being silver and copper currencies, respectively, used internally within the Swedish kingdom.[6]

ACKNOWLEDGMENTS

In writing this work, I received help from many individuals to whom I want to express my gratitude. First, thanks go to my graduate school advisor, Michael F. Metcalf, for his guidance through the research process, for his willingness to read and comment upon multiple drafts of the manuscript, and for his continuing friendship. I also want to express appreciation to other members of the University of Minnesota faculty, in particular Carla Rahn Phillips, Stanford Lehmberg, and James D. Tracy, for their insightful critiques during the dissertation phase. The revision of the manuscript would not have been possible without the helpful comments provided by members of the Scholarship Seminar sponsored by the history department at the University of Nebraska at Kearney. In particular, I owe a debt of gratitude to Carol Lilly, who read the entire manuscript and provided suggestions for revising the work. Finally, I would like to thank John Lynn of the history department at the University of Illinois at Urbana-Champaign for his continuing support.

Throughout the research process, I was fortunate to receive financial support from various organizations, without whose help the research would have been impossible. As a graduate student at the University of Minnesota, I received two Title VI Foreign Language and Area Studies Fellowships from the Center for European Studies, which funded necessary language instruction. A fellowship from the American-Scandinavian Foundation and a travel grant from the Union Pacific Foundation allowed me to pursue the research in Sweden. The Research Services Council at the University of Nebraska at Kearney funded research in the British Isles.

Many individuals made my research overseas immensely easier. In particular, I want to thank Margareta Revera of the history department at the University of Uppsala, who set aside many hours in her busy schedule to discuss the intricacies of seventeenth-century Swedish history. Additionally, I want to express appreciation to James Cavallie and Folke Ludwigs of Riksarkivet in Stockholm, who provided an extensive introduction to the material available in that archive and who helped track down many elusive sources. I also want to express gratitude to Harald Runblom of the Centre for Multiethnic Research at the University of Uppsala for providing me with an introduction to the University of Uppsala and for his insightful comments on the current state of migration studies. Finally, my research would not have been nearly as enjoyable without the help of the staff of Riksarkivet, Stockholm; Krigsarkivet, Stockholm; Kungliga Biblioteket, Stockholm; Uppsala Universitetsbibliotek; Lund Universitetsbibliotek; the British Library, London; and the Public Record Office, London.

Throughout the process of completing this work, I have enjoyed the support of many wonderful friends. I am grateful for their interest and for their willingness to listen to discussions of the lives of British mercenaries. In particular, I want to thank Pradeep Barua, whose friendship, encouragement, and editorial advice played crucial roles in my ability to complete this work. Finally, I want to thank my family for their love and support. In particular, I want to express my appreciation to my parents, Bill and Ginny Ailes. Without them, none of this would have been possible, and for that reason, this work is dedicated to them.

INTRODUCTION

Historians have long believed that the European continent experienced a profound period of social, economic, and political crisis during the seventeenth century. This era saw the last stages of the great confessional wars that racked western and central Europe until the signing of the Treaty of Westphalia in 1648. Beyond the military conflicts, problems of a more general nature, such as economic depression and population decline, also plagued most European societies.[1] Out of the ashes of the century's social, economic, and political dislocation arose a new political force, namely the centralized state, which in many European kingdoms took the form of absolute monarchy.[2] To participate in long-term warfare, expand their economies, and create strong armies, monarchs throughout Europe modernized their state apparatus. This process included expanding and centralizing government bureaucracies, creating sophisticated tax and legal systems, and developing professional military administrations.[3]

In northern and eastern Europe, this process often coincided with the immigration of foreigners. Lacking the population or resource base to reform their kingdoms, many monarchs used foreigners to supply the necessary technical skills and manpower to modernize their state apparatus and their economies. During the early modern period, the rulers of Denmark, Prussia, Sweden, and Russia created policies that encouraged the importation of skilled foreigners into their kingdoms.

The Swedish kingdom provides an interesting example of a polity that depended heavily upon foreigners to push forward the process of state centralization. As did Peter the Great of Russia in the eighteenth century, Swedish monarchs of the sixteenth and seventeenth centuries actively encouraged merchants, skilled industrial workers, and military technicians to settle in the kingdom to aid in the Swedish empire's development and growth.[4] Of all the professionals immigrating to Sweden during the early modern era, the most numerous were the soldiers. Beginning in 1563, the Swedish state experienced roughly 150 years of nearly constant warfare. As a result of battlefield victories, the Swedish crown succeeded in establishing an empire that included present-day Sweden and Finland, encompassed the eastern shore of the Baltic and the Baltic littoral, and stretched into areas of the Holy Roman Empire. To sustain and defend this expanding empire, the government needed to maintain the army and the navy. Sweden had a nationally conscripted army during this period, but because of the small population of Sweden and Finland, native conscripts could not meet the military needs of the state.[5] As a result, the crown employed foreign mercenaries to fill the army's ranks and bring expertise to the navy.

Although the Swedish crown hired mercenaries from throughout Europe, it recruited most heavily from the British Isles. Soldiers from Scotland, England, and Ireland first entered Swedish service in the 1560s to fight for the crown's interests in the Seven Years' War of the North (1563–70).[6] During the next century, other regiments followed in this group's footsteps. From 1563 until 1660, Swedish monarchs hired tens of thousands of mercenaries from the British Isles. Most of these soldiers either died during military service or returned home when their enlistment period ended. A minority of elite officers, however, remained permanently in Swedish employment and settled in the Swedish realm.

As was the case for all foreign officers in the Swedish military, the officers from the British Isles became more integrated into the kingdom's social life than did the contemporary immigrant communities of merchants and industrial workers. Rather than living in tightly knit communities like those of the Dutch merchants in Gothenburg or the Walloon iron workers in central Sweden, British officers were scattered throughout the realm. Additionally, as battle wounds and disease decimated their original regiments, the officers began to command units of Swedish soldiers. Consequently, they had greater contact with Swedes than their Dutch and Walloon counterparts and thus had to adapt more quickly to living in a foreign culture. Foreign military officers also differed from other immigrant groups in that a disproportionate number played significant roles in the Swedish military, in Sweden's political system, and in Swedish society in general. As a reward for their loyal service, the crown granted land to many of them, and those of noble background received titles of nobility. As a result, many foreign officers became members of the most powerful and elite group in Swedish society. Given their integration into the society, their wealth, and their influence, investigating the lives of the officers from the British Isles serves as a case study useful for discussing connections between state centralization and migration in early modern Sweden. In order to examine larger issues, including the military's role in promoting elite migration, the opportunities that state building provided to elite foreigners, and the roles immigrants played in expanding the Swedish state, this work will focus on what happened to the British officers and their descendants once they settled in Sweden.

Many scholars have addressed the experiences of mercenaries from the British Isles who served in the Swedish military during the early modern period. These works fall into two categories: biographies of the great commanders and discussions of military campaigns involving British soldiers. In both cases, such scholarship has followed traditional lines within military history, concentrating upon battles, recruitment, and tactics. While these works provide valuable descriptive material, they do not analyze the importance of the mercenaries either to the Swedish crown or to Sweden's military efforts.

Works in the biography category focus on the lives of some of the most important and successful British military commanders in Swedish service. In some cases, the authors are descendants whose main concern is to catalog the military and political careers of their famous ancestors.[7] These works tend to be genealogical in nature, containing detailed descriptions of the commanders and their families but little analysis of the significance of their careers or their roles as members of a foreign elite. An additional body of literature focuses on Scots in Swedish service, highlighting the careers of the most prominent officers in this group. Most of these works concentrate on the Thirty Years' War, when Scottish involvement in the Swedish military was at its peak. This scholarship portrays a parade of military heroes who significantly enhanced the Swedish crown's military successes in the Holy Roman Empire during the 1630s but again provides scanty analysis of this group's broader impact upon the Swedish military or Swedish society.[8]

The other body of literature on mercenaries from the British Isles addresses British participation in specific Swedish military campaigns.[9] As in the case of the biographies, much of this scholarship focuses on the Thirty Years' War, describing the recruitment of mercenaries in the

British Isles, the battles in which these soldiers fought, and, in some cases, their daily lives in the Swedish army.[10] Special mention should be made of James A. Fallon's Ph.D. dissertation, "Scottish Mercenaries in the Service of Denmark and Sweden, 1626–1632." Based on extensive research in archives in Denmark and Sweden, this dissertation gives an in-depth account of Scottish regiments in the Scandinavian armies during the Thirty Years' War. In addition, Fallon investigates the regions of Scotland from which the heaviest recruitment of mercenaries occurred and examines the daily lives of soldiers in the Scandinavian armies.

Two other events involving Scottish participation in the Swedish military have also received special attention from scholars. The first is the fate of the Scottish regiment under the leadership of Archibald Ruthven, which fought for John III during the Seven Years' War of the North. Campaigns in Estonia decimated the regiment, and the officers were imprisoned and executed for their involvement in a plot to execute John III and to restore his brother, Erik XIV, to the throne.[11] The second event is the attempt by a regiment of Scots to march secretly through Norway to meet the main Swedish army during the Kalmar War in 1612. The regiment did not make its rendezvous, however, because a group of Norwegian peasants massacred the soldiers as they marched through a mountain pass. Many myths and stories surround this event. In his *History of the Scottish Expedition to Norway in 1612*, Thomas Michell investigates the fate of this regiment to clarify the events and discern the true nature of the massacre from the stories that developed around it.

As these works provide many details of the military lives of the mercenaries from the British Isles, they are invaluable sources for discussing the ebb and flow of recruitment throughout the sixteenth century and the first four decades of the seventeenth century, as well as for analyzing the soldiers' experiences on the battlefield. Additionally, with their descriptions of army life they add to the already active discussion of the social history of early modern armies. They have, however, many shortcomings.

First, all discussions of British military activities end in the mid-1630s, when Swedish recruitment in the British Isles began to decline until it temporarily ended during the Civil Wars of the 1640s. Much of the previous scholarship has been based on the assumption that so few soldiers from the British Isles entered Swedish service after the late 1630s that further investigation was unwarranted. Although the intensity of recruitment in the British Isles never again reached the levels of the 1630s, the process continued until the Swedish kingdom entered a period of peace after 1660.

Second, the previous scholarship concentrates exclusively upon Scottish mercenaries in Swedish service. Although the majority of soldiers recruited in the British Isles for Swedish service were Scots, English and Irish regiments were also recruited. Excluding the English and Irish soldiers from a discussion of recruitment in the British Isles leaves out many mercenaries who came from circumstances similar to those of the Scots and who served alongside the Scots.

Finally, the third and most serious weakness of these works is that while most of them note that the British officers who settled in Sweden formed an immigrant group, they never examine the issue. Likewise, most of the scholarship mentions that officers from the British Isles made significant contributions to their new homeland, but none provides further details. While hinting at the broader implications of foreign recruitment, they fail to investigate such issues as the incentives the Swedish crown used to encourage foreign officers to pursue Swedish military careers, the factors regulating the officers' success in their careers, or the social consequences of importing so many elite foreigners. Examining these concerns moves the discussion of mercenary activities away from a narrow focus on recruitment and battlefield experiences to an expanded discussion of the impact of military migration upon the state and the society. Additionally, the Swedish example serves as an interesting case study in the growing literature addressing foreign military communities in other European areas during the early modern period.[12] As more regional studies of military migration are completed, historians will be able to create more sweeping conclusions regarding mercenary service and the impact of foreign soldiers upon their new communities.

By focusing on the British officers as immigrants and on the opportunities that Swedish military service made available to them, this work will move beyond the previous scholarship, with its heavy emphasis on military campaigns and life on the battlefield, to address the broader implications of military migration for Swedish society. Chapter 1 investigates the migration of British officers on a state level, analyzing the policies of the English and Swedish governments that regulated the migration of soldiers to Sweden. Chapter 2 discusses individual motives for entering foreign service, particularly focusing on why members of the nobility chose mercenary service over other available options. Additionally, the chapter analyzes factors unique to the British Isles that encouraged widespread migration from that region during the sixteenth and seventeenth centuries. Chapter 3 investigates the paths of the British officers' military careers as a means of discussing the professional opportunities available to foreigners through Swedish military service and the factors that regulated their ability to exercise those options. Chapter 4 analyzes the lives of the officers in Sweden. Specifically, it explores the social, economic, and professional opportunities that came through ennoblement, marriage, and landholding to illustrate the status foreign officers could achieve in Swedish society and the rewards available to them. The chapter also addresses the officers' political participation in the Swedish House of the Nobility in order to clarify their integration into the kingdom's political and social life. Chapter 5 looks into the officers' diplomatic careers to elucidate the roles of the immigrants in developing and fostering diplomatic and military ties between England and Sweden. The work concludes with a discussion of the factors leading to the end of British military migration to Sweden in the early eighteenth century and the general impact of this migration on Swedish politics, society, and the military during the early modern era.

BRITISH MERCENARIES
IN SWEDISH SERVICE

Throughout the second half of the sixteenth century and during the entire seventeenth century, the politics of the Baltic region were very unstable. The Order of the Livonian Knights that ruled the eastern shore of the Baltic collapsed, and the Hanseatic League lost control of the Baltic trade. Meanwhile, Russian, Polish, Swedish, and Danish rulers tried to expand into the power vacuum in Livonia, while the Danish and Swedish monarchies competed for political dominance throughout the region.[1] These rivalries led to a century of almost constant warfare among the kingdoms surrounding the Baltic. From the 1560s until 1660, Sweden was the most successful participant in these wars. Military victories enabled the Swedish crown to acquire a vast empire encompassing areas of the eastern and southern shores of the Baltic.[2] Because of the small size of the population living within the Swedish realm, however, the crown needed to employ foreign mercenaries to fight wars continuously and to garrison strongholds and newly acquired territory.[3]

To help fill the ranks of the army, the Swedish crown frequently turned to the British Isles for soldiers. Beginning in the 1560s, thousands of soldiers from throughout the British Isles served in the Swedish military. From this multitude, a segment of elite officers settled within the Swedish realm. The following section provides an overview of the royal policies that regulated Swedish military recruitment in the British Isles and places the experiences of these immigrants in their historical context. Investigating the recruitment's fluctuation from 1560 until 1660 illuminates the political factors that controlled the migration of soldiers from the British Isles to Sweden.

The Early Years of Recruitment, 1563–1611

Soldiers from the British Isles first appear in Swedish service during the

Seven Years' War of the North (1563–70). The earliest record of British soldiers in Swedish service is a receipt for payment, in 1563, of a Scottish cavalry unit under the leadership of the Scottish nobleman Andrew Keith.[4] Throughout the remaining years of the war, recruitment in the British Isles continued, and by 1570 the Swedish crown employed three Scottish cavalry units.

The first documented large-scale recruitment of infantry regiments occurred in the 1570s during the reign of John III. When he ascended the throne, John attempted to expand the Swedish crown's political influence into the eastern Baltic in response to the collapse of the Order of the Livonian Knights, which had ruled the region since the 1300s. At the same time, the Russian tsar, Ivan the Terrible, tried to take advantage of the region's political instability by extending the borders of the emerging Russian kingdom. The competition for control of Livonia led to warfare between Sweden and Russia throughout the 1570s. To bring the army up to full strength for the Russian campaigns, John III turned to the British Isles for the necessary soldiers. Scottish cavalry officers, who had remained in Swedish service after the Seven Years' War of the North and who were acquaintances of the king, probably influenced John III's decision to hire mercenaries from the British Isles. In 1573, the Scottish Royal Privy Council gave Archibald Ruthven, a younger son of Patrick, third Lord of Ruthven, permission to recruit sixteen hundred men for Swedish service.[5] In the summer of 1573, Ruthven's troops landed in Sweden and were joined together with the Scottish cavalry that had remained in Sweden and with other soldiers who had been recruited in Scotland. At this time, the Scottish forces totaled about four thousand soldiers.[6]

Ultimately, these mercenaries caused many problems for John III and became a strain on diplomatic relations between Sweden and Scotland. While campaigning in Estonia, the Scots pillaged the countryside in retaliation for not having been paid or given sufficient supplies. Additionally, the Scottish soldiers attacked German regiments that were also in Swedish service after these regiments received money that the Scots believed was due to them.[7] In 1574, when the war ended, John III dismissed all of his foreign mercenaries. It has been estimated that most of the Scottish infantry were dead by this time. Of those who did not die fighting the German soldiers, many died during the remainder of the campaign. By the spring of 1574, perhaps only five hundred of the original three thousand mercenaries were alive.[8]

Even after the war ended, tensions remained between the Swedish king and the officers who had led the Scottish regiments. While the soldiers were fighting in Estonia, John III had uncovered a plot among the Scottish commanders to assassinate him and to place on the throne his brother, Erik XIV, whom John had deposed in 1568. Two Scottish officers were tried and convicted for their part in the conspiracy. One died in prison, while the other was executed in August 1576.[9]

The wartime loss of so many soldiers and the trials and deaths of the officers greatly upset the Scottish regency government. In the summer of 1574, the Scottish regent, in reaction to the news, decided to stop sending soldiers overseas.[10] John III had feared that the Scottish crown might declare war over the fate of the Scottish mercenaries, but while the regency was very displeased, its main concern was to keep troops at home to fight against a threatened Spanish attack.[11] Throughout the rest of the sixteenth century, although individual officers from the British Isles entered Swedish service, there does not appear to have been any organized recruitment of mercenaries.

The next period of large-scale Swedish recruitment in the British Isles came at the beginning of the seventeenth century. In 1600, Duke Charles of Södermanland began a war against Poland with an invasion of Livonia.[12] The goal of the campaign was to drive the Poles from Estonia, a territory to which both Sweden and Poland laid claims because of its strategic position as the gateway to Russian trade. Underlying the conflict was a dynastic struggle between the Catholic king, Sigismund, who ruled both Sweden and Poland, and his Protestant uncle, Duke Charles of Södermanland, who since 1594 had acted as regent while Sigismund was in Poland.[13] In 1597, these dynastic tensions led to a civil war in Sweden between the king's adherents, who sought to preserve the power of the monarchy, and the forces of the duke, who tried to enhance the regent's ability to govern the kingdom and to preserve Protestantism within the Swedish realm. By 1599, Duke Charles's forces had defeated Sigismund's followers, thus denying the king control of the Swedish crown.[14] As a result of these events, the Swedish and Polish monarchs waged intermittent warfare against each other for the next sixty years as each branch of the dynastic Vasa family tried to assert its right to govern the Swedish kingdom.[15]

In 1608, the war spread into Russia, as Tsar Vasili Shuisky concluded an alliance with Charles IX, the former Duke Charles, who in 1604 had seized control of the Swedish throne. The early seventeenth century was a tumultuous period in Russian history, as many pretenders claimed the position of tsar. Shuisky had helped lead a revolt against one of the pretenders and had been placed on the throne by the rebels. He enjoyed little popular support, however, and in the summer of 1608 he faced an uprising led by a combined force of Russians, Poles, and Cossacks. Shuisky's alliance with Charles IX in November 1608 promised him the use of five thousand Swedish soldiers in exchange for ceding to the Swedish crown the province of Kexholm, located on the Swedish-Russian border in Finland.[16]

To bring his own army up to strength, Charles turned to the British Isles for mercenaries. James I of England approved his request and allowed recruitment to begin in Scotland and Ireland. Although the sources do not explicitly spell out the reasons for the renewal of military ties between the British Isles and Sweden, the contemporary pressures of population growth and rebellion in Scotland and Ireland probably influenced James and his councillors' decision. During the late sixteenth and early seventeenth centuries, Scotland underwent a period of rapid population growth, which led eventually to increased levels of vagrancy and unemployment.[17] Allowing the Swedish crown to recruit in Scotland served as one means for the Scottish Privy Council to control the spread of vagrancy and crime. Additionally, recruitment helped to ease unemployment as it provided job opportunities to younger sons of the nobility, who often lacked adequate job prospects, and to commoners thrown out of work by the economic woes of the kingdom.

All monarchs during the early modern period were concerned about controlling the spread of vagrancy and crime. As historian Ian D. Whyte has pointed out, however, Scotland proved to be a special case because vagrancy posed a potentially greater threat to the stability of society there than it did in other kingdoms. Instead of having large rural communities, the Scottish countryside consisted mostly of small, scattered dwellings. Consequently, bands of beggars found it easier to travel through rural areas terrorizing individual farmsteads than they might have in kingdoms with heavily settled rural communities.[18] Adding to this problem was the widespread poverty of the Scottish peasants. Because of the difficulty of raising crops in northern climes, Scottish farmers constantly lived on the edge of poverty. When crops failed, some of the Scottish rural inhabitants were forced to resort to begging or stealing because the kingdom lacked an adequate social welfare system that could support a large number of individuals.[19] As was generally true of regimes throughout seventeenth-century Europe, the Scottish government had little sympathy for individuals unemployed by downturns in the economy. Scottish law reserved charity and welfare for the elderly and the sick. The church or the government usually denied economic help to young, healthy individuals because it was believed they were making a conscious choice not to work and thus were undeserving of help.[20] Because of the general problem of poverty in the Scottish countryside and attitudes toward the unemployed, the king and the Scottish Privy Council were eager to find ways to rid society of unemployed men. Thus, sending men into foreign mercenary service acted as a safety valve on potential social unrest by helping to siphon off individuals caught in the economic problems of the early seventeenth century.

During the same time, the English crown pursued policies to suppress rebellions in Ireland that had sprung up in response to the growth of English political influence in the region. One means of bringing Ireland more tightly under the crown's control was to confiscate the lands of Irish rebels and to use the property to establish plantations for English and Scottish settlers. After the rebellions ended, the English crown also allowed foreign rulers to recruit soldiers in Ireland in order to remove defeated and unemployed men from the region. Gráinne Henry, in her work on the migration of Irish soldiers to Spanish Flanders, has stressed that the English administration in Ireland viewed the enlistment of Irish soldiers into foreign service as a prerequisite for the creation of the plantations. The administration feared that because they knew no life other than warfare, such men would be incapable of living peacefully with their neighbors.[21]

Recruitment in Scotland was overseen by the Scottish nobleman Sir James Spens of Wormiston, who was to become the most important recruiter in the British Isles for the Swedish crown during the first three decades of the seventeenth century. In 1606, Charles IX commissioned

Spens to recruit six hundred cavalry and one thousand infantry troops in Scotland for the Swedish war in Russia. In 1608, he renewed Spens's commission with the stipulation that Spens recruit an additional five hundred cavalry and one thousand infantry.[22] It is not known exactly how many soldiers these levies raised, but in 1610 Spens wrote to the Earl of Salisbury that Charles IX planned to send twenty-two hundred British mercenaries, then in Sweden, to Russia to aid in the Swedish siege of Ivangorod.[23] Recruitment began in Ireland in 1609, when Robert Stewart and his brother William received a commission from James I to levy one thousand Irishmen for Swedish service.[24] Late in 1609, a Colonel Bingley also received a commission from Charles IX to recruit a thousand men in Ireland, and by November of 1610 he had sent seven hundred Irish mercenaries to Sweden.[25]

In 1611, the conflict in the Baltic expanded once more as the Kalmar War broke out between Denmark and Sweden. Tensions had existed between the Scandinavian kingdoms for many years. Swedish wartime naval activities had disrupted trade in the Baltic, which cut into the revenues that the Danish crown collected from the Sound Dues. The Baltic wars also encouraged merchants to use alternative ports to enter the Russian trade; in particular, the route through the White Sea to Archangel became a viable option. To gain control of this trade, Charles IX declared sovereignty over the northern portion of the Scandinavian peninsula, an area over which both the Danish and Swedish crowns claimed political authority.[26] Beyond the economic tensions, Christian IV of Denmark was concerned about the expansion of Swedish influence in Estonia and Livonia. At the opening of the seventeenth century, Denmark was the most powerful state in the Baltic region. Christian feared that a continued growth of Swedish power would eventually eclipse Danish influence.[27]

As in the past, Charles IX commissioned James Spens to recruit mercenaries in Scotland for the Swedish army, but the political circumstances in the British Isles in regard to the levying of mercenaries for Swedish service had changed. James I was married to Anne of Denmark, the sister of Christian IV. At the outbreak of the Kalmar War, James I promised his brother-in-law that the recruitment of mercenaries for Sweden would be suspended for the duration of the war.[28] Despite the royal prohibition against Swedish recruitment, however, a group of 300 soldiers under the leadership of Col. Alexander Ramsay secretly sailed from Caithness in northern Scotland to enter Swedish service.[29] On or about August 20, 1612, the Scottish troops landed on the west coast of Norway and began their march to Sweden, but because they plundered the countryside during their march, the peasantry in the region viewed them as a military threat. To punish the mercenaries, the peasants set up an ambush in a mountain valley through which the regiment had to travel. On August 26, when the soldiers reached the valley, the peasants rolled logs down the hillside to crush them and shot those who tried to escape. In the ambush the peasants killed all but 134 Scottish mercenaries, whom they took as prisoners. The next day, the peasants shot most of the prisoners, leaving only 18 alive. Of the survivors, the 3 officers, Lt. Alexander Ramsay, Lt. James Monneypenny, and Capt. Henry Bruce, were sent to Copenhagen for trial while the remaining 15 soldiers were drafted into the Danish army.[30] This was the last group of Scots to enter Swedish service during the Kalmar War. James I's ban on recruitment for the Swedish army remained in effect until the Danish and Swedish crowns signed the Peace of Knäred in 1613, which brought the Kalmar War to an end.

Once the Kalmar War was over, the Swedish king turned again to the British Isles for soldiers. Until 1617, the Swedish crown continued to fight a war in Russia for domination of the eastern Baltic. In 1614 Gustavus Adolphus, who had inherited the Swedish throne after Charles IX's death in 1611, commissioned James Spens to organize the recruitment of eight hundred Scots to replace soldiers from Samuel Cockburn's Scottish regiment who had been killed fighting in Russia. According to a letter from James Spens to Gustavus Adolphus, the troops were raised and shipped to Sweden by the summer of 1615.[31]

The Height of Recruitment, 1628–1638

Throughout the rest of the 1610s and the early 1620s, the Swedish crown continued to recruit mercenaries in the British Isles on a smaller scale for its wars in Russia and Poland. The Swedish military's next large-scale period of recruitment in the British Isles began in the late 1620s, as the Swedish monarch made preparations to enter the Thirty Years' War. At the outset of the war, the new king of Bohemia, Frederick, elector of the Palatine, sought the support of other Protestant leaders, particularly that of his father-in-law, James I, for his claim to the throne of Bohemia. Even though English public opinion favored offering military support to the Protestant cause, James I chose to grant only diplomatic support. He knew that England did not possess the financial resources to back a military intervention in Germany, and he did not want to jeopardize his current pro-Spanish foreign policy.[32]

By 1624, however, English foreign policy goals had changed, as the crown's attempts to negotiate a marriage alliance with the Spanish court fell apart. As Paul Douglas Lockhart has argued, this proved to be a turning point in Stuart policy, as the king became more interested in supporting a campaign in the Holy Roman Empire to restore his son-in-law, Frederick V, to his position as elector of the Palatine.[33] Throughout 1624, English diplomats approached both Christian IV and Gustavus Adolphus with the possibility of leading a Protestant force against the Habsburgs. Although Gustavus Adolphus expressed interest in commanding the forces, he also realized that it was not in the Swedish government's best interest to embroil itself in the Thirty Years' War. Throughout the 1620s, the Swedish king led his army in the continuing war against Poland over control of the Baltic littoral. Gustavus Adolphus invaded Polish Livonia in 1617, with the hope of providing greater security for Swedish possessions in the eastern Baltic and of forcing Sigismund to renounce his claim to the Swedish throne.[34] Because of his military commitments in the eastern Baltic, Gustavus Adolphus agreed to enter the war in the Holy Roman Empire only on the condition that the English and the Dutch give him a fleet of forty-eight ships to protect the Baltic, that the allies secure a port in Prussia where he could land troops, and that he be provided an army of thirty-two thousand men, paid in advance. The allies also would have to guarantee him control of two German harbors (one on the North Sea and one on the Baltic Sea), secure the neutrality of Danzig, and give him the supreme military command of the Protestant army.[35] Additionally, Gustavus Adolphus proposed an ambitious plan for attacking the Habsburgs and their allies, which included a Swedish invasion through Poland into the eastern regions of the Holy Roman Empire with the support of simultaneous attacks from Hungary, the Netherlands, and the Italian peninsula. Such a strategy would bolster the Swedish crown's political position in Poland and shift the war's focus away from the northern and western regions of the empire and into the Habsburg hereditary lands.[36] Because James I could not meet the Swedish crown's financial demands and because he favored a smaller-scale strategy, namely the restoration of Frederick V to the Palatine, English diplomats entered more serious negotiations with Christian IV. In Christian IV, the English crown found a more compatible ally. With his vast personal resources from the Sound Dues, Christian could accept less financial and military help from his potential allies. Additionally, Christian's vision of the proposed Protestant coalition's purpose corresponded more closely with James's goals.[37]

In 1625, with promises of financial and military aid from England, France, and the United Provinces, Christian IV organized a defensive force in the Lower Saxon Circle. Because the Council of the Realm, which oversaw Danish foreign policy, opposed Danish involvement in the Thirty Years' War, Christian used his status as a German prince, namely the Duke of Holstein, to lead a military force in defense of Protestant interests in the empire.[38] The fortunes of the Protestant forces fared badly, however, due to a lack of allies, funds, and capable military leadership.[39] By 1628, the Protestant army's repeated military failures allowed imperial forces to occupy portions of the southern coast of the Baltic Sea, as well as the Jutland peninsula of Denmark. Given these new circumstances, Gustavus Adolphus entered the war in 1630 as the leader of the Protestant armies.[40]

In preparation for the war, the Swedish government again recruited soldiers in the British Isles, beginning in 1629 and continuing throughout the war, with the most intense period of recruitment lasting from 1629 until 1631. It has been estimated that as many as twenty-five thousand soldiers from the British Isles fought in the Swedish armies during this three-year period.[41] In 1629, James Spens traveled to Scotland to hire mercenaries for Gustavus Adolphus's first invasion of Germany in 1630. After having received permission from both the Scottish and the English Privy Councils, Spens organized the recruitment of one English and two Scottish regiments, which arrived in Germany in the spring of 1629.[42] In the winter of 1629, another Scottish regiment, known as Mackay's Regiment, entered Swedish service. This regiment of Scottish Highlanders had been recruited in 1626 by Donald Mackay to fight first for the Protestant military entrepreneur, Count Mansfeld, and then for Christian IV in Germany. After Christian IV exited the Thirty Years'

War in 1629, the regiment's commander, Robert Monro, sent an envoy to Gustavus Adolphus to inquire about potential service in the Swedish army. Because the regiment had gained fame during its Danish service, the king willingly accepted it into his army.[43] After his regiment entered Swedish service, Donald Mackay continued to recruit mercenaries in Scotland for Gustavus Adolphus. By the mid-1630s, Mackay had recruited ten thousand men for Swedish service.[44] The largest single group of British mercenaries to enter Swedish service was the English regiment of James, the third Marquis of Hamilton. In 1630, Hamilton raised six thousand mercenaries organized into four regiments. These soldiers arrived in Germany in the summer of 1631.[45]

The Swedish campaigns of the Thirty Years' War are well known and will not be elaborated upon here, but it is worth noting that throughout the 1630s British mercenaries played integral roles in Swedish military activities in the Holy Roman Empire. British troops fought in most of the major battles of the 1630s, including those of Breitenfeld, Nördlingen, and Lützen, to name only a few. They also garrisoned German towns conquered by the Swedish army.[46]

The recruitment of soldiers in the British Isles continued throughout the 1630s until 1638, when many British mercenaries decided to leave Swedish service. Throughout the 1630s, the troubles that would lead up to the Civil Wars of the 1640s were brewing in the British Isles. In 1639, the Scottish Privy Council decided to set up a regiment in each of the shires in Scotland. To have the most professional officers lead these new regiments, a call went out for Scottish officers in continental armies to return to Scotland.[47] In response, many officers traveled back to the British Isles to fight for the interests of their nation and king during the Civil Wars.[48]

The decade of the 1630s marked the high point of Swedish recruitment in the British Isles. Although the Swedish crown continued to hire British soldiers through the 1670s, the recruitment levels never reached the same intensity as during the first few years of Swedish involvement in the Thirty Years' War.

Later Recruitment, 1655–1660

In the 1650s, Sweden was once again fighting wars against Denmark and Poland to maintain its now dominant position in the Baltic. Both the

Dutch and the English governments were particularly interested and involved in these wars because the Baltic region was their source of naval stores. These states sought to maintain a balance of power in the Baltic and tried to prevent warfare there to ensure constant access to the markets of the region. Early in the 1650s, the English government sent a diplomat named Bulstrode Whitelock to Sweden to arrange an alliance between the Swedish and English governments. In 1655, the Swedish crown sent diplomats to England to try to conclude the alliance. On the Swedish side, one motive for the alliance was to receive permission from the English government to recruit soldiers in the British Isles for the Swedish armies in Poland.

One of the diplomats sent to England in 1655 was Sir George Fleetwood, an Englishman who served in the Swedish armies during the Thirty Years' War and rose to the rank of major general. Fleetwood was in a unique position because he was a member of a prominent English family and his brother Charles was married to Oliver Cromwell's daughter, Bridget.[49] The Swedish king instructed Fleetwood to use his connections with Cromwell to assure the English ruler of Sweden's friendship and willingness to enter into an alliance. The crown also instructed him to seek permission to recruit two thousand men in Scotland for the Swedish army.[50] Cromwell did not, however, initially support allowing the Swedes to recruit mercenaries in Scotland. Throughout 1653 and the spring of 1654, a royalist uprising had taken place in the Scottish Highlands. Given the recent turmoil in Scotland, Cromwell feared that if the Swedish crown concluded peace before the mercenaries it had hired in Scotland could be shipped overseas, he would be left to deal with large groups of armed Scots who might fight for a restoration of the Stuart monarchy.[51] In response, Swedish ambassador Peter Julius Coyet reassured the Protector that the recruitment would be beneficial as it would allow the English government to ship abroad some of its more rebellious subjects. He also promised that the mercenaries would not be armed in Scotland or assembled into large groups. Instead, they would be hired only a few hundred at a time, taken to the ships, and immediately sent overseas.[52]

Once Cromwell received these reassurances, Swedish recruitment in Scotland became a more attractive proposition to him, especially when his commanders pointed out that he could thus rid Scotland of some of his political enemies. Cromwell had already been wrestling with the problem of how to deal with Scottish soldiers who could become potential supporters of a restoration of the Stuart monarch in exile in the Netherlands. The English government tried a policy of shipping soldiers and vagabonds to the English colonies in the West Indies to work on the plantations. The government soon abandoned this plan, however, because its unpopularity seemed likely to cause even more rebellions against English rule.[53] As an alternative, Cromwell's commanders urged him to ship Scots off to a foreign country as mercenaries. As Gen. George Monck wrote to Cromwell, "The late sending of prisoners to Barbadoes takes soe ill with them that many of them are coming in, but having formerly bene souldyours, and having noe other way of livelihood, know not what course to take. If encouragement were given to some that might bee entrusted to transport them for the service of some forraigne Prince or State, I humbly conceive it would rid the Nacion of most of them, whoe will otherwise trouble the Country by robbing in small parties."[54] Mercenary service was doubly appealing because it also fulfilled the administration's goal of ridding the countryside of vagrants, criminals, and people displaced by warfare. To accomplish these objectives, Cromwell's generals concluded treaties with defeated royalist leaders and began to recruit regiments in Scotland for foreign service.[55]

Many of the royalist leaders, however, failed to fulfill their obligations, probably in part because Charles II disapproved of Cromwell's policy. For example, in August 1655, Charles II wrote to Alexander Leslie, the Earl of Leven, to dissuade him from recruiting soldiers in Scotland for foreign service and to ask him to discourage his fellow officers from accepting such offers.[56] Charles II feared that such extensive recruitment could potentially rob him of a power base in Scotland.[57] Despite the reluctance of royalist leaders to take part in the recruitment of soldiers in Scotland, the process of hiring Scottish mercenaries for Swedish service proceeded.

One of the first recruiters approved by Cromwell was William, Lord of Cranstone, a Scottish nobleman who was the son-in-law of the Earl of Leven. Despite Charles II's suggestion that Leven not recruit Scottish soldiers for Swedish service, the earl, probably due to his long service in the Swedish army and continuing contact with the Swedish king, established his son-in-law as a Swedish recruiter. In the fall of 1655, Cranstone received permission from Cromwell to hire two thousand men in Scotland for Swedish service. Cranstone and the Swedish government were to finance the process.[58]

In 1656 and 1657, further recruitment took place, with George Fleetwood receiving permission to hire two thousand men in England and Col. William Vavassour obtaining leave to recruit two thousand men in Scotland.[59] In 1657, Ludvig Leslie, a Scot who had formerly served in the Swedish army, received a commission from Charles X Gustavus to recruit eight hundred Scottish or English soldiers for Swedish service. By 1658, however, these troops had not been recruited, and it is unclear if Leslie ever fulfilled his commission.[60]

During this period, a number of English naval officers and their crews served in the Swedish navy. As the war in the Baltic became more intense in the late 1650s, Cromwell and then his successor, Richard Cromwell, allowed extensive recruitment in England for the Swedish navy in order to protect English economic interests in the Baltic and to help the Swedes provide a check on the expansion of Dutch influence in the region.[61] Throughout the seventeenth century, several Scots had served as officers in the Swedish navy. The 1650s, however, appears to be the first time that English rulers allowed English sailors to serve with the Swedish navy.[62]

The End of the Recruitment

In 1660, the wars in the Baltic came to an end, and Sweden entered a period of relative peace for the next ten years. The year 1660 also marked the end of Swedish recruitment in the British Isles. When warfare broke out again in the 1670s, the Swedish government attempted to enlist British mercenaries, but the recruiter, William Leslie, abandoned the task because he never received his recruitment pay.[63] Between 1660 and 1700, many changes occurred in Sweden that made the recruitment of mercenaries unnecessary.

From the Swedish point of view, the recruitment and financing of foreign mercenaries had become too expensive. By 1680, the Swedish government was bankrupt from trying to maintain a vast empire with a small population, poor agricultural production, and few natural resources. Until 1680, the crown financed the military and the wars by alienating crown land (in lieu of cash payment of salaries to military officers), by borrowing against future incomes from customs duties and copper exports, by obtaining foreign subsidies, and by exacting contributions from overseas provinces.[64] By the end of the 1670s, the practice of borrowing against the future income of the kingdom and of giving away crown land finally caught up with the government. Because so much crown land had been alienated, the revenues of the crown continually decreased, while the taxes on noncrown land steadily rose. When the war ended in the 1670s, the government had few resources left to pay off creditors or to rebuild the military.[65]

One means of remedying this situation was to raise taxes, which would prove to be an unpopular solution with the nonnoble estates. The other potential solution was to adopt the policy of *reduktion*, which allowed the king to reclaim ownership of land previously donated to the nobility. Such a policy would give the crown new sources of revenue and free the nonnobles from increased taxation.[66] The idea of a *reduktion* had enjoyed popular support throughout the second half of the seventeenth century, and the parliament had approved a partial *reduktion* in 1655, although this policy had never been carried out. By 1680, however, the kingdom's finances were in such a state of disarray that many commoners suffered under increasing taxation, and members of the lower nobility, many of whom were salaried state employees, were not receiving their wages on a regular basis. This situation drove these groups to call again for a *reduktion*. In 1680, Charles XI, with the support of the three nonnoble houses of parliament, forced the nobility to give up the estates they had received from the crown. At the same time, Charles XI declared himself to be an absolute monarch.[67] The king used the reacquired land to finance the army by strengthening a system of state finance called the *indelningsverk*. In this system, a set number of farmers had responsibility for the welfare of one soldier. While the soldier was off campaigning, a specified portion of the revenues produced by the farmers would provide financial support for him. In times of peace, the soldier would return to a specified farm and work the land. This system provided a stable means of financing the military and rid the government of the need to employ so many expensive foreign mercenaries.[68]

With the political and economic changes that were occurring in Sweden during the second half of the seventeenth century, the need to hire mercenaries decreased. Once the Swedish crown lost interest in recruiting mercenaries in the British Isles, the recruitment stopped. As a result, the large-scale immigration of military officers from the British Isles to Sweden also came to an end.

Conclusion

Beginning in 1563, a tradition of recruitment for the Swedish military in the British Isles began. Over the next century, thousands of men would leave their homes in the British Isles to fight for the interests of the Swedish crown. This pattern of recruitment reveals much about the relations between the two regions and the benefits that each side could garner from such transactions.

For the Swedish crown, hiring soldiers overseas had many benefits. The most obvious gain was that the importation of foreign soldiers helped to fill the ranks of the Swedish army and allowed the Swedish monarchs to engage in an expansive foreign policy throughout the first half of the seventeenth century. Second, having foreign mercenaries in their employment gave Swedish kings a bargaining chip in their relations with the native nobility. Particularly during periods of internal political strife, monarchs could use foreign soldiers to defend their interests against the nobility. In the case of Sweden, Charles IX relied upon foreign soldiers during his struggle to gain control of the throne from his nephew Sigismund. The fight for the throne caused a split within the nobility, as many sided with the lawful king, Sigismund. As the struggle dragged on, Charles IX increasingly depended upon foreigners, as he believed that he could not trust the native nobility.[69]

For the governments in the British Isles, the recruitment of mercenaries for Swedish service also held many benefits. First, during times of economic hardship, the enlistment of men for overseas military service helped to reduce the burden of unemployed people upon society. Particularly in the 1620s, when Scotland suffered from poor harvests resulting in widespread famine, the Scottish Privy Council encouraged the recruitment of the poor and vagrants into both the Danish and the Swedish armies as a means of relieving the problems of poverty in the kingdom.[70] In a letter to the Earl of Northampton, Charles I described the potential advantages to the kingdom: "Wee have undertaken this charge . . . for the benefitt which this kingdome will finde in disburdening it self of so many unnecessarie men that want imployment."[71]

Secondly, although there were other means of dealing with poverty, such as imprisoning vagrants or providing charity, foreign mercenary service was a more cost-effective solution to the problem. Creating either an effective prison system or a social welfare system was beyond the financial capacity of any of the governments in the British Isles. In comparison, foreign mercenary service offered a cheaper alternative because foreign rulers usually paid the recruitment costs. In negotiating agreements to recruit, the diplomats of the Swedish crown assured the king and his negotiators that they would not be held financially responsible for the process of hiring the soldiers.[72] Funding for recruitment came from the financial reserves of the Swedish kings, from the resources of foreign and domestic merchants, and most frequently from the pockets of the diplomats overseeing the recruitment. In fact, covering the monetary shortfalls of the Swedish crown during the recruitment process financially ruined many diplomats. As James Spens lamented in a letter to Gustavus Adolphus, "As for my personal concerns I do not know what to write, since I have written so often to no purpose and I have of all men the justest reasons for making complaint, since I have still not been paid even in part. . . . The Chancellor writes that he handed over seventy talents of copper but to date nothing has come into my hands and if it had it would scarcely have sufficed to meet the expenses which my servants have incurred, the space of two years having elapsed in procuring such a small part of such a large sum."[73] Because others incurred the financial responsibility for the recruitment process, rulers in the British Isles found that allowing their men to enlist in the Swedish army was an inexpensive way of ridding the kingdoms of undesirable segments of the population.

Finally, allowing recruitment of men from the British Isles for the Swedish army also had significant diplomatic advantages. During the early seventeenth century, English colonization of North America began. In order to expand the process of colonization and to protect the colonies, the shipbuilding industry in England had to grow. Throughout the seventeenth century, the Baltic provided the bulk of shipbuilding materials such as tar, hemp, flax, and timber for kingdoms throughout Europe. Because continued growth of the economies of England and the colonies depended upon shipping, ensuring constant access to the markets of the Baltic region became a major diplomatic priority for the English government. The English diplomat Thomas Roe described this concern in conjunction with the growing threat of Habsburg influence in the region during the Thirty Years' War: "The loss of the free trade of the Balticque sea is more dangerous to the kingdome of England and to the United Provinces then any other prosperity of the house of Austria, being the Indyes of the materialls of shipping, and, consequently, both of their strength, riches and subsistence. There is no counsell so necessarye and so pressive as the consideration of meanes to preserve it in libertye, which being subjected to the Emperor, the Hanse townes must of necessitye submitt to him."[74] To secure access to Baltic markets, the English government concluded alliances with both the Danish and Swedish rulers. Often such agreements included clauses allowing Scandinavian recruitment in the British Isles. Supporting Scandinavian recruiting activities in the British Isles thus helped to maintain these diplomatic relationships and to ensure English merchants continual access to the Baltic markets.

2

MOTIVATIONS FOR MIGRATION

In making a decision to enter foreign service, individuals were choosing to give up their homes and families and to embark on a journey with an uncertain ending. The perennial dream that recruiting officers dangled before the eyes of eager young men was that foreign service would bring adventure, wealth, and status. For the men who made up the ranks of the common soldiers, tales of booty and glory and the promise of a regular income were probably enough incentive to entice many to enlist. Did these same promises, however, serve to attract noblemen into the officer corps of foreign armies? With their greater wealth, status, and opportunities, nobles may have had other motivations for becoming mercenaries. To understand their decisions to enter Swedish service, one must consider their other opportunities for emigrating from the British Isles, what motivated individuals to enter foreign military service, and the attractions of serving the Swedish crown.

British Emigration

Becoming a mercenary was only one of many options available to ambitious individuals. Enlistment in a foreign army held more appeal to certain groups of men than other opportunities they encountered. Discussing these other possibilities reveals the factors that encouraged particular men to seek out foreign military service.

Individuals from the British Isles who were interested in expanding their horizons found many opportunities. During the late sixteenth century and the entire seventeenth century, thousands of people throughout the British Isles migrated either within the region or overseas. Some responded to new opportunities for land acquisition in other areas of the British Isles and others took advantage of opportunities overseas, while the economic and political turmoil of the era drove others away.

During the early modern period, regional migration occurred within the British Isles. As was common throughout Europe, individuals moved locally or regionally for better economic opportunities. In rural societies, men and women often spent a period during their youth working as servants on local farms.[1] Many people also left their rural communities seeking better economic opportunities in towns and cities. In the majority of these cases, the migrants probably perceived their relocation as temporary and not a permanent move away from their homes and families.[2]

During the same period, the English government created policies that also encouraged migration within the British Isles. Throughout the sixteenth and seventeenth centuries, English monarchs promoted internal colonization to expand their tenuous control over Ireland and Scotland. The process began first in Ireland during the reign of Queen Elizabeth (1558–1603), who attempted to enlarge the crown's political control beyond the English Pale around Dublin by establishing plantations in Ireland. In the 1580s, the crown made land grants to English noblemen who in turn settled English farmers upon these estates. Many English artisans also settled in Ireland during this period because of the plentiful supply of natural resources such as wool and leather from the animals raised in the region.[3] The migration of people from England and Wales to Ireland continued throughout the seventeenth century, with a temporary pause during the Irish Revolt of 1641. It has been estimated that about 170,000 individuals moved to Ireland before 1672 as a part of this process.[4]

While these policies provided new opportunities for England's growing population, they also sparked numerous revolts in Ireland against English rule, with the most serious uprising occurring in Ulster. In 1603, the English defeated the Irish, and as a means of preventing further rebellions the new king, James I, confiscated the lands of the Irish leaders in Ulster. In a continuation of Elizabeth's Irish policy, James planned to use the land to establish a colony of English and Scottish settlers who, it was hoped, would bring civilization and Protestantism to what the king viewed as the heathen and barbaric Irish. While individuals from England also settled in Ulster, the overwhelming majority of migrants to the region were Scottish farmers. It has been estimated that by 1641 between twenty thousand and thirty thousand Scots had settled in Ireland.[5]

Meanwhile, in Scotland James also pursued a policy of internal colonization to civilize the Celtic fringe. The focus of this scheme was the Western Isles and the southwestern Highlands, whose inhabitants had a long history of rebelliousness and independence. Since the collapse of the Lordship of the Isles in 1493, Scottish monarchs had sent military expeditions to the area to force the inhabitants to obey the kingdom's laws.[6] Beginning in the late 1500s, James VI sponsored attempts to create plantations on the Isle of Lewis and in Kintyre to remove the most rebellious groups and to increase the economic productivity of these regions. This plan was part of a larger policy to reform and "civilize" the local clans.[7] In comparison to Ireland, however, the creation of plantations in Scotland was not very successful. One reason for their limited success was that farmers from the Scottish lowlands, whom the king hoped would settle in the region, were attracted to the more fertile lands of Ulster. As a result, these men were reluctant to fund or take part in the continuous military campaigns necessary to subdue Lewis and Kintyre.[8] Additionally, the king and members of the Scottish Privy Council shared the opinion that, given the right circumstances, the clans along the western coast of Scotland could be civilized, unlike their Irish counterparts in Ulster, whom the king and council believed had to be removed to stabilize the region. Based on this belief, royal policy concentrated upon controlling the region through social reform, which included restricting the use of arms, abolishing personal military forces, reducing vagrancy, and requiring clan chiefs to present annual accounts of the orderly conduct of their followers.[9]

Ambitious individuals sought new opportunities not only within the British Isles but also overseas. People from various regions of the British Isles had different opportunities available to them, however, thus creating unique migratory patterns for each of the three kingdoms.

The Irish were diverse in their destinations of migration. The New World attracted many Irish, in particular the Amazon basin and the West Indies, where they engaged in the cultivation and sale of New World products such as tobacco and sugar.[10] Of more numerical significance, however, was the contemporary migration of tens of thousands of Irish men to the European continent. While some of these individuals took part in overseas trade, the majority served as mercenaries in foreign armies.[11] The recruitment of mercenaries in Ireland for foreign armies resulted from the Irish revolts against the expansion of English political power in the region. Each time an uprising took place, the English government suppressed it. Problems persisted, however, as groups of defeated and unemployed soldiers remained in Ireland. To deal with this potentially explosive situation, Queen Elizabeth and her successor, James I, allowed extensive recruitment in Ireland for the Spanish, French, and Swedish armies.[12]

The overwhelming majority of Irish mercenaries served in Catholic armies, particularly in the service of the king of Spain.[13] Although recruitment for the Swedish military took place in Ireland, the Swedish crown did not favor Irish soldiers, fearing that Catholics might not be loyal to a Protestant monarch.[14] The Irish themselves also seemed to favor military service under Catholic kings. For example, when the Swedish crown recruited Irish mercenaries between 1609 and 1613, local Catholic priests tried to persuade men in their communities that they should not enter the service of a heretic. Rumors also circulated at the time that men entering Swedish service would be thrown overboard and drowned once their ships set sail. These rumors seem to have had an impact, as many of the Irish mercenaries initially bound for Sweden defected to the armies of Spain, Poland, and the Holy Roman Empire.[15]

The recruitment of Irish soldiers for European armies developed into the romantic tradition of the "Wild Geese." This term refers to Irish soldiers in continental service, whose souls were thought to return to Ireland in the sounds and shapes of migrating wild geese. The term also came to represent the Irish men driven into mercenary service because of the plantation policies of the English crown.[16] Most of these mercenaries died during their military service. Of those who survived, many chose to remain permanently in foreign service and settled overseas.[17]

Among the English, the most common area of emigration was the colonies in North America. Beginning in the seventeenth century, the English government began to build an empire in North America that attracted tens of thousands of colonists. The situation was beneficial for the government and for individuals: England needed immigrants to settle in the American colonies, and people seeking new economic opportunities or more freedoms far from the established controls at home could find new lives in America.[18] Unlike their Irish counterparts, few English men chose foreign mercenary service as a means of migration. Although recruitment for the Swedish army took place in England, English rulers generally discouraged this practice, apparently wishing to keep potential soldiers at home to fight for the crown's interests. Particularly during the 1620s, when heavy recruitment occurred in Scotland for both the Danish and Swedish armies, the English crown recruited roughly fifty thousand men in England for expeditions to France and Spain.[19]

The Scottish migration followed a different pattern than that of the English or the Irish. Throughout the seventeenth century, very few Scots chose to migrate to North America. In 1621, the crown attempted to establish a Scottish colony in present-day Nova Scotia and New Brunswick, but the project attracted few settlers. With its rocky, unproductive soil and cold winters, New Scotland could not compete against the closer, more familiar, and more productive land available in Ulster. In 1632, the colonial experiment of New Scotland ended when Charles I granted the territory to France as part of the peace negotiations ending England's conflict with the French kingdom.[20] During the 1650s, a small-scale renewal of Scottish immigration to North America began. The vast majority of these individuals, however, were involuntary migrants who reached the English colonies in North America as prisoners of war deported during the Cromwellian invasion of Scotland. During this period, the English government also issued the Navigation Acts to restrict and control trade with England's colonies. Although these acts targeted Dutch economic competition, they also served to keep Scottish merchants from developing ties with the English colonies in North America. Scots did not gain full economic access to English colonies until the union with England in 1707.[21] In the 1680s, further small-scale attempts were made to establish Scottish colonies in New Jersey and in the frontier region between South Carolina and Spanish-held Florida. These settlements did not last long, however, because they did not have the support of their colonial neighbors or of the English crown. In New Jersey, the Scottish settlement was quickly subsumed into the Dominion of New England, while the southern community was attacked and destroyed by local Spanish forces.[22] Given the restrictions placed upon Scottish economic activities in the English colonies and the lack of royal support for the establishment of Scottish settlements in North America, most Scots chose to move to two locations within Europe: Poland and Sweden.[23]

During the first half of the seventeenth century, tens of thousands of Scots migrated to Poland in search of better economic opportunities. Perhaps as many as forty thousand Scots wandered throughout Poland as "small merchants, pedlars, and tradesmen."[24] Although most of the Scottish merchants in the Baltic plied their trade in Poland, other Scottish merchant communities in the region included settlements in the cities of Gothenburg, Stockholm, Malmö, and Elsinore.[25] These individuals moved to the Baltic region to employ their expertise as merchants and traders and to take advantage of the area's growing markets in grain and shipbuilding supplies.

The hope of better economic opportunities also drove thousands of Scots to enter Scandinavian service as mercenaries. Beginning in the second half of the sixteenth century, the Danish and Swedish crowns recruited tens of thousands of Scots for their armies. As was the case with the Irish mercenaries, most Scots died during their military service, but of those who survived many chose to remain in foreign service permanently. Although most Scottish mercenaries served in the Scandinavian armies, other European states, including France, the United Provinces of the Netherlands, Spain, Russia, and Bohemia, recruited Scots during the seventeenth century.[26]

Motivations for Entering Mercenary Service

Individuals who voluntarily enlisted in foreign military service had a different set of priorities from their counterparts who chose to settle in Ulster or the American colonies as farmers and artisans or in the Baltic as merchants and traders. For common men, life as mercenaries held the promise of stable and continuous work, a regular salary, and quick enrichment through plunder. In addition, when men signed up for foreign military service, they usually received a monetary bonus, thus immediately enriching them.[27] Finally, mercenary service offered the advantage of excitement and change from the daily routine. When recruiting in the British Isles, Swedish agents told potential recruits great tales of the heroic exploits and wealth that awaited them overseas. Once they arrived on the European continent, many of them must have been disappointed that mercenary service did not always provide them with the stable income or wealth for which they had hoped. As was the case with all contemporary armies, the Swedish monarchs often had difficulty paying their soldiers on a regular basis. For the Swedish crown, the cost of waging long-term warfare overseas often ran beyond the financial means of the state, with the result that soldiers were sometimes not paid for months or, in extreme cases, for years.[28] These problems did not, however, seem to deter men, with their perennial hopes of wealth and adventure, from willingly seeking out service in Swedish armies. Additionally, individuals who wanted to pursue employment, wealth, and excitement through the military had to travel overseas to accomplish this goal. Before the Civil Wars of the 1640s, England did not possess a standing army. Instead, each county had a militia that provided for local defense. Under the threat of war or domestic strife, the militia could be mustered, but it would be disbanded as soon as the conflict ended.[29] A similar militia system existed in Scotland. It was not until 1638, with the creation of the Army of the Covenant, that Scotland had its own army.[30] This meant that a career in the military was not an option for any man from England or Scotland unless he enlisted in one of the continental armies.

For members of the nobility, a different set of economic issues influenced their decisions to enter Swedish service. Most of these men were younger sons of noblemen or members of cadet branches of noble families. During the seventeenth century, the system of primogeniture regulated inheritance among families in the British Isles. In this system, the noble title and the family's land passed only to the eldest son. All of the other children were considered commoners by law.[31] Consequently, younger sons or men who belonged to cadet branches of noble families had to find careers to support themselves. This could prove very problematic, however, as the laws of many European kingdoms stated that nobles who practiced a trade forfeited their noble status. Additionally, in many kingdoms a religious life was no longer a path to influence and power, as the Protestant church did not offer the same opportunities for social advancement as the medieval Catholic church had. Thus, many men from noble families turned to the military, which the nobility traditionally viewed as their preserve and as a means by which they could provide valuable service to their rulers.[32]

FIGURE 1. THE HAMILTON FAMILY IN SWEDISH SERVICE

Source: Henning Adolf Hamilton, *Svenska ätterna Hamiltons engleska härstamning,* 4–5.

The experiences of the Hamilton family in Swedish service illustrate both the motivations of noblemen to enter Swedish service and the opportunities available to them there. Malkolm Hamilton, a member of a Scottish noble family, left Scotland before 1611 and moved to Ireland, where he became the archbishop of Cashell in 1623. Malkolm married twice and had six sons. By his first wife, he had three sons. The eldest, Archibald, took over his father's position as archbishop at the time of Malkolm's death in 1629.[33] In 1624, Malkolm sent his second son, Hugo, overseas to serve in the Swedish army. The third son, John, remained in the British Isles and served in the English army, but he had two sons, Malkolm and Hugo, who served in the Swedish army. Malkolm also had three sons by his second wife. The oldest, Malkolm, lived in Ireland. The second son, Ludvig, and the youngest, Alexander, followed their half brother Hugo into the Swedish military during the reign of Gustavus Adolphus.[34] The reasons that the Hamiltons signed on for Swedish service probably were similar to those of other young men of noble origin. As a member of a cadet branch of the Hamilton family, Malkolm could not inherit the family estate. To provide support for himself and his family, he pursued a religious career in the Protestant church in Ireland. While Malkolm could establish his oldest son as his successor, his other sons needed to find occupations to support themselves.

Enlisting in Swedish service turned out to be a sound decision, as all of the Hamiltons enjoyed successful military careers. Hugo and Ludvig both advanced to the rank of colonel and were ennobled by the Swedish crown for their loyal service. To further reward them for their military leadership, Sweden's king Charles X Gustavus raised them into the Swedish aristocracy, granting them the title Baron of Deserf in 1654.[35] John's sons, Malkolm and Hugo, enjoyed even more successful careers. Malkolm entered Swedish service in 1654 as a member of Queen Christina's Life Guard. From this position, he rose through the ranks to become a major general and the county governor of Västernorrland, in northern Sweden. In 1680, Malkolm enlisted his younger brother, Hugo, as a second lieutenant in the Älvsborg regiment, which he commanded. Hugo also had a successful career that culminated in his achieving the rank of general. As a reward for their service, the crown ennobled both brothers in 1689 and gave them the title Baron of Hageby.[36] Becoming a titled member of the aristocracy at one's ennoblement was very unusual and marked the crown's high esteem of them. Alexander's career, although successful, was not as spectacular as those of his relatives. He reached the rank of captain but was not ennobled.[37]

Another group that sought out foreign military service as a career consisted of illegitimate sons. As was the case with younger sons, illegitimate sons did not usually inherit family property and needed to find careers to support themselves. Serving in a foreign army could provide such men with valuable military experience and, if they had successful careers, with enhanced social status that they could not acquire in the British Isles. One such illegitimate son who used mercenary service in the Swedish army to his best advantage was Alexander Leslie.

Leslie was born in Scotland in 1582 as the illegitimate son of George Leslie, a captain of the castle of Blair.[38] In 1605, Leslie served as captain in a regiment in Dutch service, but around 1608 he entered the Swedish army. He fought in the Swedish army for thirty years and gained fame as a brave and astute military leader. During his continental military career, Leslie commanded the Swedish forces that successfully defended Stralsund in 1628, helped to organize and command the Scottish and English regiments that James, third Marquis of Hamilton, raised for the Swedish army in 1631, and received the highest rank in the Swedish army, that of field marshal.[39] In 1638, he retired from Swedish service and returned to Scotland to take a role in the formation of a Scottish army. Upon his return to Scotland, and in view of his extensive military experience, the Scottish administration named Leslie lord general in command of the Scottish Covenanters' military forces.[40] In 1641, Charles I rewarded him for his military service in Scotland, as well as his grand military exploits in Sweden and Germany, when he chose Leslie to be a member of the Scottish Privy Council and made him a peer with the titles of Earl of Leven and Lord Balgonie.[41] Although Leslie's achieve-ments were very unusual, his career in the Swedish army illustrates that serving as a mercenary could be translated into wealth and greater so-cial status.

Not every man who chose to enter mercenary service did so for economic reasons. Political problems at home also encouraged some noblemen to seek their fortunes overseas. Sometimes this occurred through the actions of an individual's relatives, which cast the entire family under the disapproval of the monarch. Particularly in cases of treason, all relatives of an offender could suffer for the crimes com-mitted. To ensure that a traitor would not continue to pose a threat to royal authority, the crown usually executed the convicted individ-ual and outlawed his family, thus prohibiting other family members from owning property or pursuing professions. Often, men who fell into this category chose to seek their fortunes overseas through foreign military service. The Ruthven family best exemplifies how charges of treason could drive individuals into foreign service and how mercenary service could, under the right circumstances, help individuals reclaim their lost status.

In the seventeenth century, the Ruthven family became established in Swedish service in the wake of its involvement in the Gowrie Plot. On August 5, 1600, James VI of Scotland rode to Gowrie House with Alexan-der, Master of Ruthven, after a hunting party. While at the manor house, Ruthven apparently assaulted James. When the king yelled for help, his attendants burst into the room and killed the Master of Ruthven and his younger brother, who was also present. As punishment for attacking the king, the crown commanded that the bodies of the Ruthvens be quar-tered and put on display, their property confiscated, and the name of Ruthven outlawed.[42] Patrick Ruthven, later Earl of Forth and Brentford, enlisted in the Swedish army shortly after the crown outlawed his family, probably sometime between 1606 and 1609, when James Spens recruited in Scotland for the Swedish crown's wars in the eastern Baltic against Russia and Poland.[43] Ruthven probably found service in the Swedish army very attractive because it offered him an opportunity to gain law-ful employment at a time when he had few legal options in Scotland.[44] Foreign military service also allowed Ruthven to develop his military skills and possibly to gain wealth through plunder.

Ruthven's career in the Swedish military turned out to be very successful. He faithfully served the Swedish crown and gradually worked his way through the ranks to become a major general in 1632. While in Swedish service, he gained a reputation as a skillful soldier and as a loyal supporter of the Swedish crown. In addition to his military duties, he served as a recruiting agent for the Swedes in Scotland and represented the Swedish crown as a diplomat at the court of Charles I in 1637.[45] In this instance, foreign service had a redeeming influence on a member of an outlawed family. So great was Ruthven's reputation as a soldier and as a diplomat that, in 1618, James I gave him a certificate proclaiming his noble birth and thereby restoring his status as a member of the Scottish nobility.[46]

Some noblemen who entered foreign service were more directly involved in the political conflicts of the era and served overseas to escape problems at home. The career of one Scottish nobleman, William, third Lord of Cranstone, fits this description. In the 1640s and 1650s, Cranstone ran afoul of the English parliamentary movement under the leadership of Oliver Cromwell. During the 1640s, Cranstone became involved in the Engagers Movement, which tried to place Charles I back on the throne of England. As part of this movement, he took part in the Duke of Hamilton's unsuccessful invasion of England in 1648. His interest in the royalist movement continued when he participated in Charles II's invasion of England in 1651. After the Scottish defeat at Worcester, Cromwellian forces captured Cranstone as well as many other Scots in Charles II's army.[47] Unlike most of his Scottish comrades, however, Cranstone was not deported to the English colonies in North America. Instead, because of his noble status, the Commonwealth held him in a London prison until 1654.[48] After his release, Cranstone faced an uncertain future. In the early 1650s, Cromwell's forces under the leadership of Col. Robert Lilburne and Gen. George Monck had successfully conquered Scotland and brought it under Cromwell's control. For the time being, the royalist movement in Scotland was dead, and Cranstone— as an avowed member of the royalist party—would have been regarded with suspicion by the occupying forces in Scotland. To make matters worse, the governing forces in Scotland had declared Cranstone's property forfeited and had confiscated his land.[49] Probably in an attempt to escape the political tensions in Scotland and to reestablish his economic fortunes, Cranstone agreed in 1655 to take a commission as a colonel in the Swedish army and to recruit two thousand Scottish soldiers.[50] As was the case for other men in similar circumstances, foreign service had a redeeming effect upon Cranstone's status with the ruling bodies in the British Isles. As a result of Cranstone's meritorious service to the Swedish crown, Charles X Gustavus wrote to Oliver Cromwell asking that the confiscation of his lands be rescinded and that he be given a full pardon. Thanks to the recommendation of the Swedish king, Cranstone received a pardon from the English Parliament in 1657 and reclaimed a portion of his property.[51]

Rewards for Loyal Service

While economic need and government policies led many men to join foreign armies, the rewards a crown gave its officers also served as incentives. Throughout the seventeenth century, when the monarchs of many kingdoms received permission to recruit forces in the British Isles, the rewards and incentives that particular rulers offered probably played a role in an individual's decision about which particular monarch he wished to serve.

In comparison with other European rulers, Sweden's monarchs were very liberal in the rewards they showered upon foreigners who provided valuable service to the state. Because the crown often could not give adequate financial compensation to its creditors and military officers, the Swedish rulers used ennoblement based on service to the state as partial payment. In addition, as a means of further compensation the monarchs usually gave land in Swedish territories to ennobled officers or the right to collect taxes on specified estates.[52]

This type of payment was quite unusual during the seventeenth century, as the nobility in many other European kingdoms did not allow the widespread ennoblement of foreigners. A case in point is the kingdom of Denmark, which also employed thousands of mercenaries from the British Isles during the same period. Although many noblemen from the British Isles enlisted in Danish service for reasons similar to those that encouraged their counterparts to join the Swedish forces, they did not find the same possibilities for advancement in Danish society. Skillful and brave soldiers and officers could expect to gain military experience and find wealth through plunder, but in Denmark, the nobility jealously guarded its privileges and vehemently fought against the monarch when he tried to reduce its influence or political power. As a result, foreigners found it virtually impossible to advance into the ranks of the nobility in Denmark during the early seventeenth century.[53] In comparison, the Swedish crown's policy of ennobling deserving foreigners met with the approval of the native Swedish nobility. The changing status of the Swedish nobility during the seventeenth century reveals the reasons behind their acceptance of the ennoblement of foreigners.

At the beginning of the seventeenth century, the Swedish nobility possessed much political influence and used this power to restrict the positions that foreigners could hold in the government and the military. During the reign of Charles IX (1604–11), the king's reliance upon foreigners and nonnoble secretaries severely weakened the political position of the nobility. After Charles IX's death in 1611, his seventeen-year-old son Gustavus Adolphus succeeded him. In reaction to Charles's policies, the nobles forced the new monarch to sign a restrictive accession charter, granting them greater political power. The nobility could enhance its political influence because Gustavus Adolphus had not yet reached the age of majority. In exchange for the nobles' recognition of the new king's authority to rule, Gustavus Adolphus agreed to restrict the influence of foreigners in the kingdom.[54] According to his coronation charter, the high offices of the realm, which consisted of the steward, the marshal, the admiral, the chancellor, and the treasurer, as well as all positions on the Council of the Realm and the Exchequer Council, were to be reserved exclusively for native-born Swedish noblemen. The Swedish nobility also received control of the positions of judge and governor of each province and the command of the main fortresses of the kingdom.[55]

The adoption of the Form of Government in 1634 further strengthened the political position of the Swedish nobility. This document, which Axel Oxenstierna claimed to have written together with Gustavus Adolphus prior to the king's death in 1632, outlined the governmental reforms created by the king during his reign. Two clauses of this document restricted the political power of foreign nobles in Sweden. The first reinforced Gustavus Adolphus's accession charter in stating that only native-born nobles could serve on the Council of the Realm. The second clause stated that nobody was to be ennobled or naturalized as a noble while the king was a minor, ill, or out of the country.[56]

While documents such as the Form of Government create the impression that the Swedish nobility was successful in restricting foreigners' access to powerful positions within the kingdom, in reality the native-born nobles were gradually losing their monopoly on these offices. The reasons behind the erosion of noble political influence were the rapid growth of the Swedish state and the acquisition of the Baltic empire, which reached its greatest expanse in 1660.[57] With these developments it became impossible for the Swedish nobles to fill all of the necessary positions in the government and military. Consequently, as many foreigners came to hold the expanding number of offices in the kingdom's bureaucracy and military, the Swedish nobility had to accept the necessity of foreigners in their ranks.

On an official level, the Addition to the Form of Government of 1660 expressed these new attitudes. In regard to the rights of foreigners to hold government and military offices, the addition stated that while a native Swedish nobleman should not be passed over for an office for which he was suitable in favor of a foreigner, neither should foreigners who had provided good service to the state be overlooked simply because of their foreign birth. The addition further relaxed the restrictions placed on regency governments by stating that ennoblements could be granted when the government lacked other means of compensating deserving people. The ennoblements, however, were to be carried out with the permission of the Council of the Realm and would be given only to deserving individuals and not to entire families.[58]

Despite the restrictions placed upon the ennoblement of foreigners, the Swedish crown during the seventeenth century ennobled and introduced into the House of the Nobility thirty-five British officers representing twenty-eight families.[59] During the Thirty Years' War, the crown ennobled both foreign and native-born officers who reached the rank of colonel. After the Thirty Years' War ended in 1648, the crown began to ennoble officers at the rank of captain in order to provide compensation for these men as they were decommissioned.[60] Despite these practices, some officers among the British immigrants served at a higher rank without being ennobled, usually because they either died or left Swedish service before being ennobled. But even if the crown did not ennoble a first-generation officer, members from the second generation of his family often received this honor. If a high-ranking officer died before he could be ennobled, his children could be given noble status based on their father's merit. In other cases, the sons of officers who followed their fathers into the military were ennobled based on their own merit. These factors led to members of another twenty-seven British military families being granted noble status in the second generation.

Most of the British military families whom the crown ennobled became members of the lower nobility in Sweden. The Swedish nobility was divided into three classes. The first class was the aristocracy, whose members held the title of *greve* (count) or *friherre* (baron). The second class consisted of untitled nobility whose families had served as members of the Council of the Realm, while the third class consisted of all other noble families. The class system was important because each noble family was required to send members to the meetings of the House of the Nobility (Riddarhus), which formed one of the four houses of the Swedish parliament (Riksdag). At the meetings of the House of the Nobility, voting was done by class, and the support of two classes was required for the approval of any measure. Even though all noble families had representatives in the parliament, the voting system ensured that the first and second classes could outvote the lower nobility, who formed the majority of the members of the House of the Nobility.[61] Generally, even though the Swedish monarchs followed a plan of widespread ennoblement of foreigners during the first half of the seventeenth century, most foreigners were taken into the third class and did not advance beyond it. Of the thirty-five first-generation British officers whom the Swedish crown ennobled, only seven became members of the first class, while none was admitted into the second class.[62]

In general, the opportunity to become a member of the Swedish nobility was probably very attractive to foreign officers. It ranked them among the wealthiest and most powerful group in the kingdom and, in some cases, allowed individuals to rise well above the social station into which they were born. One way to measure the importance of ennoblement is to look at the actions individuals took in trying to secure ennoblement. Being taken into the Swedish nobility was not a passive process whereby individuals patiently waited for the monarch to bestow noble status upon them. Instead, individuals directly petitioned the crown or had other nobles plead their case. To receive the honor of noble status, foreigners had to be members of noble families in their homelands and had to be of legitimate birth. To assure the crown of their high-born origins, officers often produced birth letters signed by the ruler of their native country stating their family history and attesting to their noble birth. If an officer could not obtain such papers, he could have other foreigners who knew his family and who were already established as members of the Swedish nobility attest to the validity of his claim to noble heritage.[63] Once the crown had bestowed noble status upon an individual, the House of the Nobility debated the validity of the person's claim and then voted upon whether to accept him as a member. If the vote was in the affirmative, the House of the Nobility would recognize his status as a member of the Swedish nobility with all the rights and privileges of native-born noblemen.[64]

The case of David Sinclair, a Scot who entered Swedish service during the Thirty Years' War and rose to the rank of colonel, reveals the benefits of the ennoblement process.[65] According to family genealogies, he was the legitimate son of Barbe Halcro and William Sinclair of Tohop and Sabay.[66] David's father was a member of the noble Sinclair family, which ruled the Orkney Islands from the late fourteenth century until the late sixteenth century.[67] His mother was also of noble origin and was a member of one of the Orkneys' oldest landowning families.[68] This depiction of Sinclair's noble background must have satisfied both the king and the members of the Swedish nobility because in 1655, when the crown ennobled him and the nobility approved his introduction into the House of the Nobility, no one questioned his status.[69] In his study of the origins of the Swedish Sinclair family, Håkan Dackman discovered, however, that the traditional depiction of David Sinclair's noble heritage was untrue. According to records Dackman found in the Orkney archives, David Sinclair was the illegitimate son of William Sinclair and thus was accepted into the Swedish nobility under false pretenses.[70] It is not possible to tell from the sources who created the lies regarding David Sinclair's legitimate birth or when this fictional account was first developed. Responsibility for the lies probably rests with David Sinclair, however, because becoming a member of the Swedish nobility would justify his position as a high-ranking member of the military and as a holder of land donations that he had received as compensation for his military service. Additionally, being accepted into the nobility allowed Sinclair to pass on noble status to his children, which he would not have been able to do under normal circumstances due to his illegitimate birth.

Beyond their obvious desire to be members of the highest social group within society, achieving noble status held other rewards. One of the most important advantages was the opportunity to receive land grants from the Swedish crown. During the first half of the seventeenth century, the Swedish crown donated land to many military officers as an alternative to remitting sums for back pay and unpaid pensions. The crown gave the officers either donations of land or the right to collect the taxes on crown estates. The land grants did not give the officers outright ownership of the land. Instead, the grant had to be reapproved at the beginning of each new monarch's reign, and the land could not be sold without the crown's permission. Despite the restrictions on the land grants, the possibility of receiving land and collecting rents from tenants of the estate appears to have been very important to the British military families. Because the Swedish government was chronically short of money to pay salaries and pensions, land grants were sometimes the most secure means of receiving the financial compensation due to military officers.

Another important aspect of land grants was that being a landowner brought prestige to an individual and set him apart from the majority of the population. Because of the system of primogeniture that regulated inheritance practices in the British Isles, becoming landowners in their homeland was virtually impossible for most of these officers. Having the opportunity to become landowners in Sweden must have been a very attractive incentive for these men to remain in Swedish service.

Conclusion

Three elements played crucial roles in influencing men from the British Isles to enter the Swedish crown's military service. First is the issue of place. The British Isles throughout the early modern period consisted of societies in which abundant opportunities existed to travel both within the islands and overseas to take advantage of new economic opportunities. These movements of population occurred not only at the grassroots level but also were encouraged through royal policies designed to bring greater stability and wealth to the region. The migration of noblemen from the British Isles into the officers' corps of the Swedish crown can be seen as part of a much larger flow of people out of the British Isles to the American colonies and to the European continent.

Secondly, the characteristics and outlook of the nobility in the British Isles led individual noblemen to choose foreign mercenary service over other opportunities overseas. While possibilities existed for men and women to engage in trade or farming once they had settled in new lands, these prospects probably held little appeal to nobles. By tradition, the privileges of the nobility throughout Europe were defined by military service. In many kingdoms, a nobleman who engaged in trade lost his noble status, thus making the military one of the few avenues open to noblemen who needed careers to support themselves. Another important characteristic of noble society, which was particular to the British Isles, was the system of primogeniture. This inheritance system drastically limited the size of the nobility in the British Isles and created a pool of younger sons who had little hope of finding prosperity at home. Finally, the political upheaval that took place in the British Isles during the seventeenth century led many noblemen to find refuge overseas in the military service of foreign kings.

Third, the incentives and rewards that the Swedish crown offered to its military officers probably attracted some individuals to Swedish service and encouraged those already in Swedish employment to remain. In the military, there were many opportunities to rise to the highest ranks of command. In comparison to individuals serving in many other armies in Europe during the seventeenth century, officers in the Swedish army below the rank of colonel did not have to be members of the nobility, and they did not have to purchase ranks and commissions in the army. Instead, soldiers and officers advanced through the ranks based on their own merit. Military service also provided the possibility of ennoblement, as officers were usually ennobled at the rank of captain. These two factors gave ambitious foreigners opportunities to become high-ranking officers and nobles, opportunities not generally available to the British officers in their homeland. As high-ranking officers and nobles, the foreign mercenaries could gain wealth and prestige and perhaps could marry into the Swedish nobility. Taken together, these factors allowed some foreign officers to found noble families that still exist today.

3
MILITARY CAREERS

Once they made the commitment to pursue a career in Sweden, mercenaries from the British Isles were found in every regiment and at every rank within the Swedish military. Naturally, the success of individuals' careers varied. Some British soldiers had long careers that saw a steady rise through the ranks, while others quickly achieved the highest levels of command. Generally, an individual's success in reaching the higher levels of command can be attributed to two factors: patronage and skill. Investigating the recruitment of soldiers in the British Isles, the branches of the Swedish military in which British officers served, and their progression through the military ranks will illustrate the extent to which these factors controlled their careers and how these factors differed from or were similar to the circumstances that shaped the careers of native-born officers.

Recruitment

An officer's first commission in the Swedish military often depended upon his role in the recruitment process and his personal connections with the men who organized these operations. When the Swedish crown wanted to hire soldiers in the British Isles, a representative of the monarch requested permission from the English ruler to recruit. Once the kingdom's Privy Council approved the petition, the Swedish crown hired local British noblemen to serve as colonels and organize the regiments. Even at this early stage, patronage played an important role, as the colonels chosen for these positions often were acquaintances or relatives of Swedish diplomats or had other personal connections with the Swedish crown. An especially clear example of this practice is the role that James Spens played in placing his relatives and associates as colonels overseeing recruitment.

During the first three decades of the seventeenth century, Spens, a Scottish nobleman, negotiated and oversaw the recruitment of soldiers in the British Isles for Gustavus Adolphus. Frequently in his letters to the king Spens discussed the men whom he had chosen to serve as commanders of Scottish regiments. In April 1629, during the Swedish crown's preparations for entering the Thirty Years' War, Spens wrote to Gustavus Adolphus, "I have put Sir John Meldrum in command of one regiment commissioned by Your Majesty, and in command of the other Alexander Hamilton, brother of the Earl of Melrose, who will be better than 10,000 men to Your Majesty."[1]

Spens's use of his influence in hiring commanders extended not only to acquaintances but also to his family members. Earlier in the 1620s, Spens used his position as a diplomatic representative of the Swedish crown to place his son as a recruiting officer in Scotland. At the same time, Spens established his younger son as a captain in the same regiment. In writing to the Swedish chancellor, Axel Oxenstierna, in 1624, Spens described his reason for employing his son: "I have sent my youngest son with one company of his brother's regiment; he has had three years' good experience in Holland, both in adequate military training of his own and in giving others military instruction. Although he is over twenty three he is not given to say much, but he has a stout heart all the same and I hope will give the King satisfaction. I must commend him to Your Lordship's most worthy favour. I certainly have no greater proof to offer of my loyalty to His Serenity and his realm than those two only sons of mine."[2] The extensive patronage power that James Spens enjoyed over the recruitment process allowed him not only to place friends and associates in positions as recruiters and colonels of the newly created regiments but also to establish his sons in Swedish service.

Once recruiting officers had been selected, the Swedish crown drew up a contract stipulating the officers' and soldiers' pay and the conditions under which the regiment would serve. These contracts, which outlined the duties of the regiment's colonel and soldiers, as well as the responsibilities of the Swedish crown, followed a standard form. The colonel's obligations included overseeing recruitment, equipping the soldiers, and commanding the regiment. The soldiers' duties included obeying their officers' orders, building and defending earthworks when necessary, and observing the Swedish Articles of War. In turn, the Swedish crown committed to paying the soldiers once a month and to supplying ransom for any officer or soldier whom the enemy captured. In addition, the crown promised to provide a temporary home within the Swedish realm or one month's pay for overseas travel to any soldier disabled during military service.[3]

After the Swedish crown issued the contracts, the colonels proceeded with the enlistment of officers and soldiers. Colonels generally had the freedom to hire whom they pleased, and they had extensive powers to dole out patronage benefits within the regiment. Frequently, colonels hired officers from among their family members, friends, or supporters. This practice allowed them to have under their command men upon whose fighting skills and loyalty they could depend and to reward or support individuals with whom they were closely connected.[4] The career of Alexander Craufurd provides an example of the importance of having familial connections with recruiting officers. Craufurd was born into a noble family in Anachie, Scotland. Although his grandfather was George Craufurd, Baron of Fedderet, his father was a younger son and thus did not inherit the family title or property. Consequently, Alexander needed to find a career befitting his noble status. Such an opportunity arose in 1612, when his father-in-law, Patrick Rutherford, received a commission as a colonel to recruit soldiers for the Swedish army. In setting up his forces, Rutherford appointed Craufurd to be a captain in his regiment, probably to provide employment for his son-in-law and to give Craufurd a rank appropriate to his noble status. From this position, Craufurd could proceed to build a career as an officer in the Swedish army.[5]

Beyond a desire to create career opportunities for their relatives, colonels also used their patronage power to reward and preserve the loyalty of their tenants and political supporters. This practice was particularly common among colonels who were leaders of Scottish Highland clans. Traditionally, a mixture of kinship and tenancy ties defined the membership of the clans. Throughout the early modern period, a Highland clan was defined as a kinship group that possessed control over particular geographical areas of the Scottish Highlands. Sometimes the group's landholding centered upon the property of its chief, while other clans defined their territory through the land that was owned by many of its members.[6] The mixed nature of the ties that drew the clan members together also created a system of dependency among members of the group. Clans maintained control over their property by having relatives of the group's leaders living as tenants upon the land. The tenants' responsibilities included providing food for the clan and, in the case of senior families of the group, providing fighting men to defend the clan's property and interests. In exchange for these services, the clan chiefs stored a surplus of supplies in their homes to help clan members during times of dearth and gave protection to their followers.[7]

When clan chiefs chose to take commissions in foreign armies, they usually filled their regiments with members of their clans. This allowed them to provide support for the young men of the clan, to establish their followers as officers who might enjoy the booty of foreign conquests, and to have loyal kinsmen under their command. When establishing his regiment for Swedish service in 1630, Alexander Forbes, later to become eleventh Lord of Forbes, recruited twenty-six hundred Scots.[8] As the leader of the Forbes clan, Alexander enlisted many members of his family and clan to fill the ranks. The autobiography of his brother, William Forbes, provides a typical description of many clan members who followed their chief into Swedish service. William wrote that he entered Swedish service in 1634, when his brother Alexander returned to the wars in Germany after having been imprisoned for debts incurred in the recruitment process.[9] Another brother, John Forbes, Baron of Puittachie, had already entered Swedish service in 1633. Two younger brothers, Arthur and James, together with their half brother John, served in the Swedish armies during the Thirty Years' War. Other members of the Forbes clan, whom William listed as officers in the Swedish army, included John Forbes of Corse, who was the colonel of a regiment; Alexander Forbes of Ardmurdo, who recruited a regiment in Germany and later died there; Arthur Forbes of Corse, who was a lieutenant colonel; John Forbes of Tulloch, who died during the battle of Nördlingen; George and Alexander Forbes, brothers who both served as majors; and Arthur Forbes of Towis, who was a lieutenant colonel.[10]

Besides employing their own kinsmen, clan leaders sometimes granted positions within their regiments to individuals from allied clans. To achieve control over as much territory as possible, clan chiefs formed ties to their neighbors through marriages, bands of friendship (agreements to provide aid in lawful transactions), and fostering the children of allies.[11] The decision to grant potentially lucrative officer commissions to members of allied clans could be seen as an attempt both to reward and to preserve loyalty between the clans. The creation of Donald Mackay's regiment illustrates this point. Mackay, who was the chief of the Mackay clan, received permission in 1626 to recruit three thousand soldiers in Scotland for Danish service. After three years fighting for the Danish army, the regiment transferred to Swedish service in 1630 to support the Swedish crown's entrance into the Thirty Years' War.[12] In recruiting soldiers, Mackay relied upon members of his clan and of clans with which he was closely allied. In particular, many infantrymen and officers came from the Monro clan, which had a long history of ties to the Mackays through marriages among the leading families. The most recent marriage had occurred in 1619, when Hector Monro, brother of Robert Monro, chief of the Monro clan, married Mary Mackay, sister of Donald Mackay.[13] Officers from the Monro clan included Robert Monro, eighteenth Baron of Fowlis and head of the Monro clan; Robert's brother Hector, who served as a captain in his brother's company; John Monro of Obsdale, who rose to the rank of colonel in Swedish service; John's son George, who took part in the battle of Lützen in 1632; and John's younger brother Robert, who also became a colonel in Swedish service and who wrote an account of the regiment's action in *Monro, His Expedition with the Worthy Scots Regiment (called Mac-Keys Regiment)*.[14]

Military Service

Once regiments from the British Isles entered Swedish service, they usually did not retain their British composition for very long because of the high death rates in the armies. As was the case for all contemporary European armies, soldiers in the Swedish army were underpaid, poorly fed, and furnished with inadequate supplies. While on campaign, soldiers either lived out in the open or in squalid military camps. These unsanitary living conditions allowed diseases to reach epidemic proportions in the armies. For example, in July 1631, James, the third Marquis of Hamilton, landed in Germany with 6,000 soldiers he had recruited for the Swedish crown in England and Scotland. Within fourteen days, plague swept through their camp, leaving 2,000 soldiers either sick or dead. Six months later, in February 1632, Hamilton estimated that only 700 of the original 6,000 soldiers were still alive. The others had died of disease and battle wounds.[15] Unfortunately, these death rates do not appear to have been unusual. In comparison, in June 1631 James Lumsdain's Scottish regiment consisted of 133 men, 79 of whom he reported as suffering from various illnesses.[16]

Contributing to the malnutrition and poor living conditions of the mercenaries was the lack of adequate local supplies. As one Scottish mercenary, M. Wroughton, wrote to an official in the English government,

> It is the affliction of five thousand, besids my self that I now truly write wee are not yet in action, and that wee are in a country, where, after one month more, men can not live without Glorifyed bodyes, and where a wider Fatality is threatened from hunger, than a coward can apprehend, or a Jesuite wish us from the Warre to which wee are going. This desolate land for three years together, hath suffered a miserable defloration by the arymes of two Kings and an Emperor; and now nothing but Doomsday can make it worse. . . . neyther is here plenty of anything but of grasse, for with it the highways are covered and lost, and wee see nothing likely to consume it besides our army and the Grasshoppers.[17]

Because supply lines were often inadequate, soldiers often had to live off of the land or commandeer goods from surrounding villages. When there were no crops or peasants to grow crops in a particular region, the plight of the soldiers could become very serious.

As soldiers died, new recruits from the British Isles replaced them to bring the regiments back to full strength. When recruiting in the British Isles was not possible, the remaining soldiers would be joined together with other depleted regiments. This practice caused the national character of individual regiments to be lost, as soldiers from the Holy Roman Empire, the British Isles, and the Swedish empire served together. For the officers of British regiments, this meant that they eventually came to command non-British soldiers.

The sources very rarely speak of problems occurring between officers from the British Isles and their soldiers who were from different areas of Europe. Probably the greatest potential problem was the language barrier between the soldiers and the commander. The sources, however, say very little about the language problems that must have occurred on the battlefield. Only one reference was found that addressed this issue. In 1642, Johan Oxenstierna, a member of the Council of the Realm and the son of Axel Oxenstierna, wrote to Queen Christina regarding the troubles that Alexander Gordon had commanding his troops. Gordon, a Scot, served as the colonel of a regiment of Finnish soldiers who were garrisoning the fortress of Driesen. Oxenstierna wrote that the garrison had experienced many difficulties because Gordon could not speak Finnish and his troops could not understand him. As a remedy, Oxenstierna suggested that Swedish troops, who could presumably understand Gordon's commands, be sent to the fortress.[18]

Although most of the officers from the British Isles could not speak Swedish or German when first entering Swedish service, few seemed to experience problems similar to those that Gordon encountered. Usually the language of command was German, and most officers from the British Isles probably acquired enough German phrases to lead their troops.[19]

Once officers became established in the Swedish military, tracing their career paths is not difficult. The crown and the College of War, after its establishment in 1634, kept meticulous records of Sweden's soldiers.[20] From these sources it is evident that men from the British Isles served in the three different branches of the Swedish military—the navy, the cavalry, and the infantry.

Of the three divisions, the men who served with the navy constituted the smallest group, since the English crown seldom allowed the recruitment of sailors or naval officers for foreign powers. Traditionally, the defenses of the British Isles had been based on the navy. Allowing the fleet or its sailors to serve under a foreign crown was not an option most English rulers endorsed, as it would weaken the defenses of the island. In regard to Swedish affairs, the one exception to this rule occurred in 1659, when the English Lord Protector Richard Cromwell sent a fleet of forty-one ships under the command of Adm. Edward Montagu to the Sound.[21] This reversal in policy came about as an attempt to aid the Swedish navy in its struggle against Danish and Dutch fleets during the Baltic wars of the 1650s. Beyond safeguarding his Swedish allies, Cromwell hoped to preserve the economic interests of English merchants in the Baltic and to prevent Dutch merchants from gaining control of the Baltic markets in naval stores.[22] This fleet remained in the Baltic for six months, helping to defend the Swedish forces. It returned to England in August 1659 after peace negotiations had begun.

Despite the reluctance of English rulers to allow sailors to enter foreign service, a handful of British men became officers in the Swedish navy during the seventeenth and early eighteenth centuries.[23] These men became some of the most decorated naval officers of the period. During the seventeenth century, naval officers from the British Isles included four captains, one vice admiral, and three admirals.[24]

A larger group of British officers served in the cavalry. All of the officers from this group entered Swedish service before 1611. Throughout the Swedish crown's wars against the Poles and the Russians during the late 1500s and first decade of the 1600s, the Swedish crown actively recruited cavalry regiments in the British Isles. After the end of the Kalmar War in 1613, however, there is no archival evidence to suggest that the Swedish crown continued this practice. Probably the major reason behind the decline of British cavalry forces in Swedish service was Gustavus Adolphus's reorganization of the Swedish cavalry. During the early years of his reign, Gustavus Adolphus revamped the domestic recruitment of cavalry to ensure a constant supply of adequate forces. Before this time, the cavalry consisted of foreign mercenaries, volunteers from Sweden, and Swedish noble units. The bulk of the cavalry was supposed to come from the resources of the nobility, who supplied horsemen through an institution called *rusttjänst* (knight service). According to the system, each noble landowner provided the crown with a specified number of cavalrymen based upon the amount of land an individual owned. The more land a nobleman possessed, the more men he supplied. In exchange, the nobility enjoyed such privileges as exemption from taxation and from conscription of the peasants who lived upon the nobleman's demesne. Throughout the sixteenth century, this system declined, as the nobility, in an effort to exert its influence over the monarchy, refused to fulfill its obligations.[25] By the early seventeenth century, it was obvious that *rusttjänst* was inadequate for the defense of the realm. To fix the problem, Gustavus Adolphus divided Sweden and Finland into eight districts, each of which was responsible for producing one squadron of horsemen. This system was more reliable, as it placed the burden of recruitment and supply on whole regions and not on individual nobles.[26]

The other reason for the decline in recruitment of cavalry regiments abroad was their decreasing importance on the battlefield. The introduction of infantry tactics based upon the use of firearms and pikes in the fifteenth and sixteenth centuries caused a decline in the percentage of heavy cavalry found in armies throughout Europe. As more commanders employed these new tactics, the traditional weapons of the knight, such as the lance, became less important. Commanders still needed cavalry as offensive units to aid in attacks, but over time they played a less important role in the army as a whole.[27]

The vast majority of soldiers from the British Isles were members of infantry regiments. The Swedish crown began recruiting infantry regiments in England, Scotland, and Ireland in the 1570s. Recruitment proceeded continuously until the 1640s, when the men began to stay at home to fight in the Civil Wars. Recruitment resumed in the 1650s, but it never reached the levels of the early decades of the seventeenth century.

Progression through the Ranks

Officers from the British Isles were found at every level of the Swedish army and in all of the army's regiments. Once regiments recruited in the British Isles became amalgamated with other regiments in Swedish service, their officers were spread throughout the army. There does not appear to be a particular regiment that contained a concentrated number of British officers. As commanders of non-British regiments, the success of the British officers' careers became governed by the same circumstances that governed the success of native-born Swedish officers. The College of War, which regulated all administrative affairs of the army, oversaw promotion within the Swedish military. At the rank of colonel and above, the College of War approved promotions based on *meritförteckningar* and recommendations from individuals of noble standing. At ranks below colonel, a regiment's commanding officers recommended individuals for promotion.[28] This meant that having close connections with a member of the Swedish aristocracy was of crucial importance because such a patron could encourage members of the College of War to grant to his clients influential positions within the military.[29]

Among the officers from the British Isles, one individual whose career reflected the importance of patronage was George Fleetwood. Fleetwood was an Englishman who entered Swedish service in 1629 as a major in a regiment recruited in the British Isles. He became a lieutenant colonel in 1629 and returned to England in 1630 to recruit an infantry regiment, which he commanded as a colonel from 1631 until 1635.[30] In 1640, he became the colonel of the Jönköping regiment. He reached his highest rank in the army in 1656, when he was promoted to the rank of lieutenant general.[31]

Early in his career, Fleetwood's superiors recognized his military expertise. In 1632, while campaigning in the Holy Roman Empire, Fleetwood met Gustavus Adolphus and Axel Oxenstierna. At this meeting, Oxenstierna spoke of how Fleetwood's leadership skills had greatly impressed him. He also promised to act as Fleetwood's patron and do what he could to support him. In a letter to his father in November 1632, Fleetwood described this promise in writing: "I am confident of the rex-chancellour's favour, and doubt not but soe longe as he lyves he will be my patron."[32]

Oxenstierna's promise to Fleetwood developed into a meaningful relationship that benefited both parties. Besides promoting Fleetwood's progression through the military ranks, Oxenstierna also established him as a Swedish diplomat. In 1636, Oxenstierna sent Fleetwood, as a representative of the Swedish regency, to the court of Charles I to request military aid for Sweden's continuing campaigns in the Holy Roman Empire.[33] In England, Fleetwood presented Charles I with a memorandum requesting permission to recruit six regiments of infantry in England and Scotland.[34] Establishing Fleetwood as a diplomat not only helped to further Fleetwood's career but also proved valuable to the Swedish crown. George Fleetwood was a member of a prominent English gentry family. His father, Miles, served as a member of the House of Commons from 1614 until his death in 1640.[35] His older brother, William, was a cupbearer for both James I and Charles I and later became the comptroller of Woodstock Park.[36] His younger brother, Charles, pursued an army career and achieved prominence during the Civil Wars, in part because he was married to Oliver Cromwell's daughter, Bridget. During the 1640s, Charles Fleetwood served as Cromwell's lord deputy in Ireland.[37] Fleetwood's familial connections with the court and Parliament helped to develop ties between the Swedish and English courts.

Officers, however, were not the only individuals from the British Isles to use their connections with the Swedish aristocracy to promote the careers of their family, friends, and associates. The wives of officers also occasionally used their husband's ties to members of the Swedish aristocracy to further the careers of their family members. Margareta Foratt, a Scottish woman who married two officers from the British Isles, used her first husband's close ties with the Swedish chancellor, Axel Oxenstierna, to promote her son's career. Foratt's first husband was James Spens, who organized the recruitment of mercenaries for the Swedish crown during the first decades of the seventeenth century. In this capacity, Spens became acquainted with Oxenstierna as they worked together to enlist soldiers for the Swedish army. After Spens's death in 1632, the friendship between the families continued as Axel Oxenstierna took on the role of guardian for Spens's five-year-old son, Jacob. Margareta Foratt's second husband, Col. Hugo Hamilton, a Scots-Irish officer in Swedish service, later took over this role.[38] When Jacob became a young adult, he decided to continue the family tradition and pursue an army career. To help him become established within the officer corps, Margareta Foratt turned to Oxenstierna for help. In 1650, she wrote to Oxenstierna, requesting that he speak to the field marshal and see if an officer's position could be made available to her son. She based this appeal on their long friendship and the interest that the chancellor had always expressed in her children.[39] With the chancellor's support, Jacob became a lieutenant with the artillery. From this position, he would move quickly through the ranks, becoming a colonel of his own regiment in 1657 at the age of thirty.[40]

A system of patronage existed not only between British officers and members of the Swedish aristocracy but also among the officers themselves. Frequently, officers from the British Isles implored their Swedish patrons to promote their subordinates. Just as George Fleetwood enjoyed the privileges of having an important patron, he in his turn used his influence to promote the careers of his junior officers. For example, in the 1650s Fleetwood enjoyed a close relationship with another member of the Swedish aristocracy, Carl Gustaf Wrangel. Wrangel had a spectacular military career leading forces in the Thirty Years' War and in the Baltic conflicts of the 1650s. He held the rank of field marshal and served as the Admiral of the Realm, presiding over the College of the Admiralty. Fleetwood and Wrangel knew each other professionally from having served in the army together. In addition, they had a close personal relationship because Wrangel was the nephew of Fleetwood's wife, Brita Gyllenstierna, and probably attended Fleetwood's wedding in 1640.[41] Throughout the 1650s, Fleetwood maintained a regular correspondence with Wrangel and often referred to him as his patron. Included among the letters are requests that Wrangel support the promotion of two captains, Brian Stapleton and Daniel Goodrick, who served under Fleetwood's command.[42] This petitioning does not seem to have been an unusual practice, as other prominent officers from the British Isles, including Robert Douglas, James Spens, Alexander Leslie, and James King, wrote to members of the Swedish aristocracy recommending the promotion of lower ranking officers serving in their regiments.

The patronage power of British officers extended not only to forming connections between lower ranking officers and members of the Swedish aristocracy. Officers who held the rank of colonel or higher had the right to appoint low-ranking officers within their regiments.[43] Often colonels appointed their sons, or the sons of their colleagues, as officers under their command. The military careers of the Thomson family, which migrated from Scotland to Sweden in the 1590s, provide a particularly clear example of this practice. Tomas Thomson, who entered Swedish service during the 1590s, was the quartermaster colonel with the Närke-Värmland regiment by 1623. In 1622, Thomson's son, Eskil, became a second lieutenant with the same regiment. In 1631, another son, Samuel, joined the regiment as a second lieutenant. In 1633, the crown appointed Tomas Thomson as colonel of this regiment. Eskil continued to serve with his father at the rank of captain until 1635, when he transferred to another regiment. During Tomas Thomson's tenure as colonel of the regiment from 1633 to 1643, three of his other sons served under him. Jakob became a second lieutenant in 1633, Patrick became a second lieutenant in 1638, and Alexander became a second lieutenant in 1641. Jakob served with his father until 1637, when he was killed in battle. Patrick also remained with his father's regiment, where he rose through the ranks to become a lieutenant colonel in 1658. Alexander served with the regiment for five years, until he became a captain with a dragoon regiment from Västergötland in 1646. His tenure with the Närke-Värmland regiment was not over, however. From 1652 until 1658, he was a captain of the regiment, and he ended his military career as a lieutenant colonel, serving with the regiment at that rank from 1669 until 1677.[44] Just as having connections with a recruiting officer in the British Isles could establish an individual's career in the Swedish officers corps, having similar connections with colonels of Swedish regiments could bring comparable benefits to the sons of mercenaries from the British Isles.

Beyond needing friends in high places, a British officer also needed skill in military affairs to pursue a successful career in the Swedish army. During the early modern era, the Swedish monarchy was unique in allowing qualified nonnobles to rise to the highest ranks of the army. Technically, the Swedish nobility held a monopoly over the ranks of colonel and above. However, because of Sweden's small population and the massive scale of warfare that the crown engaged in throughout the seventeenth century, it was beyond the capacity of the native Swedish nobility to fill the necessary positions within the officer corps. To address this problem, the monarchs ennobled individuals at the rank of colonel, thus allowing foreigners and nonnobles to serve at all levels of command.[45]

Despite the crown's recognition of a need to reward the military prowess of skilled foreigners and nonnobles, the success that these groups enjoyed in acquiring high-ranking commands differed. Generally, the College of War granted more commands at the level of colonel or higher to foreign officers than to nonnoble Swedes. In his study of the officer corps of the Södermanland, Uppland, and Västmanland regiments, Klaus-Richard Böhme clearly illustrated this point. According to Böhme, between 1626 and 1682 thirty colonels commanded these regiments. Twenty-two were members of the Swedish nobility, six were foreigners, and two were nonnoble Swedes.[46] The reason why more foreign officers held the rank of colonel than nonnoble Swedes was that some foreigners began their careers as high-ranking officers within the regiments recruited in their homelands. Once these men moved into commanding Swedish forces, they held ranks at the same level or higher than the position they had originally held. Additionally, foreign noblemen often received commissions as colonels of regiments they had recruited in their homelands. If they displayed good leadership skills, the crown often moved them into higher levels of command. For example, Robert Douglas enlisted in Swedish service in Scotland in 1627. Because he was sixteen years old, he spent a number of years serving as a page for various noblemen in Swedish service. In 1632, Douglas received his first commission in the army as a major in a Scottish regiment. Because of his leadership skills, Douglas advanced to the rank of lieutenant colonel in 1634 and in 1635 received a commission to return to Scotland as a colonel to recruit more soldiers. Upon returning to the continent, his superiors continued to recognize Douglas's leadership skills. The College of War awarded him the rank of major general in 1643, general in 1651, and field marshal in 1657.[47] In comparison, many nonnoble Swedes began their careers as ordinary soldiers. Over time, they worked their way up through the ranks into the officer corps. However, because they began their careers at such low ranks, most did not have the opportunity to move into the highest levels of command.

Slow progression through the ranks was a problem that not only plagued nonnoble Swedish officers but was also a factor regulating the careers of many sons of British officers. As the sons of army officers, many second-generation immigrants began their military careers as low-ranking officers in their fathers' regiments. Because the sons started their careers in an established military system, they did not have the same opportunities as their fathers to enter the army as colonels in command of individual regiments. Instead, they had to serve many years in order to progress to the ranks of high command.

Another factor hampering the careers of many second-generation officers was that they came of age during a time when opportunities for professional advancement in the military were disappearing. The height of military migration from the British Isles into the Swedish kingdom occurred during the 1630s. This meant that many sons of officers from the British Isles grew to adulthood during the second half of the seventeenth century, when the Swedish crown fought fewer wars. To gain professional military experience, many of these sons of ennobled British officers served in foreign armies. For example, Axel Douglas and his brother Adolf fought in both the French and the Dutch armies during the 1670s; Gustaf Miles Fleetwood served in the life guard of Charles II of England during the 1660s; Hugo Johan Hamilton found employment in the French and Dutch armies during the 1690s, while his first cousins Henrik, Jakob Ludvig, Fredrik, and Claude Archibald were in French service during the 1720s and 1730s; and Jakob David Montgomery returned to the British Isles in the 1640s to fight for Charles I during the Civil Wars of that decade.[48] The practice of young men entering foreign military service before beginning a military career in Sweden was not just restricted to the sons of foreign officers. Because the later decades of the seventeenth century afforded few opportunities for a military career in Sweden, the sons of native-born nobles also fought for other monarchs to gain military experience and to establish themselves in military careers.

Beyond leading troops on the battlefield, a handful of officers from the British Isles served as bureaucrats in the Swedish military administration. During his reign, Gustavus Adolphus (1611–32) began to reform the government bureaucracy, creating for the first time in Sweden's history a centralized administration located in the capital city, Stockholm. He based the organization upon a system of colleges, each of which oversaw a particular aspect of the kingdom's affairs. The Swedish parliament formally established and recognized this system with the adoption of the Form of Government in 1634.[49] In regard to the army, the College of War, under the direction of the Marshal of the Realm, oversaw all administration of this institution and acted as the supreme court in regard to army affairs.[50] The College of the Admiralty, under the direction of the Admiral of the Realm, undertook similar duties for the navy.[51] During the seventeenth century, two first-generation British officers, George Fleetwood and Robert Douglas, served on the executive board of the College of War. Later in the century, the crown appointed a second-generation officer, Lt. Gen. Robert Lichton, to be a member of the board.[52] Individuals from the Clerck family served on the executive board of the College of the Admiralty. These included Lt. Adm. Hans Clerck and his son, Adm. Hans Hansson Clerck.[53] Sitting on the colleges' boards was one of the most prestigious positions any officer could achieve. The crown's willingness to appoint foreigners to these positions illustrates both the prestigious careers available to skillful and ambitious foreigners and the high esteem in which the Swedish monarchs held such individuals.

Conclusion

Throughout the second half of the sixteenth century and the first half of the seventeenth century, thousands of soldiers from the British Isles fought for the Swedish crown. Generally, officers from the British Isles were quickly integrated into the Swedish command structure, and their advancement through the ranks came to be controlled by the same factors as those affecting native Swedish officers. Although the native Swedish nobility continued to hold most of the influential positions in the military, the careers of the British officers illustrate that foreigners who could successfully utilize patronage and their own skills had the potential to advance to the highest levels of command within the Swedish army.

Their careers also suggest, however, that the factors allowing them to enjoy great success in their profession were of a temporary nature. Most military immigrants from the British Isles entered Swedish service during the first half of the seventeenth century when the massive scale of warfare expanded the opportunities for advancement in the military. In comparison, their sons came of age in an era of military contraction when the same possibilities for advancement and wealth through military service no longer existed.

4

IMMIGRANT MILITARY SOCIETY
IN SWEDEN

Once officers from the British Isles decided to settle permanently in the Swedish realm, they began to enjoy the fruits of their successful military careers. The high-ranking positions in the army and the navy that many of them held opened windows of opportunity for social advancement, wealth, and political power in their new homeland. As was the case with their military careers, however, the status of individual officers in Sweden and the opportunities available to them differed. To analyze the opportunities that success in military affairs brought to foreign officers and the factors that regulated their abilities to take advantage of these opportunities, this chapter will discuss three aspects of life for the British officers in Sweden. First, to discover the elements controlling the status of the officers within Swedish society and the attitudes of the Swedish nobility toward the newly ennobled foreigners, the investigation focuses upon the marriage patterns of British officers. Secondly, the discussion turns to an exploration of the practice of royal land donations to reveal the opportunities available to foreign officers for acquiring wealth within the Swedish realm. Finally, to illustrate the potential political power and influence that successful foreigners could exercise in seventeenth-century Sweden, the chapter analyzes the political lives of the British officers, in particular their role in the Swedish parliament.

Marriage

Measuring the attitudes that immigrants had about their place in Swedish society and the opinions of native Swedes toward the newcomers is exceptionally difficult. Few personal sources exist in which individuals reflect upon their new homeland or their circumstances within their new society. Since the written opinions of the immigrants are too scattered to provide meaningful insights into their social status, another means of analyzing their place in Swedish society is to investigate their social interaction with each other, with other foreigners in Sweden, and with native-born Swedes. Marriage patterns provide a means of exploring this issue. In transacting a marriage, men and women took many factors into consideration. Although arranged marriages were no longer customary in the seventeenth century, an individual's social background, economic status, and religious convictions still played important roles in determining the suitability of a potential spouse.[1] Given these circumstances, examining the criteria British officers used to select a potential spouse provides a means of discussing the factors regulating their social interactions with each other and with other members of the Swedish community.

Among the families of the first generation of British immigrants, many created close connections with each other through marriage. Of the 119 officers who settled in Sweden, about 90 percent were married, with about 25 percent having married women in the British Isles before they entered Swedish service and another 25 percent marrying women of British descent who already lived in Sweden.

In regard to the men who were married before they entered Swedish service, many brought their wives along on campaign or sent for them after they were established in Sweden. Many probably engaged in this practice because maintaining family life was a priority. In a letter to Gustavus Adolphus, James Spens discussed this concern:

> When the bearer of this letter, John Hay, a Scotsman and a great expert in naval matters arrives he will report to Your Most Serene Majesty that I have promised and assigned to him command of some of your ships. I have also dispatched five other Scots, gunners, to whom I have given sealed accounts for settlement of pay; if there were the necessity for such action and occasion demanded and offered, they would be capable of taking over personal command and filling the role of captain in a masterly and suitable manner. Since they have wives, if the condition of their service and pay corresponds to and comes up to their expectations, they will arrange for their wives to be brought to Sweden.[2]

The practice of women following their husbands into the military was not unusual. Throughout Europe, women went with their husbands on campaigns. They tended to their husbands' needs by finding and preparing food, taking care of their husbands' clothing, and helping the sick and wounded.[3] In the account of his regiment's employment by the Swedish crown during the Thirty Years' War, Robert Monro described the experiences of a woman who accompanied her husband on campaign. While Monro's troops sailed across the Baltic to rendezvous with the Swedish army, they encountered a storm and were shipwrecked on the north coast of Germany. Monro wrote that the wife of one of his men gave birth to a baby boy during the storm. He commented that it was remarkable that the woman had delivered the baby under adverse conditions and then the next day had marched four miles with the rest of the troops "with that in her Armes, which was in her belly the night before."[4]

Although the wives of some soldiers accompanied their husbands to the battlefield, many officers sent their families to live in towns nearby so as not to expose them to the actual fighting. Robert Monro espoused this practice as the wisest way to ensure that the men would not be distracted from their duties on campaign. When he traveled to Germany, Monro brought his wife and children with him but settled them in Stettin, where he knew they would be safe and he would not have to worry about them becoming caught in a battle. Monro described the problem of women accompanying the army when he discussed Gustavus Adolphus's concerns for his wife, Maria Eleonora, during her visit to his military camp in Germany:

> In the discharge of the former dutie we see his Majestie
> [Gustavus Adolphus] was troubled with a double care; the
> one for his Queene, the other for his Armie; being diligent
> in bringing both forwards, as also carefull to put them
> both in assurance; for having left the Queen at Donavert,
> he marched on Rhine to subdue his enemies. Where we
> see, that it behooved him first to put his Impedimenta in
> assurance, teaching thereby Cavaliers, that followed him
> in time of service, to quit their wives, whereby their care
> might be better employed in discharging the points of their

> Calling; which shews us, that such impediments at such
> times were better away than present: for our nature is ever
> to grieve much for the losse of things we love.[5]

Recognizing, however, that it was difficult, if not impossible, to prevent
women from following the army, the crown allowed soldiers and officers in Swedish service to bring their wives with them on campaign. The
roles of women in the Swedish army were outlined in the Articles of War,
which allowed soldiers to have their lawful wives accompany them on
campaign but prohibited unmarried women and prostitutes from following the army.[6] The king and chancellor realized that lawfully married
women could provide valuable support to the soldiers, but they feared
that prostitutes and other single women could cause problems within
the ranks and upset the discipline of the army. To combat this problem,
the Articles of War stipulated that if an unmarried woman was found in
the company of a soldier, he had a choice of marrying her or putting her
aside. The king and chancellor also wanted to prevent discipline problems arising from soldiers mistreating women. Accordingly, the Articles
of War stated that if a soldier abused a woman and if the victim could
provide proof to substantiate this claim, the offending soldier would be
put to death.[7] Women who tried to invoke this clause probably found
the process to be difficult, as the articles never defined what constituted
abuse nor the proof needed to support such a charge. The inclusion of
such a statement, however, showed the seriousness with which the king
and chancellor regarded the need to prevent soldiers from harassing local women and the necessity of protecting the women who followed
the army.

Wives were not the only female relatives who followed British mercenaries overseas. In some cases, the sisters of British officers also settled
in Sweden and found husbands among their siblings' comrades. These
instances, however, differed from the immigration of wives in that the
sisters seemed to travel to Sweden after their brothers had established
homes in the kingdom, thus making it unlikely that they accompanied
the army on campaign. According to Gustaf Elgenstierna, there were at
least two such cases. One was Isabella Kinninmond, who was born and
raised in Scotland. In the 1620s, three of her brothers entered Swedish
service, where they joined their uncle, Col. Johan Kinninmond. Some-

time after her brothers left Scotland, Isabella married a Scottish no-
bleman, Johan Urqvard, who was also serving in the Swedish military.
Although it is unknown when they were married, it seems likely that
Isabella and Johan met through Isabella's brother, Thomas, who was
Urqvard's commanding officer.[8]

An even clearer example of a sister following her brothers to Sweden
is the case of an Irish woman, Lilian Hamilton. Her brothers Hugo,
Ludvig, and Alexander entered Swedish service in the 1620s and the
1630s. All three brothers decided to remain permanently in Swedish
service and married and settled in Sweden. On December 30, 1655, Lilian
Hamilton married Johan Macklier, a prominent Scottish merchant who
traded out of the port at Gothenburg.[9] This union was Hamilton's first
marriage, but it was Macklier's second. Macklier had established himself
as a merchant in Gothenburg in 1629, when he formed a partnership
with another Scottish merchant, Jacob Macklier. Johan cemented the
partnership by marrying the sister of Jacob Macklier's wife in 1629.[10]
Johan Macklier's first wife died in 1653, and although it is not known
when he met Lilian Hamilton, it is likely that they became acquainted
through her brothers, because Macklier maintained close connections
both with the British Isles and with the British officers who served in
the Swedish armies.

Even though only two known instances of sisters following their
brothers to Sweden exist, both examples suggest that wider family immigration among the British soldiers occurred. The phenomenon of
female family members accompanying their brothers, sons, fathers, or
uncles into Swedish military service was probably more common than is
portrayed in the sources. Because the published genealogies of Swedish
noble families often list only the male founder of the family, other members of his immediate family who also immigrated to Sweden usually
are not listed. The lives of Isabella Kinninmond and Lilian Hamilton
show that not only wives but other female relatives of foreign mercenaries journeyed to Sweden in search of a better life, and their experiences
suggest the possibility of additional but unrecorded occurrences among
other families.

Beyond finding wives among the sisters of their comrades, officers
from the British Isles also found spouses among the daughters and
widows of fellow British officers. In regard to the daughters, it would be

natural to assume that they would find spouses among the friends and colleagues of their parents. Although women in the seventeenth century enjoyed greater control over their choice of marriage partners than their counterparts in earlier periods, many women still led sheltered lives and had little opportunity to meet men of whom their parents did not approve. Additionally, because of the legal restrictions placed upon the rights of single women to own or oversee property, unmarried women still depended upon their parents for financial support and upon their fathers for a dowry.[11]

Like the daughters of British officers, widows from this group also tended to find spouses among the associates of their late husbands. Although widows usually enjoyed more legal rights over their property than married women, many probably chose to remarry to avoid the stigma attached to single, adult women who lived alone.[12] In the case of women living in a foreign land, finding a new husband upon the death of their first spouse was probably of the utmost importance. While living overseas, they had little or no contact with their parents or siblings who could provide them with the necessary financial and emotional support after the death of their husbands. Without their male relatives to safeguard their property, economic survival could depend on their success in finding another husband. It would not be unusual for these women to turn to family friends and associates in their time of need, nor would it be unusual for these relationships to develop into marriages.

The marriages of daughters to their fathers' British comrades and of widows to their late husbands' British associates led to an extensive network of social ties among the immigrants. Investigating these kinship groups reveals the intimate ties that many of the immigrants maintained with each other once they settled in Sweden. Although many instances of these social connections exist, one of the best examples concerns the marriages between members of the Sinclair, Hamilton, and Spens families.

The Sinclairs, a family from the Orkney Islands and Caithness in northern Scotland, had many representatives in Swedish service. The officers in this family married extensively within the British community in Sweden, thus developing ties to many British immigrant families. In the early 1630s, David Sinclair and his older brother John entered Swedish service. At the time of their enlistment, neither of the brothers

FIGURE 2. THE MARRIAGES OF JOHN AND DAVID SINCLAIR

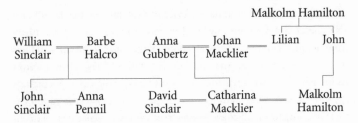

Source: Gustaf Elgenstierna, *Den introducerade svenska adelns ättartavlor med tillägg och rättelser,* 3:457–58, 7:273.

was married. In 1641, John married an Irish noblewoman named Anna Pennil, whose first husband, also an officer in Swedish service, had been killed in a duel.[13] In 1651, David married Catharina Macklier, the daughter of the previously mentioned Scottish merchant, Johan Macklier. Their marriage, however, was of very short duration because David Sinclair died in 1656 from a cannonball wound he received while leading his regiment in a battle in Poland.[14] In 1661, Catharina Macklier married another British officer, Malkolm Hamilton. Macklier and Hamilton had a close family connection as Malkolm was the nephew of Lilian Hamilton, who was Catharina Macklier's stepmother.[15]

Another member of the Sinclair family who served in the Swedish army was Frans Sinclair, a distant cousin of John and David Sinclair. Frans Sinclair was a member of two very prominent families in northern Scotland. On his mother's side, he was the nephew of Patrick Stewart, Earl of Orkney, and on his father's side he was the nephew of George Sinclair, Earl of Caithness.[16] Frans Sinclair enlisted in the Swedish army in 1628 as a member of MacKay's Highland regiment. At the time of his enlistment, he was already married to a Scottish woman named Joanna Sutherland. Sometime after they settled in Sweden, Joanna Sutherland died and Frans Sinclair married a woman named Regina Hendersen. With his first wife, Sinclair had a son named Jakob, who was born in Scotland.[17] With his second wife, Sinclair had two daughters, Regina and Christina. Frans Sinclair's children continued the tradition of marrying into British military families. Jakob Sinclair married Elisabet Clerck, the daughter of Johan Clerck, a Scottish officer in the Swedish navy. This was a second marriage for Elisabet Clerck because she had previously been married to Jakob Drummond, a Scottish officer in the Swedish army who died during military service in 1645. Jakob Sinclair and Elisabet Clerck did not have any children, but Elisabet had three children from her previous marriage who were ennobled under the name of Dromund in 1649 based on the merit of their father, Jakob Drummond.[18] As for Jakob Sinclair's half sisters, Christina married twice, both times to officers of German background in the Swedish navy. Regina married Johan Burdon, a Scottish nobleman who became a colonel in the Swedish army.[19]

Closely related to the Sinclairs were the Hamilton and Spens families. As previously mentioned, two members of the Hamilton family, Malkolm and Lilian, married members of the Sinclair family. Other members of the Hamilton family also found spouses within the British community in Sweden. Hugo, Lilian Hamilton's brother, was unmarried when he came to Sweden in 1624, but in 1637 he married Margareta Foratt, the Scottish widow of the general and diplomat, James Spens.[20]

Margareta Foratt was James Spens's second wife. His first wife had been another Scottish woman named Agnes Durie. The children of James Spens and Hugo Hamilton married extensively into the British community in Sweden. With his first wife James Spens had three sons—James, David, and William—none of whom married, and three daughters, all of whom married Scottish officers in Swedish service. With his second wife, Margareta Foratt, James Spens had two sons. The elder son, Axel, married a Swedish noblewoman, Sofia Rytter, while the younger, Jakob, never married.[21]

During her marriage to Hugo Hamilton, Margareta Foratt also gave birth to a daughter named Brita Margareta, who, in 1659, married Gustav Adolf Skytte, a descendant of an earlier British immigrant to Sweden. Skytte's mother, Maria Neaf, was the daughter of James Neaf, a Scot who had fought in the armies of John III in the late 1500s.[22] Even though Gustaf Adolf Skytte was a third-generation descendant of a Scottish immigrant, his family maintained close contact with other British families in Sweden and with the British Isles. His father, Johan Skytte, who was a native-born Swedish nobleman, was ambassador to England in 1604, 1610, and 1635. His brother, Johan Skytte the younger, was a chamberlain of James I of England and was knighted by Charles I in 1632.[23] Members of the Skytte family apparently spoke some English because their collection of family papers contains letters written in English from their

FIGURE 3. THE MARRIAGES OF FRANS SINCLAIR

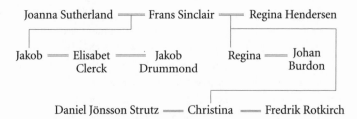

Source: Gustaf Elgenstierna, *Den introducerade svenska adelns ättartavlor med tillägg och rättleser*, 1:535–36, 7:272–73.

friends in the British Isles and a pamphlet written in English that details the commands for the regiment under the control of Johan Skytte the younger.[24]

Another Hamilton who married a descendant of an earlier Scottish immigrant was Hugo Hamilton, the nephew and namesake of Col. Hugo Hamilton. Through the encouragement of his brother Malkolm Hamilton, Hugo immigrated to Sweden and entered Swedish service in 1680. In 1688, while stationed in Gothenburg, Hugo married Anna Margareta Henriksdotter. Her parents were Henrik Arvidsson, a Gothenburg merchant, and Margareta Jacobsdotter Lindsay, who was probably the daughter of Jacob Lindsay, a Scottish officer in Swedish service.[25]

The marriages among the Sinclairs, Hamiltons, and Spenses illustrate the extent of intermarriage among the British military families in Sweden. Among the three families, there were eight first-generation officers. Of these eight officers, seven married women who were either born in the British Isles or were descendants of earlier British immigrants to Sweden. Among the second generation of the families, there were sixteen daughters, six of whom never married. Of the remaining ten daughters, five married Scottish officers or the descendants of earlier Scottish military immigrants. Two other daughters were born and raised in Ireland after their father, Hugo Hamilton, returned to his homeland to claim an inheritance. They also married men of British descent, but their marriages took place in the British Isles. The three remaining daughters married either Swedish noblemen or men of German descent who had been ennobled by the Swedish crown. In these families, there were also twenty-two sons, twelve of whom never married. Of the other ten sons, only three married women of British de-

FIGURE 4. THE BRITISH MARRIAGES OF THE HAMILTON FAMILY

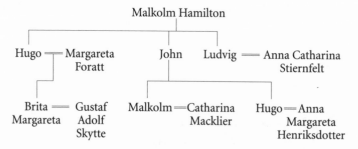

Source: Gustaf Elgenstierna, *Den introducerade svenska adelns ättartavlor med tillägg och rättleser,* 3:453, 457–58.

scent, while the others married women of Swedish or German background.[26] Although the amount of intermarriage with other British families in Sweden was higher among these families than was usual for the community as a whole, their marriages show the extensive network of ties that formed among these immigrants.

There are many reasons why individuals from the British Isles would seek each other out as marriage partners. Probably the most common factor was a shared sense of identity. Possessing a common native language, having similar religious beliefs, and growing up in comparable environments could lead individuals to find many commonalities with each other. The practice of intermarriage among members of an immigrant community who share a common background is not unusual. A contemporary example is the frequency of intermarriage among Irish soldiers and women of Irish descent who settled in Spanish Flanders during the late sixteenth century and early seventeenth century. In her study of this community, Gráinne Henry cites the frequency of Irish weddings occurring in Flanders as an example of "the close interaction of Irish families."[27]

Beyond the positive reasons for British immigrants to seek marriage partners among individuals from their homeland, such marriages may have occurred because of characteristics of the first generation that decreased their appeal as appropriate spouses for native-born Swedes. The first factor limiting their options was their social status. The majority of the British officers came from noble backgrounds, but at the time of their first marriages, most of them had not been ennobled by the

FIGURE 5. THE BRITISH MARRIAGES OF THE SPENS FAMILY

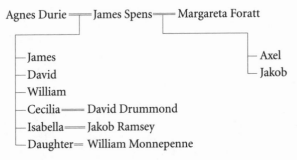

Source: Gustaf Elgenstierna, *Den introducerade svenska adelns ättartavlor med tillägg och rättleser,* 7:427–28.

Swedish crown. This meant that they did not hold recognized status as members of the Swedish nobility, and a potential spouse would have only their word to rely upon for assurance of their social background. For members of the elite, maintaining the social status of their family was of the utmost importance. Throughout Europe, nobles held fast to the tradition that individuals who married commoners lost their noble status.[28] As a result, parents wanted their children to marry partners of an equal, if not higher, status than themselves. In the case of the British officers, this concern was not just one of the matters to be considered by the relatives of Swedish women with a potential marriage to a foreign officer, but it was also a pressure that members of an officer's own family could exert. With their relatives fighting overseas, members of the family who remained in the British Isles did not have much influence over the officers' marital decisions. In order to ensure that an individual did not conclude a marriage that could dishonor the family, relatives of the officers would sometimes express their concerns.

An example of the concerns that were common to nobles throughout Europe is provided by the letter that M. Drummond wrote to his brother, who was serving in the Swedish army, regarding the brother's upcoming wedding. Drummond wrote, "Brother tho you have wrot nothing to me of your marriage yit by mr. Hum and others I understand you ar about one: I wish you good succes: bot if it fall out that your fancie domin abouv resson: in chusing basly I shall forget you are my brother; and shall in my affection prefes strangers befor you: . . . and give not occassion to your childring if god send you aney to curse you heir efter in matching basly. Brother as I have wrot in my former lettors so do I in this: if your match be honorable and that it pleasie god to call me lehv you: I have assneid on you and your childring me estate."[29]

It is not known whom the brother married, but the letter writer's attitudes toward marriage are very clear. If the soldier made a good and honorable match, he would remain his brother's heir to the family estate in the British Isles. If, however, he chose to marry "bas[e]ly" or beneath his status, his brother would disown him and the social status of the family could potentially be destroyed as the children of such a union would continue to marry beneath the status that the family once held.

Given these circumstances, it is not surprising that of the first-generation British officers who did not marry British women, those of noble background often found spouses among noblewomen from other immigrant groups, while nonnobles often married the daughters of foreign merchants. Those who married Swedish women either took spouses who were commoners or who were members of the lower Swedish nobility. British officers who hoped to use marriage as a means of upward social mobility usually were frustrated in their attempts. With their unconfirmed social backgrounds, most foreign officers could not expect to marry into the Swedish aristocracy.[30]

The second factor limiting the opportunities of first-generation British immigrants to marry native-born Swedes was the immigrants' religious beliefs. The mercenaries from the British Isles were either Anglican, Presbyterian, or Catholic. Problems arose, however, because Sweden was a Lutheran kingdom, and, throughout the seventeenth century, the Swedish crown strictly enforced Lutheran orthodoxy. Given the perceived threat of the Counter-Reformation in Sweden during the 1590s and the political struggles with the Catholic king, Sigismund, during the early seventeenth century, the Swedish elite feared the potential strife arising from conflicting religious interests in the kingdom. To prevent future instability, the king and the Council of the Realm upheld the legitimacy of Lutheranism as the only viable religion in Sweden throughout the early modern period. Such opinions were expressed in the Form of Government of 1634, which stated that the foundation of Sweden's political stability came through agreement on religious practice and belief.[31]

Because maintaining religious conformity was a high priority, the crown forbade most immigrants from holding non-Lutheran worship services, even in the privacy of their homes.[32] Occasionally, the Swedish monarchs granted dispensations from this rule to particular groups of foreigners who lived in concentrated communities and who provided valuable economic benefits to the crown. Such was the case with the Walloons, who worked the iron mines in central Sweden, and with the Dutch merchants in Gothenburg.[33] These instances were, however, very rare.

Another way to prevent foreigners from spreading their religious beliefs was to place restrictions upon immigrants who wished to marry Swedes. When such a marriage took place, the foreigner had to sign a document promising not to convert his or her spouse and promising to instruct any children of the union in the Lutheran faith.[34] While Swedish rulers recognized that it would be difficult to force foreigners to change their religious beliefs, the kings and the members of the Council of the Realm hoped that requiring immigrants to sign contracts regarding the religious upbringing of their children would curb the perpetuation of non-Lutheran theologies in the Swedish realm.

Throughout Europe during the early modern period individuals based their choice of spouse partly on issues of compatibility and love. At the same time, however, men and women considered the social background, wealth, and religious beliefs of their potential spouses to ensure their financial stability and to preserve their social status.[35] The factors governing the marriages of the British officers in Sweden reveal that the state regulations regarding marriages between Swedes and foreigners together with the unrecognized social status of the officers probably made the relatives of most Swedish women reluctant to promote a union with an officer from the British Isles.

In comparison, the sons of the British officers more frequently found spouses outside the confines of the British community than had their parents. Having been raised in Sweden and having learned to speak Swedish, the sons probably held more appeal as marriage partners to Swedish families than had their fathers.

Beyond their familiarity with the social life of the Swedish kingdom, the sons also might have had more opportunities to marry into the Swedish nobility because of their higher social status. Out of the 119 officers from the British Isles who settled in Sweden, 35 were ennobled and introduced into the Swedish House of the Nobility. In comparison, 131 out of 160 sons were ennobled and introduced into the Swedish House of the Nobility. More sons possessed noble status because they inherited their positions from their fathers or were themselves ennobled based on their father's or their own merit. Additionally, all of the children of Swedish noblemen inherited the family's noble status. This created a situation whereby the number of nobles in a given family potentially could increase in successive generations.

The higher social status of the sons not only opened the way for them to marry extensively into the Swedish nobility, but it also meant that some had the opportunity to marry into the Swedish aristocracy. Officers who rose to the highest positions in the military often received titles of nobility from the crown, thus raising them into the ranks of the aristocracy. When this happened, the newly titled noble often tried to conclude marriage alliances between his children and those of other aristocratic families in order to confirm his newly acquired aristocratic status. These unions held advantages for both families because they secured the position of the British families among the Swedish aristocracy and provided wealth to the Swedish families through the plunder and land donations gained via the military careers of their in-laws.

One example of this practice may be seen in the marriages of the children of George Fleetwood, an Englishman who had a long and distinguished career in Swedish service. Fleetwood enlisted in the Swedish army in 1629 and rose through the ranks to achieve the position of lieutenant general in 1656. He also went on two diplomatic missions to England, in 1636 and in 1655. For his loyal service, the monarch raised him into the Swedish aristocracy in 1654 and granted him the title of baron (*friherre*).[36]

As the children of an aristocrat, Fleetwood's sons perpetuated their family's status by marrying into the Swedish aristocracy. His oldest son, Gustaf Miles, married Baroness Märta Stake, whose father was Baron Harald Stake, a lieutenant general who served on the Council of the Realm. Fleetwood's youngest son, Adolf Jakob, also concluded a union with an aristocratic family when he married Baroness Christina Maria Siöblad, whose father was Gen. Carl Siöblad.[37] Without their recognized status as members of the titled nobility, Gustaf Miles and Adolf Jakob would have been unable to marry the daughters of aristocrats. These marriages also illustrate that although many members of the Swedish nobility probably were unhappy with the massive ennoblement of foreigners that took place in the seventeenth century, once these individuals officially had been granted this status, they became acceptable spouses, even at the highest levels of Swedish society.

Royal Land Donations

While a few British officers achieved upward mobility through marriage ties to members of the Swedish nobility, more officers gained standing in Swedish society by acquiring wealth, in particular from the assets that came from royal land donations. Beginning in the late sixteenth century, Swedish monarchs alienated crown land or the right to collect taxes upon particular pieces of property. The disposal of crown property occurred because the kingdom possessed a weak economy and few monetary resources, thus making it difficult to pay, in a timely fashion, the salaries of the growing military establishment. Land donations also provided the monarchs with a means of rewarding these individuals for their loyal service and provided foreign officers with places to live when they settled in Sweden and Finland. Investigating the success of foreign officers in acquiring royal land donations reveals two issues regarding the opportunities for foreigners to acquire wealth in Sweden. First, as a result of receiving land donations from the crown, many officers came to have extensive land holdings within the Swedish empire. The prosperity that particular men gained from their property ranked them among the wealthiest group within the Swedish realm. The crown's willingness to shower foreigners with such extensive riches suggests that the monarchs greatly valued the military prowess and leadership of these officers. Second, once individuals had gained control of property, they devised schemes to expand the amount of land they held. To achieve this goal, officers employed such strategies as marrying well, attempting to inherit the land of their relatives, and buying and trading land with their neighbors to consolidate their holdings. These activities illuminate the factors that affected the officers' abilities to maintain control of their land and to build upon their property.

Although officers from the British Isles received land grants throughout the Swedish empire, this investigation focuses on a comparison of their landholding patterns in two regions of Sweden—Uppland and Småland. These areas have been chosen for many reasons. Uppland and Småland provide a contrast between the center of political power and a peripheral region on the border of Swedish territory. Uppland, the province immediately to the north of Stockholm, was one of the most desirable locations within which to acquire land in Sweden. The region is close to the center of political power, has good agricultural land, and is accessible to the capital by water along the coast and the interior lakes, an important factor in the seventeenth century.[38] In comparison, Småland was not as attractive. The region has few natural resources. It is heavily forested, has sparse mineral resources, and has rocky soil that makes agriculture difficult.[39] Moreover, until 1660 the region was located on the border of the Danish realm and was exposed to possible Danish invasions.[40] Traditionally, this region of forests served as a barrier between the core of the Swedish realm located around Stockholm and the Danish provinces to the south.[41]

Although the granting of lands to noblemen as a reward for their service to the monarch dated from the Middle Ages, the practice of giving land to military officers to replace unpaid salaries developed in Sweden during the late sixteenth century out of a need to finance the many wars in which the crown was engaged. Because the crown frequently lacked the cash to pay salaries, receiving land from the monarchs became very important to military officers because it gave them a more stable income than the government could provide.[42] For foreign officers who wished to settle in Sweden, land donations held particular importance because as landowners the officers could become naturalized Swedes and maintain their permanent residence within the Swedish realm. Royal donations did not always consist of land grants, however. Sometimes the crown gave officers the right to collect taxes levied on a region or on a specific group of farms. In such cases, ownership of the land remained with the peasants, but the nobleman received the taxes rather than the crown.[43]

Even though foreign officers had received land grants throughout the second half of the sixteenth century, the number of donations increased dramatically during the 1590s and early 1600s under the rule of Charles IX. Throughout the 1590s, Charles had fought against his nephew Sigismund for control of the Swedish throne. After Sigismund was deposed, Charles declared that the nobles who supported Sigismund had forfeited control of their property, thus allowing the crown to confiscate their land. The newly crowned king then granted these estates to military officers to reward them for their help during his bid to take over the throne. Since many of the Swedish nobles had sided with Sigismund, Charles gave much of the forfeited land to foreign officers upon whom he had relied heavily. He hoped that these rewards would help maintain their support of the new regime.[44]

During the reign of Charles IX's son and successor, Gustavus Adolphus, the financial demands on the state increased as the Swedish crown continued to expand its influence in the eastern Baltic and became involved in the Thirty Years' War. With the increasing military costs, Gustavus Adolphus expanded his father's policy of alienating crown resources to the nobility in order to pay the military officers. He also continued this process as a means of speeding up the development of a cash economy. Up until this time, crown revenues came from the produce of royal property and taxes, most of which were paid in kind. Gustavus Adolphus believed that a cash-based economy could be created if royal revenues were based on taxes paid with specie and if crown land were sold or given to members of the nobility to compensate them for their service to the kingdom.[45] The king justified the disposal of royal assets with the idea that the nobility had more resources with which to manage the land than did the crown. Gustavus Adolphus also mortgaged crown land as security for loans from noble financiers to fund the war effort.[46]

There were restrictions, however, on the king's ability to give away the crown's assets. According to Magnus Eriksson's Land Law, a monarch was not allowed to dispose permanently of the crown's resources.[47] If such a practice occurred, the successor to the throne had the right to reclaim what had been alienated.[48] To prevent illegal donations from taking place, the Riksdag in 1604 adopted the Resolution of Norrköping. According to this document, the holder of a land donation had to have the grant confirmed by each new monarch, the donation could only be inherited by direct male heirs, and the crown had the right of first refusal when the property was to be sold or mortgaged.[49] The Riksdag's acceptance of the Form of Government in 1634 placed further restrictions on the alienation of crown property. According to that document, "While the King is abroad, or ill, or a minor . . . no crown land, no freehold land, nor any other of the crown's rights and sovereignties, shall be either sold, exchanged, donated, or in any other way alienated by the government; and a King may, upon his return home, or his recovery, or his majority, revoke and resume at pleasure any such alienations."[50] This clause was to be problematic after the death of Gustavus Adolphus as the Swedish kingdom continued its involvement in the Thirty Years' War. It resulted in the regency needing to maintain the practice of granting land donations to finance the war effort. After much debate, the Council of the Realm decided that it had no alternative but to proceed with the alienation of land to the nobility, even though the practice was technically illegal.[51] The chancellor, Axel Oxenstierna, particularly supported this policy because, like the late king, he believed that the Swedish economy would grow stronger by converting the crown's income from the produce of the royal estates to direct or indirect taxes paid in cash.[52] After Gustavus Adolphus's daughter Christina achieved her majority in 1644, she did not punish the Council of the Realm by invoking the Form of Government and reclaiming the property alienated during her minority but instead expanded the amount of resources donated to the nobility. She did so, in part, to continue her father's economic policies of converting the crown's income to indirect taxes to secure more ready cash. Christina also dramatically increased the number of donations as a means of rewarding military officers who were returning from the wars in Germany.[53]

Christina's reign marked the height of donations to the nobility. Although this practice would continue until 1680, the number of donations never again reached the levels of the late 1640s and early 1650s. The late-seventeenth-century downturn in land donations came about as a result of the opposition of the nonnoble estates to the process. Throughout the first half of the seventeenth century, as royal resources decreased due to the expansion of donations, the crown had to increase the taxes levied to make up the shortfall. Because members of the nobility and their tenants, who lived on farms attached to the noble residences, were exempt from taxation, the burden of taxation fell more and more heavily upon the freehold peasants and trade.[54] The nonnoble estates also united against further alienations because they believed that their political influence was threatened as the nobility grew wealthier and more powerful through the continuing practice of land donations.[55]

In 1654, when Charles X Gustavus ascended the throne, the crown finances needed to be strengthened and the grievances of the nonnoble estates had to be addressed. As a result, the new monarch presented the nobility with an ultimatum that they would either have to pay taxes or agree to a *reduktion,* the process enabling the crown to reclaim some of the donated land. Although many members of the nobility opposed both schemes, the House of the Nobility chose to support a partial *reduktion* as the best means of preserving the nobility's traditional privileges. Such a solution gained particular support from the aristocracy when it was realized that a partial *reduktion* would have the most impact upon those individuals whose status as landowners depended upon receiving donations, namely, foreigners and newly created nobles.[56] The lands retaken were to include all property in areas seen as indispensable to the crown, such as the iron mining region of central Sweden, and one-quarter of the donations granted since the death of Gustavus Adolphus in 1632. In addition, all donations that had not been granted under the stipulations of the Norrköping Resolution were to be changed to fall within the restrictions of that resolution. This *reduktion* was not carried through, however, as fighting wars against Denmark, Poland, and Russia consumed Charles X Gustavus's reign, leaving little time for domestic matters. The grievances of the nonnoble estates would wait until 1680 and the reign of Charles X Gustavus's son, Charles XI.[57]

In 1679, with the end of the war against Brandenburg and Denmark, Charles XI realized that the crown did not possess the economic capacity to rebuild the state and the military. At the same time, the nonnoble houses of the parliament again raised the cry for a *reduktion* to address the same grievances they had expressed in the 1650s. Unlike his father, Charles XI successfully carried out a total *reduktion* in 1680 because he enjoyed the support not only of the nonnobles but also of a portion of the nobility. During the second half of the seventeenth century, a split between the high nobility and the lower nobility had been developing. Although all noblemen were supposed to have access to state offices, a small number of aristocrats usually controlled the most powerful positions. Many members of the lower nobility resented the aristocracy's monopoly over political appointments.[58] In addition, the massive number of ennoblements earlier in the century had greatly increased the membership of the third noble class. Most of these men were civil servants or military officers who depended upon salaries from the crown for their livelihood. The alienation of crown lands, most of which went to members of the aristocracy, threatened the crown's ability to pay the salaries of its servants on a regular basis. Many members of the lower nobility believed that only a strong monarch would be able to save them from the expanding political power of the aristocracy and thus were willing to band together with the nonnobles and the king to break the power of the aristocracy.[59] As a result, the nobility agreed to a *reduktion* in 1680. On the basis of stipulations in Magnus Eriksson's Land Law, the parliament agreed that Charles XI possessed the right not only to grant land but also to take back the property. This process allowed the crown to regain ownership of about three-quarters of the alienated land.[60]

The process of receiving land donations that involved the officers from the British Isles corresponds to the general pattern outlined above. They began to receive royal land donations as soon as they began immigrating to Sweden in the late 1500s. The earliest donations were granted during the reigns of Erik XIV and John III, which corresponds to the period of the Seven Years' War of the North (1563–70), when mercenaries from the British Isles began to enter Swedish service. Between 1569 and 1571, two Scottish officers, Andrew Keith and Hugh Cahun, received donations in Sweden.[61] Donations to officers from the British Isles would continue until the 1670s, but the majority of the officers received their grants between 1620 and 1655. Looking into Johan Axel Almquist's work on noble lands in Uppland and Småland shows when the donations occurred. According to Almquist, twenty-one officers from the British Isles received donations in Uppland and twenty-one received donations in Småland. From the graph (figure 6), it can be seen that officers received the most donations during the middle of the seventeenth century, which corresponds to the period of the heaviest of military immigration to Sweden. Additionally, the middle decades of the century also marked the height of royal land donations, particularly as the Swedish crown sought to compensate the vast number of officers it had employed during the Thirty Years' War. As a result, this period provided the greatest opportunity for officers from the British Isles to receive land grants.

It is also interesting to note that the majority of donations in Uppland were made earlier than those in Småland. Several factors help to

FIGURE 6. NUMBER OF INDIVIDUALS
WHO RECEIVED DONATIONS BY DECADE

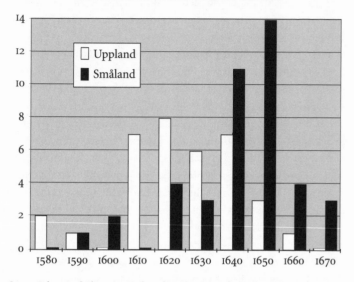

Source: Johan Axel Almquist, *Frälsegodsen i Sverige under storhetstiden,* part 1, *Stockholms och Uppsala län,* and part 4, *Småland.*

explain this phenomenon. First, the officers probably preferred having land in Uppland because of the close proximity to the center of political power, Stockholm, and because of the region's high agricultural quality. Consequently, officers may have been more likely to request land in Uppland than in a more marginal area such as Småland. Second, the rapid increase in the number of donations during the 1640s and 1650s probably caused the government to turn to donating lands of poorer quality to meet the financial obligations of the state. As the amount of high quality land available for donations decreased, Queen Christina and her government may have relied more heavily upon less attractive lands in more marginal regions, such as Småland. Third, because the crown owned more land in Småland than in Uppland, the monarchs probably drew more heavily upon their resources in Småland during the middle decades of the seventeenth century, when they granted most of the donations.[62]

Although the number of donations that officers from the British Isles received appears quite small, the amount of land actually granted was in some cases very extensive. In comparing the land donations of the

British officers in Uppland and Småland, it can be seen from tables 1 and 2 that the location of the land and the military rank of an officer influenced the size of the holdings given to individuals. The tables show that higher ranking officers generally received larger land donations than lower ranking officers. The differences in the size of the donations between men holding the same rank can be attributed to two different factors. First, because officers received land grants throughout the Swedish realm, an individual with a small amount of property in one province may have held more land in another area of Sweden or Finland. As a result, the differences in the size of donations in a single province between officers of similar rank may not reflect the total amount of land that officers of a certain rank held. Second, the quantity of land given to members of the military decreased dramatically during the second half of the seventeenth century. Officers who received their donations in the 1660s or the 1670s probably received much smaller amounts of land than had their counterparts in the earlier decades of the seventeenth century.

The tables also illustrate that the location of the land donations influenced the size of the grants. Although most officers received a small quantity of property, the total area or number of *mantal* of land given to British officers was much larger in Småland than in Uppland. It is important to note, however, that the small grants awarded to British officers were not unusual. Most individuals who received land donations received a small amount of land. According to Almquist, the average amount of land donated to first-time holders in Uppland was nine *mantal*. The crown granted larger quantities of property to very few people. Of the 260 individuals who received land donations in Uppland, only about 10 of them, including James Spens, held more than thirty *mantal* of land.[63] In comparison, the average amount of land donated to first-time holders in Småland was sixteen *mantal*. In addition, a larger number of people received land donations in Småland than in Uppland, and individuals held extensive amounts of property. In Småland, there were 337 first-time recipients of property from the crown. Within this group, 16 men received donations of more than thirty *mantal* of land.[64]

Among the officers from the British Isles who received property in Småland, one individual, Robert Douglas, stands out as having received more land than any other officer from this group. The amount of land

TABLE 1. LAND DONATIONS IN SMÅLAND

NAME	FINAL RANK	LAND DONATION (MANTAL)[1]	ANNUAL RENT (RIKSDALER)
Robert Douglas	field marshal	145.875	3186.17
James King	lieutenant general	65.5	1439.27
Patrick Ruthven	field marshal	45	892.01
George Fleetwood	lieutenant general	24	433.31
Johan Kinninmond	colonel	18.5	396.13
Thomas Muschamp	colonel	18.5	374.28
Frans Sinclair	lieutenant colonel	15	261.27
Patrick Traill	lieutenant colonel	11	286.21
Johan Lowrie (Lagergreen)	major	9.5	203.07
Johan Burdon	colonel	8	165.25
Alexander Irving	colonel	8	169.30
Jakob Drummond	lieutenant colonel	7.5	161.29
Alexander Thomson	colonel	3.75	69.04
Georg Ogilvie	lieutenant colonel	3.5	95.08
Jakob Keith	major	3	52.24
Hans Clerck the younger	*holm amiral* (navy)	2.25	43.28
Carl Campbell	captain	2	52.08
Patrick Monnepenne	captain	1	20.25
James Neaf	*ryttmästare*	?	?
David Ramsay	colonel	?	?
William Ogilvie	?	?	?
	TOTALS:	391.875	8299.53

Source: Johan Axel Almquist, *Frälsegodsen i Sverige under storhetstiden*, part 4, *Småland*, vols. 1–3.

1. The *mantal* was a uniquely Swedish measurement of land. It was developed in the sixteenth century during the reign of Gustavus Vasa and represented the "normal" amount of land an individual freehold peasant owned. It was not supposed to equal the average holdings of peasants but instead what was a "normal" allotment. The Swedish crown regulated the size of a *mantal* of land, and the measurement changed during the seventeenth century. See Göran Ohlin, trans., "Translator's Note," in Eli F. Heckscher, *An Economic History of Sweden*, 127.

TABLE 2. LAND DONATIONS IN UPPLAND

NAME	FINAL RANK	LAND DONATION (MANTAL)[1]	ANNUAL RENT (RIKSDALER)
James Spens	general	34.5	1598.29
Patrick Rutherford	colonel	13	672.26
Jakob Forbes	colonel	12	574.22
James Seton	colonel	11	550.12
William Grey	lieutenant colonel	7.5	297.9
Simon Stewart	lieutenant admiral (navy)	7	311.24
William Barclay	major general	6.5	172.28
William Philip	colonel	6.16	146.27
Tobias Duwall	colonel	6	140.5
Robert Douglas	field marshal	5.5	376.21
James Neaf	ryttmästare	5.5	?
William Borthwick	captain	5	196.20
Axel Duwall	colonel	5	205.28
Johan Urqvard	colonel	5	217.04
Mauritz Duwall	colonel	4	159.37
Vilhelm Nisbeth	lieutenant colonel	4	159.25
Hans Clerck the elder	vice admiral (navy)	2	?
Albrekt Duwall	fortress commander	2	?
Jakob Hamilton	major	2	108.4
Richard Clerck	vice admiral (navy)	1	60.2
Robert Lichton	lieutenant general	0.5	11.25
	TOTALS:	145.16	5956.28

Source: Johan Axel Almquist, Frälsegodsen i Sverige under storhetstiden, part 1, Stockholms och Uppsala län.

Douglas obtained was not only unusual among his British comrades but also in comparison to all officers in Swedish service, both foreign and native. The extensive land donations to Douglas made him one of the largest landowners in the province. The quantity of land that Douglas held in Småland clearly shows that the military rank and prowess of an individual could influence the extent to which the crown showered an officer with land grants.

Douglas entered Swedish service during the Thirty Years' War and worked his way up the army hierarchy until he reached the rank of field marshal. He also had an important political career, which included serving as a member of both the Council of War and the Council of the Realm. Throughout the 1650s, Douglas received vast donations, which were scattered over seven *härader* (regional administrative districts) throughout Småland and totaled 145.875 *mantal* of land.[65] These land donations made Douglas the fourth largest landowner in Småland. The only individuals who held more land were Axel Oxenstierna, Per Brahe the younger, and Lennart Torstensson, all of whom were members of aristocratic families and very powerful politicians.[66] To understand the extraordinary nature of Douglas's land donations it is necessary to look briefly at the careers of the comparable landowners in the province.

Axel Oxenstierna was the most prominent politician of his day, serving as chancellor for both Gustavus Adolphus and Christina. During Gustavus Adolphus's reign, he helped the king restructure the government, and after the king's death in 1632, he headed the Swedish war effort in Germany and led the regency government for Queen Christina.[67] Per Brahe was a member of a very powerful family that played a leading role in Swedish politics throughout the sixteenth and seventeenth centuries. His grandfather, Per Brahe the elder, had been an advisor to both Gustavus Vasa and Erik XIV and was the author of *Oeconomia eller Hushållbok för ungt adelsfolck* (Economy or housekeeping book for young noble folk), which described the lifestyle of the Swedish nobility. Per Brahe the younger served as a member of the Council of the Realm and for a period of time was the governor of Finland, where he was instrumental in the establishment of the University of Turku.[68] Lennart Torstensson was one of the most prominent Swedish military officers in the later stages of the Thirty Years' War. He served as commander-in-chief of the Swedish army in Germany beginning in 1641, presided over the Swedish victories at Breitenfeld in 1642 and Jankov in 1645, and helped lead the successful Swedish invasion of Denmark in 1643. In 1641, he was named a member of the Council of the Realm.[69] In comparison with these members of the aristocracy, Douglas obtained an amount of land comparable to that possessed by Brahe and Torstensson. This fact reflects the high esteem in which the Swedish crown held him and the prominent position he attained both in the Swedish military and in the Swedish political system.

The decisions regarding who received land donations were strictly controlled by the Swedish government in order to allow the rulers to maximize their resources and prevent undesirable interlopers from gaining possession of crown resources. There were, however, times when the crown set aside the regulations governing the dispersal of donations to meet the financial demands of the military. A rule that the crown often ignored was the practice of reserving land donations exclusively for members of the Swedish nobility. Because the Swedish crown at times had no other means of compensating military officers and war financiers, nonnobles received land donations and thus came to possess the same rights over the land as the nobility. As a noble landowner, the holder of a donation was free from taxation. This factor was particularly important to foreigners whom the Swedish House of the Nobility had not naturalized because acquiring estates gave them the same privileges as the native Swedish nobility.[70] The case of the Muschamp family illustrates the benefits that nonnoble foreign officers enjoyed from receiving land donations.

Thomas Muschamp was an Englishman who entered Swedish service in 1621 as the captain of a regiment that James Seton enlisted in the British Isles. He quickly worked his way through the ranks, becoming colonel of the Kronoberg regiment in 1626. Muschamp continued to serve in this capacity until his death in 1629.[71] Although the king had not ennobled Muschamp, in 1627 Gustavus Adolphus decided to give him a land donation in the province of Småland consisting of eighteen farms and six manors, which totaled 18.5 *mantal* of land.[72] This reward for loyal service was quite remarkable as it was the fourth largest land donation in Småland among those given to British officers and the fifth largest in terms of value. The British officers who possessed more property in the province held at least the rank of lieutenant general (see table 1).

These lands proved to be beneficial after Muschamp's death, as Gustavus Adolphus granted control of the property to Muschamp's widow, Elin Lindsay, and her daughters Margareta and Isabella. They were to administer the property until Margareta or Isabella had sons who could legally inherit the land.[73] Sometime after 1629, Margareta married a Scottish officer, Robert Bruce, with whom she had four sons—Rudolph, Thomas, Anders, and Robert. Although Robert Bruce reached the rank of lieutenant colonel in the Swedish army, the Swedish crown did not ennoble him. Despite his nonnoble standing, control over the Muschamp property did not revert back to the crown. In fact, Margareta and her family lived at the manor of Skiverstad, which they had built in 1645 upon some of the land donated to her father. The family did not receive noble status until 1668, when the crown ennobled Rudolph, Robert, and Anders, all of whom were army officers, for the long military service of their family.[74] The crown's willingness to allow three generations of foreign officers who had not been ennobled to hold land donations is remarkable. As the holders of the property, the Muschamps and the Bruces had the same rights and privileges over the land as members of the nobility, despite their nonnoble status. This example shows that the crown's need to provide support for its officers and the need to reward officers for their loyal service caused it to allow many individuals who were not members of the Swedish nobility to gain the privileges of noble landownership.

The case of the Muschamps was not unusual, however. Because the Swedish crown constantly experienced difficulties financing its military, a majority of the officers from the British Isles had not yet been naturalized as Swedish noblemen when they received land donations from the crown. Of the twenty-one officers who received donations in Uppland, only five officers, or about 23 percent, were naturalized Swedish noblemen at the time they received their land grants. In comparison, among the officers who received donations in Småland, six of twenty-one officers, or about 28 percent, were naturalized Swedish noblemen at the time they acquired their donations. These low percentages of ennobled foreign officers reflects the Swedish government's need to provide financial compensation to its foreign officers regardless of whether they fit the criteria for receiving a donation.

Another instance in which the crown disregarded the rules governing donations was in granting land to the wives and the widows of officers. Although only men were supposed to hold royal land donations, women sometimes received donations based on their husbands' merits. The experiences of Elisabet Clerck, the daughter of a Scottish naval officer in Swedish service who married another Scottish officer, Lt. Col. Jakob Drummond, provides an illustrative case. After her husband's death in 1645, the Swedish crown granted Elisabet Clerck a donation in Småland to provide support for her and her children. In 1650, Clerck married another Scottish officer, Jakob Sinclair, but she was allowed to keep the donation even after her second marriage.[75]

The process allowing widows to maintain control of their family land often was initiated by the women involved. Rather than passively waiting to see what would happen to them after their husbands' deaths, many of these widows took an active role in gaining confirmation of their husbands' estates. For example, shortly after her husband died in 1636, Catherine Guthrie wrote to Queen Christina asking for confirmation of land recently donated to her husband. To strengthen her claim to the property, Guthrie pointed out that her husband had faithfully served the Swedish crown for seventeen years and had held the rank of lieutenant colonel. Additionally, she tried to play upon the sympathy of the queen by emphasizing that the untimely death of her husband had left her as a poor widow with many small, fatherless children. Guthrie promised that if she received confirmation of the land, she would raise her children in a manner that would allow them to serve the Swedish crown.[76] Family papers do not reveal if Guthrie received confirmation of the property, but her attempts to maintain control of the land suggest that women, in particular widows, could take very active roles in safeguarding the economic interests and welfare of their families.

The Swedish royal practice of extending land donations to the widows of foreign officers is particularly significant because it challenges the traditional interpretation of the roles of mercenaries in European armies and the attitudes that their employers had toward them. Scholars traditionally have portrayed mercenaries as men who did not owe allegiance to the ruler for whom they fought. In addition, they have argued that since mercenaries possessed no personal interest in the causes for which their employers fought, they could simply be paid off and sent away at the end of the war. They would not leave behind widows or children who could become burdens to their employers.[77] The Swedish case disproves the universality of these ideas. The granting of land donations to the widows of foreign mercenaries can be seen as official recognition by the Swedish crown of a need to reward the loyalty of its officers and to provide for the welfare of their families regardless of whether the officers were native born or foreigners.[78]

Beyond land donations, officers gained control of land through marriage, inheritance, and purchase. Investigating these practices reveals the other opportunities that military officers had to acquire property and some of the factors regulating their abilities to build up their holdings.

Marriage was one of the most common and the easiest means for foreign officers to acquire land. When a marriage occurred, the father of the bride provided his daughter with a dowry, which sometimes included land or the rent from specific properties. After the marriage took place, the bride received a morning gift from her husband, which could consist of land or money.[79] The land that a woman brought to her marriage and the property she received as her morning gift technically belonged to her, but her husband managed them for the duration of the union. Upon the husband's death, the wife's property was supposed to revert back to her biological family to provide for her financial support. Unfortunately, this did not always happen, as men's families sometimes attempted to maintain control of the property even after the marriage had ended.[80] An example of this was the fight that occurred between Hugo Hamilton and the family of Gustaf Adolf Skytte over the right of Hamilton's daughter, Brita, to her morning gift after the death of her husband, Gustaf Adolf Skytte. Brita and Gustaf Adolf were married in 1659. As part of her dowry, Brita brought to the marriage seven hundred *riksdaler* in annual rent from her father's land. In exchange, her husband gave her a morning gift that included a manor house and the surrounding property. The marriage, however, was very short as the crown executed Skytte for piracy in 1662.[81] After her husband's death, Brita Hamilton claimed her right to maintain ownership of both the land included in her dowry and the estate given to her as a morning gift. Skytte's heirs disputed her right to the property and tried to prevent her from taking it away from the family. Hamilton had to enlist the aid of her father, who had reimmigrated to Ireland, to fight for her ownership of the land.[82] Although the result of the dispute is not known, the fight over Brita's right of ownership illustrates that marriage could be a means for officers to attain property rights but that once the property came under the control of a man's family, it could be difficult for a woman to regain her claims to her land.

Another way that marriage allowed the officers to gain control of property was that they could inherit land from their fathers-in-law in the absence of a direct male heir. According to the Norrköping Resolution of 1604, unmarried women were not supposed to inherit property that their fathers had received as donations from the crown. When a man died without a male heir, the property was to revert back to the crown. If he had a married daughter and her husband was acceptable to the monarch, however, the daughter's husband could inherit the donation and then pass it on to his sons.[83] Usually, men who received donations tried to ensure that the property remained under the control of their families. As a result, it was quite common for sons-in-law to inherit property from their wives' families. The practice of sons-in-law inheriting land was not a passive custom whereby the son-in-law merely waited for his in-laws to die before he discovered if he would inherit the property. In many cases, the sons-in-law actively urged the crown to confirm upon them the donated property of their in-laws while the owners were still living on the property. An illustrative example of this practice was the attempt of one Scottish officer, Johan Lichton, to acquire the property of his father-in-law, another Scottish officer, Robert Guthrie.

In 1632, Lichton traveled to Germany to meet with Gustavus Adolphus, who was leading military campaigns there, to receive confirmation for the estate of Wesby Nygård located in Borgo parish in Finland. The crown had donated the estate to Lichton's father-in-law, Robert Guthrie, as a reward for Guthrie's forty years of service in the Swedish army. At the time of Lichton's request, Guthrie's widow still lived on the estate. The death of the king, in November 1632, prevented Lichton from meeting with him. In addition, during his journey in Germany all of Lichton's money and papers, including the deed to the property, were stolen. After this occurred, Lichton wrote to some members of the government explaining the situation and inquiring as to whether he could still expect to receive the estate. Lichton further backed up his case by stating that he had faithfully served in the Swedish army for fourteen years and that his entire inheritance had been spent trying to receive confirmation of Wesby Nygård.[84] It is unknown if Lichton received control of the estate, but his attempts to guarantee his ownership of the property show the effort officers would exert to ensure that they would inherit the land of their in-laws.

The practice of sons-in-law inheriting property also benefited foreign officers if they were able to marry into Swedish noble families because they might be able to inherit allodial land that would have more secure landownership rights than donated land. When the *reduktion* occurred in the 1680s and the 1690s, the only noble land that had secure tenure was property of which the nobles originally had complete ownership.[85] As a result, if an officer had married into a noble family that possessed their land outright, the crown could not repossess the property that the officer might inherit from his father-in-law.

Among members of the second generation of British officers, gaining access to more secure landholding was particularly important because most of them came of age in the second half of the seventeenth century, when the crown reduced the number of donations granted. Comparing the land donations in Uppland and Småland reveals that the majority of the British officers who received donations were members of the first generation. In Uppland, sixteen of the twenty-one officers who held donations were members of the first generation. In Småland, the number was similar; seventeen of the twenty-one officers who received donations were members of the first generation. In both provinces, the members of the second generation who acquired donations were mostly the sons of officers who had entered Swedish service in either the late 1500s or the first decade of the 1600s. This meant that they were born in the early 1600s and thus reached adulthood in the middle decades of the seventeenth century, when the crown granted most of the donations. During the second half of the seventeenth century, as the alienation of crown revenues to the nobility decreased, a more common way for sons to acquire property was through inheritance either from their parents or from their wives' families. According to Almquist, the majority of British officers who inherited land in Uppland and Småland were members of the second generation. In both counties, a total of sixteen officers inherited land, twelve of whom were members of the second generation.

Acquiring land through the practice of buying and trading property was also very common among the British officers. When the crown granted land donations, the recipients received property that was scattered over a large area. This careful dispersal was done to prevent nobles from gaining large, concentrated tracts of land that could be used as a base to threaten the power of the monarchy. To build up consolidated property, all landowners bought and traded land. Many individuals bought land from the crown or purchased family property that had reverted back to the crown with the death of the original owner.[86]

Within the British community, another means for officers to obtain larger tracts of land was to lend money to fellow officers and receive property as security on the loan. One of the most prominent financiers among the British officers was Robert Douglas. Throughout his career, he lent money to many British officers and often held their property in exchange. His most advantageous loan was one given to the Scottish officer, Lt. Gen. James King.[87] As reward for his service to the Swedish state, King had received 65.5 *mantal* of land in Småland, which had an annual rent of 1,439 *riksdaler*. In 1651, King mortgaged all of his property in Småland to Douglas for twenty years to borrow 8,000 *riksdaler*. Unfortunately for King's family, he died a few months later and the property passed to Douglas.[88]

Starting in the late sixteenth century, officers from the British Isles who immigrated to Sweden could receive land donations throughout the Swedish empire. Although all officers in the Swedish military received this benefit, the fact that British officers were recipients as well points to some interesting conclusions about the custom of royal land donations in Sweden. First, the ability of the British officers to acquire what were in some cases vast tracts of land shows that the crown was willing to alienate resources not only to its own noblemen but also to foreigners who had not been naturalized as Swedish noblemen. Their success also suggests that the crown often granted land to individuals as a reward for their military leadership and that receiving property was not always dependent upon social status or native birth. Second, the number of donations that British officers received in Uppland suggests that foreigners were eligible to receive land throughout the Swedish empire and that their land donations were not always located in peripheral areas.

Political Careers

Once they became established military officers in Sweden, many of the British military immigrants began to pursue political careers. Military officers from the British Isles who became members of the Swedish nobility had a right and a duty to participate in the meetings of the Swedish parliament (Riksdag). During the early modern period, the Riksdag consisted of four houses that represented the estates of the nobility, the clergy, the burghers, and the peasants. In addition, representatives of the military officers attended the Riksdag. Throughout the seventeenth century, because it became more common for military commanders to be ennobled, most officers attended parliament as members of the nobility. As a result, the military officers as a distinct group within the parliament gradually lost importance as the century progressed.[89] In view of this development, the discussion here focuses on the political activities of the officers from the British Isles as members of the House of the Nobility.

The House of the Nobility consisted of representatives from each of the noble families in Sweden and Finland. Members of the nobility from the Baltic provinces did not participate in these meetings. Instead, they served as representatives at the meetings of their own regional assemblies.[90] Not all members of the Swedish and Finnish nobility attended the parliamentary meetings in Stockholm, however. Instead, the head of each family served as a representative at the meetings, with this individual usually being the oldest member of the oldest branch of the family. Occasionally, if the normal representative could not attend, another member of the family or a person from outside of the family would be present as a proxy at the meetings.[91] Many of the officers from the British Isles attended the meetings of the Riksdag, took active roles in the debates of the House of the Nobility, and held important roles in the Swedish government. Investigating their political careers illuminates the roles that foreigners played in the Swedish government and the importance of foreigners to the government during this period.

In analyzing the position of foreigners in the Riksdag during the seventeenth century, some problems arise. The first concerns the sources available for tracing the participation of individuals in the meetings of the House of the Nobility. The main source for studying the meetings is the minutes from the House of the Nobility, which have been published for the meetings since 1627.[92] The earliest volumes, however, give only a list of the members in attendance and a brief account of the issues addressed. Few detailed records of the debates have been recorded. The scanty nature of the minutes can be attributed to the fact that the Riksdag was not organized or given a permanent structure until the first two decades of the seventeenth century. Gustavus Adolphus and the Council of the Realm established guidelines for the workings of the parliament in 1617 with the *riksdagsordning* and for the workings of the House of the Nobility in 1626 with the *riddarhusordning*.[93] The *riksdagsordning* set forth where the parliament should meet and how the estates should deliberate. The *riddarhusordning* created the office of *lantmarskalk*, or speaker, for the meetings of the nobility, and it divided the nobility into three classes based on social status, namely, the titled nobility, the members of the Council of the Realm and their families, and the untitled nobility.[94] The purpose of the class system was to organize the nobility based on their social status and to preserve the political power of the aristocracy against the lower nobility. Throughout the 1630s and 1640s, the procedures for running the meetings of the House of the Nobility were being organized, and as a result the minutes from these meetings provide few details of the debates. Accordingly, participation of individuals in the meetings is often unrecorded. For the period up to about 1660, the minutes allow one to track only the men who attended each meeting of the Riksdag and to obtain an overview of the issues debated. As the seventeenth century progressed, however, the minutes became more detailed and the participation of some individuals can be traced.[95]

Another problem with studying the participation of foreigners in the Riksdag is that foreigners usually appear in the minutes of the House of the Nobility only at the time of their ennoblement or if they had a particularly spectacular grievance with the government that the members of the nobility needed to discuss. This situation creates the impression that foreigners only occasionally participated in the debates of the parliament. Although it is often impossible to trace the involvement of individual nobles, it could be assumed that by attending the parliament meetings, the officers kept themselves apprised of issues facing the nobility and voiced their opinions on issues of importance to them and their families. One factor that might have decreased participation among the British officers in the debates of the House of the Nobility was the language barrier. During the seventeenth century, few members of the native Swedish nobility spoke English and probably none spoke Gaelic. In most cases, it is impossible to know the extent to which individual British officers learned to speak Swedish. Most of them, however, must have learned to speak some German, which was the lingua franca of the battlefield, and those who married Swedish women presumably developed a good command of the Swedish language. In addition, throughout the seventeenth century many men from other parts of Europe were introduced into the House of the Nobility and attended the meetings of the Riksdag. As a result, it appears that it was quite common for foreigners to address the assembly in their native language or a foreign language, such as German, that would have been understood by many of the others in attendance.[96]

A third issue is to establish a time frame for studying the political careers of the officers from the British Isles. This investigation concentrates on the minutes from the period 1620 to 1660. The search for British officers' participation ends in 1660 because this was the last year of large-scale military migration from the British Isles to Sweden. In addition, by 1660 many of the first-generation officers had died or were too elderly to attend meetings of the House of the Nobility. In the second half of the seventeenth century the foreign element at the meetings consisted of sons and grandsons of the original immigrants. Because of the rapid assimilation of the immigrants from the British Isles, this study investigates the political careers of the first generation, who truly represented potentially foreign views or opinions in the Swedish government.

Social status regulated an individual's attendance and participation in the meetings of the parliament. Most foreigners came to parliament as members of the nobility, and therefore, for most of them, access to political power began with the process of ennoblement. The Swedish crown ennobled thirty-five first-generation officers from the British Isles. Another thirty-four officers were ennobled in the second generation, and five were ennobled in the third generation. These seventy-four officers represented fifty-four families from the British Isles.[97] Ennoblement generally was awarded later in the careers of the officers once they had established themselves as successful military officers and had established a permanent connection to the Swedish realm either through landownership or marriage.

Once the crown had ennobled an individual, he was supposed to attend the meetings of the House of the Nobility or send a member of his family in his place. Attendance among the military officers from the British Isles reflected both the ebb and flow of ennoblement within the group and the involvement of the Swedish crown in overseas warfare. Looking first at the trends in ennoblement over the course of the seventeenth century, one can see that the largest number of officers from the British Isles were ennobled in the middle of the century. In comparison, the number of officers from the British Isles who attended the meetings of the House of the Nobility was very small at the beginning of the period but steadily increased throughout the middle decades of the seventeenth century as more officers were ennobled.

Another factor that regulated attendance was the scale of overseas warfare in which the Swedish crown was actively engaged. Because the newly ennobled foreign officers held high-ranking positions in the military, they would have been involved in military campaigns overseas and could not have participated in parliamentary meetings. According to the graph (figure 8), few officers were present at the parliament throughout the 1620s, 1630s, or 1640s. During these decades, the Swedish crown fought wars first in Poland and later in the Holy Roman Empire, which meant that officers from the British Isles were leading troops either in Germany or Poland as part of the Swedish war effort. Once peace was concluded in 1648, however, most of the ennobled officers returned to Sweden to begin to build lives in their new homeland. The peak in attendance during the 1650s probably can be attributed in part to the peaceful state of affairs during the first half of the decade that allowed military officers to remain at home and take an active interest in domestic matters. In addition, many of the officers who entered Swedish service during the Thirty Years' War were becoming elderly by the 1650s and 1660s and were reaching the end of their military careers. Having

FIGURE 7. ENNOBLEMENTS BY DECADE

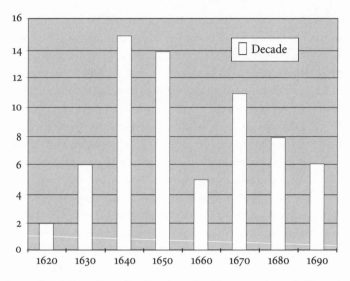

Source: Gustaf Elgenstierna, *Den introducerade adelns ättartavlor med tillägg och rättelser.*

left military service, they probably had more opportunity to fulfill their obligations as members of the House of the Nobility.

During the meetings, the House of the Nobility addressed royal resolutions and debated issues of concern to the noble estate. The minutes of the House of the Nobility reveal that issues of prime importance included land donations, performance of knight service, restrictions on noble privileges, and conscription of the nobility's tenants. One issue in particular stands out as being of great concern to the members of the nobility, namely, the ennoblement of foreigners and native-born commoners. Many debates in the House of the Nobility focused upon who could or could not be ennobled. For foreigners, naturally, the ennoblement process was of great importance because it brought not only political power but also access to royal land donations and higher social status. As a result, foreigners appear in the minutes of the House of the Nobility most often in connection with the issue of ennoblement, either when they were being ennobled or when they were supporting friends or family members who were going through the process. Investigating this issue helps to reveal the participation of foreigners in the debates of

FIGURE 8. PARLIAMENTARY ATTENDANCE BY DECADE

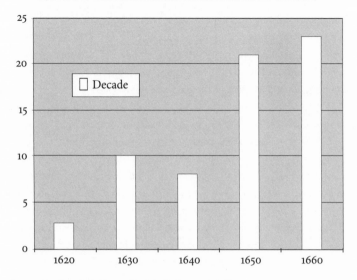

Source: Sveriges ridderskaps och adels riksdags-protokoll.

the parliament, illustrates the active role that foreigners played in promoting the ennoblement of their friends and family members, and displays some of the attitudes of the native nobility toward the massive ennoblement of foreigners during the middle decades of the seventeenth century.

In many cases, the process of ennoblement went very smoothly and deserving individuals became members of the nobility. In some cases, however, problems arose and ennoblement was either delayed or not granted. The cases where problems occurred illustrate the lengths to which people went to receive noble status, the factors that regulated who was ennobled, and the roles that foreigners played in the meetings of the House of the Nobility.

One problem that foreigners often encountered was the questioning of their noble heritage. For example, in 1630, Jakob Forbes, a Scottish colonel in the Swedish army, was naturalized and introduced into the House of the Nobility. According to the minutes of that body, there was no opposition to his ennoblement.[98] In the following years, however, some members of the nobility began to question Forbes's noble heritage and spread rumors that he was a commoner by birth and that he had bought his noble status. To stop the rumors, Forbes presented a letter at the meeting of the House of the Nobility on February 22, 1633, that attested to his noble birth.[99] The letter must have been enough proof to stop the rumors because the validity of his noble birth was not questioned again at a meeting of the House of the Nobility.

The recognition of Forbes's noble status in Sweden was further strengthened during a meeting of the Riksdag in 1638 when the House of the Nobility was debating the crown's desire to ennoble Mauritz Duwall. Duwall was born in Sweden, but he was the son of a Scottish mercenary, Albrekt Duwall. Both Albrekt and Mauritz Duwall had had long and distinguished careers in the Swedish army, but some members of the nobility had misgivings about the validity of the Duwalls' noble heritage. During the debate, the *lantmarskalk* asked Jakob Forbes if he would attest to the Duwalls' noble heritage. Forbes responded, "Yes, he did not know anything else than that they were a noble family in Scotland." With Forbes's testimony, the members of the House of the Nobility approved Mauritz Duwall's status as a Swedish nobleman and promised that he would be naturalized and introduced into the House of the Nobility at its next meeting.[100]

Undoubtedly, some foreigners made untrue claims regarding their noble heritage. To guard against bestowing the title of nobility upon foreigners of common status, the Swedish nobility debated foreigners' claims to noble heritage. Other foreigners who were already ennobled often took an active role in these debates as supporters of their friends and comrades from their homelands. As was seen in the case of Jakob Forbes, they often testified to the truth of their countrymen's heritage. As a result, foreigners often played an active role in encouraging the House of the Nobility to bring other foreigners into its membership.

Even if the noble status of a family had been proven, other factors could hamper the efforts of individuals to be ennobled. In particular, entering into a marriage with a commoner could either strip a nobleman of his status or prevent a noble foreigner from being granted the status of nobility within the Swedish realm.[101] In such cases, foreigners needed strong patrons within the Swedish nobility to help them receive recognition of the legitimacy of their marriages and of the worthiness of their children to inherit the family's noble status. Among the military immigrants from the British Isles, there was a particularly spectacular case involving a family that split apart over a marriage between a member of the family, which was newly ennobled, and a commoner. The case illustrates the potential problems a family could face during the ennoblement process, the necessity of having a strong patron who could support the goals of the family, and the ability of the Swedish nobility to exclude from its ranks individuals deemed to be unworthy of noble status.

The case concerned the Stuart family, who had immigrated to Sweden from Scotland during the 1560s. Hans Stuart entered Swedish service during the reign of Erik XIV (1560–68) as a *ryttmästare* in a Scottish cavalry unit. He remained in Swedish service and became general over all foreign soldiers in Swedish service in 1609. Stuart made a very profitable marriage by wedding Brita Eriksdotter Soop, a member of a prestigious Swedish noble family. From this marriage Stuart had two sons, Anders and David. Anders was born in Sweden in 1589 and became a chamberlain to Queen Christina the elder, mother of Gustavus Adolphus. David was also born in Sweden, in 1595, and served in the Swedish navy, where he rose to the rank of major. At some point he left the navy and also entered Queen Christina's service. The two brothers were ennobled and introduced into the House of the Nobility in 1625.[102] From 1625 until the 1650s, both brothers regularly attended the meetings of the Riksdag. In the 1650s, however, a crisis occurred in the family when Anders Stuart decided to marry a woman of nonnoble status with whom he had been having an affair. According to the document that David Stuart submitted to the House of the Nobility in 1652, Anders had been engaged in an affair with a married woman named Margareta Heideman, whom he had met while in the service of Queen Christina. At some point, the queen resided in Nyköping and Anders had been lodged with a goldsmith, Daniel Raf, and his wife, Margareta Heideman. The affair lasted many years, and Margareta had two children, Johan Anders and Brita, with Anders Stuart. In February 1652, shortly after Raf's death, Anders and Margareta were married. The scandal appeared even worse because Anders Stuart supposedly had been involved with another woman whom he had set aside in order to marry Heideman.[103] Anders Stuart sought permission from Queen Christina to marry Margareta and for his children to be legitimized and recognized as members of the nobility. On February 17, 1652, the queen granted Stuart's request and bestowed upon Johan Anders Stuart and Brita Stuart the rights and privileges of nobility.[104]

At the meeting of the House of the Nobility in November 1652, Hans Stuart, who was representing his father David, presented a memorial against his uncle, Anders Stuart. The document asked the House of the Nobility to seize Anders's property and to prevent Johan Anders from being recognized as a member of the nobility.[105] A discussion of the memorial ensued. During the debate, Hans stated that his cousin should not be considered a member of the nobility because of his illegitimate birth, and he asked that the House of the Nobility and the queen, now that they had been informed of the truth, help him to remove this stain of shame from his family. Johan Anders countered this argument by stating that the account presented in his legitimization letter was true. His father had been involved with his mother since 1627, and the couple had been secretly engaged for many years. Even though Johan Anders and his sister had been born before their parents' marriage, their parents had promised to marry each other as soon as the opportunity arose. Therefore, the children could be more easily recognized as legitimate after their parents' wedding took place.[106]

The matter ended on November 16, 1652, when a resolution was read, revealing that the queen and the House were displeased with the matter at hand and that if any wrongs had been committed, the guilty parties should be punished. Johan Anders and Brita Stuart's noble status was not stripped, however. Instead, the monarchs reconfirmed their status in 1655, 1662, and 1675.[107] Their status was reconfirmed on these occasions because the House of the Nobility was unwilling to introduce the younger Stuarts into its membership despite the crown's willingness to uphold their noble rank. In fact, the siblings never received acceptance by the House of the Nobility. In 1664, Johan Anders's matriculation into the assembly was denied, and the regency government of Charles XI demanded an explanation for this decision. The regents sent a message to the House of the Nobility stating that the mistakes of Stuart's father were known but that the scandal had been rectified when Anders Stuart received permission from Queen Christina to marry the children's mother. In addition, since the marriage had taken place according to religious prescriptions, the children were considered legitimate and thus had the right to inherit their father's noble status. The regents then asked if there was some other reason why Stuart had not been introduced, and they demanded a full account of why Stuart's recognition as a member of the nobility had been thwarted.[108] In 1667, Stuart tried once more to have his status as a member of the nobility (which had been granted by his legitimization letter) bestowed upon his wife and children. The request was not granted.[109]

Although many members of the nobility and of his family opposed Johan Anders Stuart's ennoblement, he could continue to fight for his recognition as a member of the Swedish nobility because of the support he received from the Swedish crown. As a member of the royal household, Anders Stuart had close connections with both Queen Christina and her mother. Although it is not stated explicitly in the sources surrounding the case, it may be assumed that his years of service to the royal family helped Anders Stuart gain in Queen Christina a strong patron whom he could depend upon later to support him in his quest for recognition of his children's legitimacy. Johan Anders Stuart also enjoyed close connections with the royal family. From 1657 until 1660, he served as the chamberlain of Charles X Gustavus. His loyal service to the king helped him maintain his family's ties to the monarchy and gave him a royal supporter who would help him in his fight with the House of the Nobility.

Once individuals had been ennobled and introduced into the House of the Nobility, another issue they faced was their status among the nobility. At the time of ennoblement, each family was assigned a number. Usually the numbers represented the order in which the families had been ennobled. Therefore, the older the family, the lower the number assigned to them. These numbers were then used to seat individuals during the parliamentary meetings. Members sat in numerical order, with the oldest families sitting at the front. This provided a very visible sign of the ranking and status of the noble families. The minutes of the House of the Nobility reveal, however, that not every individual or family was pleased with the position of rank given to newly introduced members of the estate. Occasionally arguments broke out regarding the ranking within the nobility. Investigating the discussions of where new nobles should sit during the meetings shows the fear that native noble families had about the ennoblement of foreigners.

At the 1649 meeting of the Riksdag, the issue of status within the nobility came to the forefront during the ennoblement of two military officers from Ireland and England, Hugo Hamilton and George Fleetwood. On January 27, 1649, the *lantmarskalk* stated that the queen commanded that both men be admitted into the House of the Nobility because of their merit and the extensive lands that they owned within the Swedish realm. Once their admittance had been approved, the *lantmarskalk* said that Hamilton and Fleetwood should take their seats behind Mauritz Duwall, who had been admitted into the House of the Nobility eleven years earlier and held the family number 241 within the third class.[110] This placement sparked a long debate among members of the third class. Over the years, some noble families had died out, thus leaving gaps in the numerical rankings of the families. Instead of moving existing nobles into these gaps, the monarchs often gave the noble number of families that had died out to newly ennobled families. Consequently, individuals recently introduced into the House of the Nobility sometimes were seated in front of men whose families had older claims to noble status within the Swedish realm. The debate focused upon the opinions of some members of the House that existing noble families should move into the vacant spaces and that new nobles should be seated behind all previously seated families.[111] The subsequent discussion of the issue thus illustrated the apprehension of many Swedish nobles that the dramatic increase in the ennoblement of foreigners was occurring at the expense of the influence and prestige of the existing noble families.

On January 29, 1649, George Fleetwood addressed the House of the Nobility. He stated that the queen had commanded the parliament to rank Hamilton and himself behind Duwall and asked those who opposed this decree to come forward and address the meeting. Two individuals arose and stated that they also had risked their lives and their blood for the fatherland and that they did not want to lose status in the future when their comrades came back from Germany. Because the practice of ennobling military officers as a means of compensation and as a reward for loyal service was becoming commonplace, these noblemen feared that many more individuals would be taken into the nobility as officers returned to Sweden at the end of the Thirty Years' War. Such a practice would inevitably lead to a continuing decline in the visible prestige of the existing members of the House of the Nobility. A vote was held on the matter, with twenty-two voting in favor of Hamilton and Fleetwood and seven voting against them. After the vote, a compromise solution was reached; Fleetwood and Hamilton would be seated between Forbes, who held number 249, and Lillieström, who held number 250.[112]

Although the debate surrounding the seating of new members of the House of the Nobility may not appear to be of great importance, the experience of Fleetwood and Hamilton illustrates the attitudes of many members of the nobility toward new nobles and the threat that they posed to the status of the original nobles.

Once foreigners were introduced into the House of the Nobility, they were supposed to attend the meetings on a regular basis and voice their opinions on the matters that concerned the assembly. Investigating the involvement of the officers from the British Isles in the meetings of the House of the Nobility helps to reveal the attitudes and concerns of this particular group of foreigners. In general, it appears that most of the officers from the British Isles shared the same concerns as other members of the Swedish nobility. From their participation in the parliament, these commanders seemed to identify themselves not as a separate foreign group with its own interests and agenda but instead as members of the Swedish nobility with whom they shared common interests. Many of the issues that were important to members of the native-born Swedish nobility, such as knight service, were also of great concern to the newly ennobled officers from the British Isles.

Knight service was an institution that had grown out of the medieval feudal system. In exchange for receiving a land donation from the crown, a nobleman was supposed to provide a specified number of armed knights for the regional cavalry. Throughout the seventeenth century, with the growth in the size of armies and the changes in battle tactics, knight service as an institution for recruiting cavalry disappeared throughout Europe.[113] In Sweden, however, the monarchs tried to maintain knight service as a form of taxation on the nobility. Throughout the first half of the seventeenth century, the nobility debated the extent of their privileges during parliamentary meetings, including their desire to be free from the burden of knight service. One means of showing their opposition to this practice was simply not to perform the service demanded or pay the taxes expected of them. To combat this trend, the government periodically released to the House of the Nobility lists of nobles who were delinquent in performing their knight service. Each of these lists contained names of officers from the British Isles who had received land donations from the Swedish crown. For example, at the parliamentary meeting in January 1647, the crown brought to the attention of the House of the Nobility that many of its members had not performed their knight service in 1644 or 1645. Among those listed as being delinquent in this duty were Mauritz Duwall, Tobias Duwall, Alexander Irving, and George Fleetwood. The list of those who contributed less than they should have included Hugo Hamilton, Herbert Gladsten, and William Spens.[114] Surprisingly, of the officers listed above only Mauritz Duwall and William Spens had been naturalized as Swedish noblemen and introduced into the House of the Nobility. The rest of the officers, except for Tobias Duwall, would be naturalized and introduced either at the meeting of the Riksdag in 1647 or in 1649.[115] Although they had not been naturalized as Swedish noblemen, as landholders in Sweden they were given the same rights as native-born, noble landholders and in return were expected to fulfill the same obligations as other members of the Swedish nobility.

The House of the Nobility discussed not only issues that were of importance primarily to the elite but also the most pressing political concerns of the day. In particular, the House of the Nobility debated resolutions concerning the adoption of the Form of Government in 1634, the adoption of the Addition to the Form of Government in 1660, and the *reduktion*. Apparently, few British officers contributed to these discussions. Because of the scanty nature of some of the minutes from the House of the Nobility, it is impossible to know if their participation was simply not recorded or if they never voiced their opinions on these issues. Their lack of participation in the larger political debates suggests, however, that the officers from the British Isles were assimilated into the political life of the kingdom only on a superficial level. Their attendance at the meetings of the House of the Nobility shows that they must have been aware of the important issues of the day, but their infrequent contributions to the political debates implies that most of them were concerned only with issues that affected them personally.

In comparison, their sons appear to have been more integrated into the political system. Throughout the rest of the century, the sons and descendants of ennobled officers continued to attend meetings of the House of the Nobility. In contrast to their fathers and grandfathers, the descendants of the immigrants took more leading roles in the parliament and the government. For example, Gustav Duwall, the grandson of the Scottish officer Albrekt Duwall who had immigrated to Sweden in the 1590s, served as the lantmarskalk of the House of the Nobility at the 1675 meeting of the parliament. This particular parliamentary session was significant, as Charles XI's coronation occurred in conjunction with the meeting.[116] Duwall's selection for this prestigious position illustrates his acceptance by his peers.

Throughout the 1670s and into the 1680s, Duwall continued to be active in the meetings of the House of the Nobility. Particularly during the debates at the 1680 meeting surrounding the *reduktion* and the establishment of absolutism, Duwall spoke out against the investigation of the regency government and the creation of a commission to carry through the *reduktion*.[117] As a member of the aristocracy whose family had served the crown for nearly one hundred years, Duwall potentially stood to lose the property his family had received as land donations throughout the century. Duwall's opposition to the crown's new policies was shared by another descendant of British immigrants, Anders Erik Ramsay.[118] As was the case with Duwall, Ramsay's family immigrated to Sweden in the 1570s when Anders Erik's grandfather, Hans Ramsay, enlisted in a Scottish regiment in Swedish service. Over the course of the century, the Ramsay family served as officers in the Swedish military, sat as members of the House of the Nobility, and received land donations as compensation for their service.[119] A *reduktion* would also affect the Ramsay family, as they stood to lose the property they had built up over the course of one hundred years.

Not all descendants of British officers opposed the creation of an absolute monarchy and the establishment of a *reduktion*. Robert Lichton, whose father Johan Lichton came to Sweden as a member of a Scottish regiment in the 1620s, apparently favored the new royal policies. In 1681, Charles XI appointed him president of the commission overseeing the *reduktion* in Livonia. Lichton's administration met with the king's favor, and his position was renewed in 1682. In contrast to Duwall and

Ramsay, Lichton's family did not have the same opportunities to build up landholdings, wealth, and prestigious government positions. Johan Lichton served in the Swedish army until he was killed at the Battle of Wittstock in 1636. Robert was born in 1631 and came of age in the 1650s and 1660s, when the opportunities for advancement in the military and gaining wealth through land donations were declining.[120] Consequently, Robert Lichton had much to gain from supporting the establishment of absolutism, as this system of rule served to break the power of the aristocracy and open government positions to members of the lower nobility.

The political activities of Duwall and Ramsay suggest that the sons and grandsons of the British officers actively participated in the debates of the parliamentary meetings and that they contributed to the discussions not only in regard to their own narrow interests but also in regard to the broader political concerns of the kingdom. Lichton's political activities suggest that toward the end of the seventeenth century the descendants of the British officers also moved beyond the confines the House of the Nobility and became active in the kingdom's other political institutions. These individuals' political careers suggest that members of the second and third generations of immigrant families were more integrated into the Swedish political system than the first generation. As in the case of their marriages, the sons of the British officers played more active roles in the political system probably because of greater familiarity with Swedish culture and Swedish language and greater social acceptance among the Swedish nobility and aristocracy.

Conclusion

When officers from the British Isles settled in Sweden, they gained many opportunities to advance to the highest social levels of the kingdom and to acquire great wealth and political influence within the Swedish realm. Investigating their marriage patterns, landholding practices, and involvement in the meetings of the House of the Nobility reveals the factors that regulated an individual officer's ability to take advantage of these opportunities. In regard to the first generation of immigrants, success in their military careers brought great wealth and status in the form of royal land donations, noble rank, and seats in the Riksdag. Despite their status, many of these immigrants seem to have been poorly assimilated into the social life of the kingdom. This failure to assimilate fully can be attributed to the royal policies regulating marriages between foreigners and native-born Swedes. In addition, the close-knit community that the immigrants formed may have prevented some of them from branching out beyond the circle of their friends, family members, and associates from the British Isles. In comparison, members of the second generation seem to have been more widely assimilated into Swedish society. More frequently the sons sought marriage partners beyond the British community, enjoyed more success in concluding marriages with members of the Swedish nobility, and played more active roles in the kingdom's political system. With their native birth, ability to speak Swedish, and recognized status as ennobled foreigners, the sons enjoyed more acceptance among the Swedish nobility. Unlike their fathers, however, the sons did not possess the same opportunities to build upon their position within the society. Because most of them came of age in an era of peace, the opportunities for social advancement and land acquisition that had existed earlier in the century began to dry up. This meant that while the sons enjoyed greater social status and greater social acceptance than their parents, the options available to them for increasing their wealth and status were declining.

5
MIGRANTS AND DIPLOMACY

During the early modern era the practice of modern diplomacy developed, with permanent embassies, professional diplomats, and diplomatic immunity. This mode of foreign relations evolved in the Italian states during the Renaissance, when the warring city-states of the Italian peninsula needed to strengthen communication among themselves. From southern Europe, these customs spread north and came to shape diplomatic practice throughout Europe by the sixteenth century.[1] Although the characteristics of modern diplomatic systems took shape during this era, a national diplomatic corps, which relied upon a monarch's native-born subjects to represent the ruler's interests, was slow to develop. Instead, rulers frequently sent foreigners abroad to represent their interests. Monarchs often used skilled foreigners as diplomats, relying in particular on military officers or bureaucrats who had been naturalized in their new homeland. As immigrants, these individuals probably possessed a wealth of international experience and had useful connections with the nobility and the courts of other European kingdoms. Throughout the seventeenth century, the Swedish monarchs engaged in the practice of using foreigners as diplomatic representatives. In most cases, they served as low-ranking diplomats and envoys, while the crown reserved for native-born nobles the most important ambassadorial missions.[2] Nonetheless, the importance of these foreigners to the development of Swedish foreign relations can be seen in the course of the kingdom's relations with the rulers of the British Isles.

Throughout the seventeenth century, both the Swedish and English monarchs used British officers in Swedish service as diplomatic representatives. For official appointments, the crown chose these individuals because of their knowledge of the respective societies and because of their connections with members of both governments. Below the level of official diplomacy some officers engaged in another range of semiof-

ficial activities. These individuals fell within the realm of spies and in-
formants whose diplomatic overtures were recognized only by their employers. The officers were also engaged in developing foreign relations
on a third level that can be classified as unofficial diplomacy. After set-
tling in Sweden, these officers maintained contact with their families
and friends in their homelands. As members of noble families, their
contacts in the British Isles often were individuals of some standing. In
sustaining these associations, they informally helped to develop diplomatic ties between the two regions by keeping nobles in the British Isles
apprised of Swedish political activities, having their families provide aid
to Swedish diplomats visiting the British Isles, and giving help to British
diplomats at the Swedish court. Moreover, throughout the seventeenth
century many of these officers decided to resign their commissions and
seek their fortunes in their countries of birth. Some were men who had
spent their entire careers in the Swedish military and, as they reached
old age, decided to retire in the British Isles. Others returned to their
homeland because of family obligations, new economic opportunities,
or changing political circumstances. Once they returned home, many
continued their friendships with members of the Swedish nobility or
their military comrades still in Sweden. Like their counterparts who remained in Sweden, these individuals helped to preserve Anglo-Swedish
diplomatic ties by keeping individuals in the Swedish government informed of English policies, helping to organize the further recruitment
of soldiers in the British Isles, and on occasion accompanying English
ambassadors to Sweden. Over time the connections that officers both
in Sweden and in the British Isles built up created an informal diplomatic network that allowed information to flow between the English
government and the Swedish crown. Investigating the official and informal diplomatic roles that these officers played provides insight into
the nature of diplomacy during the early modern period, the role of
migrants in building diplomatic ties, and the abilities of these military
officers to influence policies of both the English and Swedish crowns.

British Officers as Swedish Diplomats

The Swedish crown began to engage military officers from the British
Isles in official diplomatic functions in the late sixteenth century. The
earliest recorded account of such activities was the diplomatic mission

of Andrew Keith. Keith was a Scottish nobleman who entered Swedish service in 1563 and served as captain of a Scottish cavalry regiment fighting for the Swedish crown.[3] He had a very successful military career, which led to his appointment as commander of Vadstena Castle in 1574 and to receiving the title of baron, also in 1574, as reward for his loyal service. In 1573, he formed a close connection with the Swedish court when he married Elisabeth Birgersdotter Grip, a cousin of King John III.[4] Keith's diplomatic career began when the king appointed him as Sweden's ambassador to the court of Queen Elizabeth of England in 1583. The purpose of the mission was to negotiate a favorable trade agreement between England and Sweden that would abolish the tariffs charged on cloth exported from England.[5] Unfortunately, the sources do not reveal why the crown chose Keith for this assignment. He probably was an ideal candidate, however, because of his status as a Swedish baron, his close connections with the Swedish court, his ability to speak English, and his status as a member of a Scottish noble family who owed loyalty to the Scottish king, James VI, but not to the English queen, Elizabeth. Shortly after this mission, he temporarily left Swedish service and returned to Scotland. During this period, his diplomatic activities continued as he took part in the marriage negotiations between James VI of Scotland and Anne of Denmark. He maintained his connection with Sweden, however, and was appointed a court counselor to King Sigismund in 1587. His political career ended when he followed Sigismund into exile in Poland after Duke Charles took control of the Swedish regency in the 1590s.[6]

The practice of using military officers from the British Isles in diplomatic appointments to their homeland continued in the seventeenth century. Unlike the case of Andrew Keith however, the major focus of these men's assignments was developing military ties between the two regions.

The most prominent of all the British officers who served as diplomatic representatives of the Swedish crown was the Scottish nobleman James Spens. Spens's career was unusual because during the first three decades of the seventeenth century, he represented both the Swedish crown in England and the English crown in Sweden.[7] Although it is unknown when he entered Swedish service, he first came to the attention of Charles IX in 1605 when his brother David wrote to the king, saying,

"James should not be unwilling to be employed in our service and lead a troop of men to our use."[8] This letter was followed by a commission from Charles IX empowering James Spens to raise a unit of six hundred cavalry and one thousand infantry troops, whom he was to transport to Sweden and for whom he would serve as commander.[9] Problems arose during the recruiting process, however, and Spens never fulfilled this commission. The king renewed the contract in 1608, while Spens visited the Swedish court. Probably to encourage him to enlist the men, Charles IX named Spens general over all Scottish and English soldiers in Swedish service on condition that he recruit five hundred cavalry and one thousand infantry troops in the British Isles and transport them to Sweden by the following May. Unlike his earlier attempt at recruiting, this endeavor was successful.[10]

Spens's diplomatic career began in 1611, when Charles IX sent him to the court of James I of England. His purpose was to ask James I for permission to recruit three thousand soldiers, to inform the king about British soldiers who had deserted the Swedish crown while fighting in Russia, to ask that James punish these men if they returned to their homeland, and to open discussions about developing markets in Sweden for British merchants.[11] While Spens was in England, James I asked him to mediate an end to the Kalmar War, which had broken out between the kingdoms of Gustavus Adolphus of Sweden and Christian IV of Denmark in 1611. Although this attempt to reestablish peace between the northern powers was unsuccessful, Gustavus Adolphus chose Spens to serve as one of the Swedish negotiators at the Peace of Knäred in 1613, which ended the war. Interestingly, Spens's half brother, Robert Anstruther, served as one of the Danish negotiators at the same peace conference.[12]

In 1613, Spens became the resident Swedish ambassador in the British Isles. He remained in London, overseeing the further recruitment of soldiers for the Swedish crown, until 1621, when he returned to Sweden as a representative of the English crown. While in Sweden, his purpose was to encourage Gustavus Adolphus to form an alliance with other Protestant princes to guard against the growing might of Ferdinand II, the Holy Roman Emperor, as a result of his recent victories in the Thirty Years' War.[13] In 1623, Spens again crossed the North Sea, this time as a Swedish representative to the English court to ask that James I forbid the recruitment of mercenaries in the British Isles for Polish service. Gustavus Adolphus feared that these soldiers would be used against the Swedish army in its current war against Poland.[14] After giving Spens assurances that he would not allow the Polish crown to recruit in the British Isles, James I sent Spens back to Sweden to continue pressuring Gustavus Adolphus to join a Protestant coalition against Emperor Ferdinand. In 1624, Spens returned to the British Isles with the Swedish king's military requirements for entering the Protestant alliance. This alliance never came to pass, however, because the English crown concluded an agreement with Christian IV of Denmark regarding Danish leadership of a Protestant coalition.[15] From 1624 until 1627, Spens remained in the British Isles organizing the recruitment of soldiers for Swedish service. In 1627, he traveled to the European continent with the designation "ambassador extraordinary to the King of Sweden" with the purpose of presenting the Order of the Garter to Gustavus Adolphus. Spens returned to England in 1629 to oversee the recruitment of forces to aid the Swedish crown in its entrance into the Thirty Years' War. His career ended with his death during a visit to Stockholm in 1632. Tradition has it that news of Gustavus Adolphus's death on the battlefield came as such a shock to Spens that he died a short time later.[16]

After Spens's death in 1632, the positions of Swedish ambassadors to the English court were usually filled by native-born Swedish noblemen. Only in the 1650s, when George Fleetwood became a Swedish ambassador in England, was this position again held by a military officer from the British Isles in Swedish service. However, Fleetwood enjoyed neither the longevity in office nor the influence that Spens had during his tenure. The difference between Fleetwood's and Spens's status and influence within the Swedish diplomatic corps can be attributed to the Swedish crown's increasing use of native-born nobles to fill the most important ambassadorial positions. As the seventeenth century progressed, Swedish rulers gradually abandoned the practice of using foreigners as ambassadors to the courts of their homeland. This nationalization of the Swedish diplomatic corps reflected the growing internationalization of the Swedish elite during the seventeenth century.

Until the seventeenth century, Sweden was a relatively isolated kingdom. At the beginning of the century, Sweden had few cities, a poorly developed economy, and few international trade connections. When

Gustavus Adolphus began to encourage the settlement of foreign merchants, architects, and entrepreneurs in the kingdom, the economy began to develop and have a more international focus.[17] Internationalization also came through warfare. Swedish involvement in foreign conflicts, in particular the Thirty Years' War, exposed both the nobility and commoners who served in the army to other cultures and other ways of life. When they returned home, the officers in particular brought back with them a taste for the more luxurious living of western Europe. Their exposure to wider European culture and their new wealth through booty and land donations allowed them to adopt the latest fashions in manners, clothing, music, architecture, and art that western Europe had to offer. The war veterans have thus been credited with establishing a new culture in Sweden during the mid–seventeenth century.[18]

A wider sense of the world also came through improvements in Swedish education during the seventeenth century. Before the 1620s, rigorous higher education in Sweden was difficult to find. The kingdom's only university was located in Uppsala, but before Gustavus Adolphus reformed the university in 1620, it did not have a sufficiently stable income to ensure quality education for its students. As a result, most men seeking training in fields requiring advanced learning traveled overseas for their education.[19] With the expansion of the Swedish state during the seventeenth century, the need for trained bureaucrats increased, and in part to meet this demand the crown founded new universities in Turku, Tartu, Greifswald, and Lund. To address the needs of the students, the Swedish rulers encouraged the universities to employ foreign scholars and to emphasize more practical subjects such as rhetoric, languages, and science.[20] These changes led to an increased awareness among the Swedish elite of the academic issues being debated across Europe.

Finally, the great influx of foreigners into the kingdom during this period challenged the mental horizons of the Swedish elite. Working together with foreign officers in the army, making economic contacts with other areas of Europe through foreign merchants, and serving in the Riksdag with newly ennobled foreigners must have increased the Swedish nobility's awareness of the outside world. Given these new international opportunities, the Swedish elite of the mid–seventeenth century were more worldly and perhaps better equipped to represent their crown overseas than their earlier counterparts.

The changing diplomatic roles of the British officers during the seventeenth century can be seen particularly in the Swedish embassy to England in 1655, which included George Fleetwood, who after James Spens had the second most significant Swedish diplomatic career in the British Isles of all the British officers. In 1655, a diplomatic mission was sent to England with a twofold purpose. First, the diplomats were to inform the Lord Protector, Oliver Cromwell, of the coronation of the new Swedish king, Charles X Gustavus. Second, they were to conclude an alliance with the English Commonwealth to gain military aid and an ally against the growing economic influence of the Dutch in the Baltic region.[21] The Swedish crown sent three men to represent its interests.

Christer Bonde served as the principal representative, holding the rank of ambassador. The crown chose him for this position because of his high aristocratic birth and his acquaintance with England after having studied at the University of Oxford. With Bonde's ability to speak English and his status as a member of the most powerful and wealthy social group within the kingdom, Charles X Gustavus believed that Bonde would make the most suitable impression upon Cromwell.[22]

Second in rank on the embassy and holding the title of diplomat was Peter Julius Coyet. Coyet was also a member of the Swedish nobility, but his family did not have the ancient lineage of Bonde's family and he did not possess the strong connections with England that Bonde had. Being the first member of the embassy to arrive in the British Isles, he was to present Charles X Gustavus's plans to Cromwell and to pave the way for Bonde, who would oversee the formal negotiations.[23]

The third individual was George Fleetwood, whose purpose was to establish contact with Oliver Cromwell and encourage the Lord Protector to conclude an alliance with the Swedish crown. Rather than holding the status of an official diplomat, Fleetwood was ordered by the king to travel to England under the guise of a pleasure trip. While in England, he was to act as a concerned native-born Englishman and use his connections at the English court (in particular his brother Charles, who was Cromwell's son-in-law and lord deputy in Ireland) to establish contact with the Protector. In addition to the mandate to pursue an alliance, Charles X Gustavus also gave Fleetwood the assignment of encouraging the Protector to approve recruitment of Scottish soldiers for the Swedish army.[24] The crown chose Fleetwood for this secret diplomatic position based on his family's connections with Cromwell and his loyal service to the Swedish crown as both army officer and diplomat. Fleetwood had entered Swedish service in 1629 and worked his way successfully through the ranks, achieving the position of major general in 1653. In addition to his military career, Fleetwood had previously handled some diplomatic activities for the Swedish crown. In 1636, he traveled to the court of Charles I to request permission to enlist six regiments of infantry in the British Isles to help the Swedish army continue its involvement in the Thirty Years' War.[25] His success in this endeavor had helped him to gain favor with the Swedish rulers.

Fleetwood's status on the embassy is a particularly good reflection of changing attitudes about using foreigners in diplomatic positions. In contrast to the early seventeenth century, when James Spens directed diplomatic affairs between the British Isles and Sweden, Fleetwood did not hold the highest ranking position on the 1655 embassy. Instead, the king chose a Swedish aristocrat to oversee the alliance negotiations, while Fleetwood held the unofficial position of concerned subject. In 1656, the crown recalled Coyet and Bonde to Sweden, and Fleetwood received an official commission as ambassador.[26] This position legitimized the work he was already engaged in, that of recruiting soldiers for the Swedish army. In comparison to James Spens, Fleetwood fulfilled a more circumscribed role as a Swedish ambassador in England. His primary duties continued to be the same as they were when he held an unofficial position, namely recruitment and establishing connections with Cromwell. In 1660, with the end of the war in the Baltic and the restoration of the Stuart monarchy in the British Isles, the Swedish regency recalled Fleetwood to Sweden because his specialized qualifications no longer fit the prevailing circumstances.[27]

Other individuals from the British Isles also engaged in diplomatic activities for the Swedish crown in the British Isles, but they did not hold the rank or status that Spens and Fleetwood did. For example, the regency government of Queen Christina sent Patrick Ruthven, a Scottish officer in Swedish service, to the court of Charles I in 1636 to get the English crown's help in supplying the Swedish army for its ongoing efforts in the Thirty Years' War. In reply, the king supplied Ruthven with a copy of a treaty recently concluded between the English and French kings to invite the Swedish crown as well as the Estates General of the United Provinces of the Netherlands to form a confederacy of states to fight against the Habsburgs. Charles I also informed Ruthven that he would allow the continued recruitment of soldiers in the British Isles for the Swedish military.[28] In this capacity, Ruthven fulfilled an important role as messenger between the kingdoms, but he did not play a role in the negotiations.

From 1580 until 1660, Swedish rulers engaged military officers from the British Isles already in their employment to be diplomatic representatives to the monarchs in England. In the early part of this period, the officers held the highest ranking position of ambassador and were involved in negotiating and directing foreign policy between the kingdoms. After James Spens's death in 1632, the Swedish crown increasingly relied upon native-born aristocrats to fill the most important positions and used the British officers in more minor roles as messengers and recruiters. Despite the decreasing status of the officers in this area, their diplomatic activities remained important. Their connections with family and friends among the nobility of the British Isles and their familiarity with the language and culture of the British Isles allowed them access to members of the English court and helped pave the way for the Swedish aristocrats who oversaw the kingdom's foreign relations.

British Officers as English Diplomats

In 1638, the Scottish Privy Council voted to establish a domestic standing army to defend Scotland against the possibility of an English invasion. In order to obtain professional officers to lead this army, a call went out for all Scottish officers serving in continental armies to return to their homeland.[29] As a result of this mandate, many Scottish officers left Swedish service to fight in the new army.[30] The end of the 1630s and the beginning of the 1640s marked the most dramatic period of return migration to the British Isles among mercenaries in Swedish service. This was not the only time when such a phenomenon occurred, however. Throughout the seventeenth century, many officers from the British Isles decided to resign their commissions in the Swedish military and seek their fortunes in their places of birth. Once they arrived home, many officers did not forget their time in Sweden and tried to maintain contact with members of the Swedish government or their comrades still in Sweden. These connections proved to hold diplomatic value, linking these individuals to members of the Swedish court and in some cases to the monarchs. With their knowledge of Swedish society, their reputations as loyal military leaders, and their personal familiarity with members of the Swedish nobility, the rulers in the British Isles viewed the officers as useful men to send on diplomatic missions to Sweden.

Former Swedish officers most frequently served as diplomatic representatives during the Civil Wars of the 1640s, when both the English Parliament and the Stuarts sent men who had formerly served in the Swedish military to Sweden to gain support for their causes. Patrick Ruthven, James King, William Bellenden, and Alexander Forbes all traveled to the court of Queen Christina to gain support for the Stuarts. Christopher Potley, who semiofficially represented Parliament, worked to thwart their efforts. Investigating the diplomatic activities of these men reveals the potential political influence that former officers held in the Swedish realm and illustrates the importance of foreign officers in developing diplomatic ties between the kingdoms.

On March 4, 1646, Charles, the Prince of Wales, fled England to take refuge in the Scilly Isles. This incident marked a change in Stuart politics. With the escape of the Prince of Wales, the new court that had sprung up around him became an alternative focal point for the royalist cause throughout the last years of the Civil Wars in the British Isles. As the position of Charles I declined in England, the court of the Prince of Wales became the diplomatic focus of Stuart politics. In 1649, the prince launched a number of foreign missions to gain aid from various European monarchs to strengthen his ability to reclaim his father's thrones. In most cases, the rulers expressed outrage at the execution of Charles I but were unwilling to aid his son's attempts to reclaim the crowns of England and Scotland. One of the kingdoms where the Prince of Wales's diplomats were successful in obtaining military aid was Sweden.[31] Although Queen Christina of Sweden publicly maintained a policy of nonintervention in Stuart plots, she secretly allowed weapons to be exported to the Stuarts and permitted a royalist invasion of Scotland to be launched from Gothenburg. The queen's support of the Stuart cause was based upon two factors. First, the Stuarts' practice of allowing extensive recruitment for the Swedish army during the first three decades of the seventeenth century had created a congenial diplomatic relationship between the two crowns. Based on this relationship, the queen and the Council of the Realm wished to provide help to the Stuarts in their time of need. Second, Charles II's diplomats, many of whom had formerly served in the Swedish army, were able to use their connections at the Swedish court and their own resources in Sweden to organize the aid provided.

Diplomatic contact between the Stuarts in exile and the Swedish crown began in January 1649 when the Prince of Wales sent Patrick Ruthven to Sweden. Ruthven was a good choice for this position because he was well known in Sweden, having served in the Swedish army for twenty-five years before retiring in 1637 at the rank of major general.[32] After leaving Swedish service, Ruthven returned to Scotland, where he became involved with the royalist forces fighting for Charles I. In March 1642, Ruthven traveled to Germany and returned in the fall of the same year with a number of officers for the king's service. In October 1642, he joined Charles I and took part in the Battle of Edgehill, after which he was appointed general-in-chief of the royalist army. He held this position until 1644, when he was gravely injured at the Battle of Newbury. Since Ruthven could no longer lead troops, the king's nephew, Prince Rupert, took over command of the royal army. After leaving active military service in 1644, Ruthven became chamberlain to the Prince of Wales, and in 1646 he accompanied the prince to the Stuart court in exile in France.[33]

Because Ruthven was known at the Swedish court and had proven his loyalty to the Stuart cause, Charles I sent him to obtain help from Queen Christina. Ruthven's instructions stated that he was to acquaint the queen with Parliament's imprisonment of the king and to urge her to use her authority to save the life of Charles I. He was also to ask Christina for military assistance in the form of men, horses, arms, and gunpowder and for humanitarian assistance in the form of grain to be sent to Ireland to relieve the famine there.[34] The execution of Charles I on January 30, 1649, however, made these instructions obsolete. On February 25, Ruthven received a letter to present to Queen Christina from the king-in-exile, Charles II. In it, the king discussed his father's execution, hoping to enrage the queen at the injustice of the regicide.

He also hoped that news of the execution would encourage the Swedish queen to provide aid to the Stuarts for an invasion of Scotland.[35]

After having received Ruthven and read Charles II's letters, the queen and the Council of the Realm debated about what aid should be sent to help the Stuart cause. Members of the council agreed that something should be done to help Charles II because Scotland and Sweden had always had such good relations. Ties between the two kingdoms had been particularly strong in the last two decades, with so many soldiers from Scotland fighting for Sweden during the Thirty Years' War. The council could not decide how to proceed, however, fearing that the English Parliament would view aid given to Charles II as a statement of support for the Stuarts.[36] Despite her cordial relations with the Stuarts, Queen Christina could not afford to alienate the English Commonwealth, because in 1649 the Danes and the Dutch were negotiating an alliance. Once they concluded the alliance, the Danes, who controlled both sides of the Sound, would be in a stronger position to threaten Swedish trade in the Baltic.[37] As a result, Queen Christina needed the might of the English navy to counterbalance the naval power of the Danes and the growing influence of the Dutch in the Baltic.[38]

A month later, at the end of March 1649, the council resolved to supply Charles II with arms and ammunition. The weapons would be sent to a Scottish merchant in Gothenburg, Johan Macklier, who would then distribute them to the king's military commanders. Council members hoped that this plan would allow the Swedish crown to help Charles II without raising the suspicions of the English Commonwealth.[39] The Council of the Realm and the queen decided to send a sizable amount of material to Macklier, including six thousand muskets, five thousand pikes, three thousand bandoliers, four thousand swords, fifty drums, eighteen hundred pistols, six hundred cavalry swords, and two thousand sets of cavalry armor.[40] The weapons had been originally intended for the use of the Marquis of Ormonde in support of his campaigns in Ireland. After the Marquis of Montrose received a commission to establish an invasion force for Scotland, Ruthven informed Macklier that the arms should be split evenly between Ormonde and Montrose.[41]

In June 1649, Ruthven returned to the Stuart court, which had moved to The Hague. There he met with Montrose to discuss the recruitment of men for Montrose's invasion of Scotland and the distribution of the arms that Ruthven had organized in Sweden.[42] Although Ruthven remained in charge of Swedish affairs, James King now became more directly involved in the recruitment of Montrose's forces.

King was a Scot from the Orkney Islands who had served in the Swedish army for twenty-four years, achieving the rank of lieutenant general. In 1639, he decided to leave Swedish service after receiving the terrible news that his wife, two children, grandmother, and father-in-law had died during the summer. He wanted to return to Scotland to arrange for their burials.[43] After attending to his family affairs, King became embroiled in the politics leading up to the Civil Wars in the British Isles. He remained in his homeland, where he became one of the commanding officers in the royalist army. In 1640, Charles I sent King to Denmark to raise two regiments of cavalry for the royal army. Although Christian IV of Denmark was interested in the scheme, nothing came of it because Charles I had neither the money to recruit the troops nor the ships to transport them.[44] In 1641, King, frustrated with Charles I's unfulfilled promises to pay his pension, left royal service and retired to Stockholm. Charles I urged him to rejoin the royal cause with a pledge of regular payment of his pension. With these assurances, King returned to active service in 1643, and in that year he was present at the siege of Leeds. King continued to serve Charles I during his campaigns through the Battle of Marston Moor, when he was in command of the center of the royal army. He then resigned his military commission after a disagreement with Prince Rupert over the leadership of the army. He traveled to Germany and then to Sweden, where he retired.[45]

In November 1649, Montrose arrived in Gothenburg to begin mustering his forces for the invasion of Scotland. During his journey from the Low Countries where he had been meeting with Charles II, Montrose had stopped in Hamburg and Denmark, where he received permission to recruit soldiers. While in Hamburg, he also met with James King, whom he later chose to be his lieutenant general. King was supposed to recruit another invasion force that would follow Montrose's army after it had established a base in the Orkney Islands.[46] Although an attempt was made to recruit the additional forces, nothing came of the project, probably due to King's lack of financial resources. After King had retired in Sweden, Queen Christina granted him vast land donations in Småland, which he mortgaged to Robert Douglas for a loan of 8000 riksdaler.[47]

Throughout 1649 and 1650, King also acted as Charles II's representative at the Swedish court. His purpose was to link Queen Christina and the Council of the Realm more directly to the Stuart cause. He tried to accomplish this goal by negotiating to bring Charles II to Sweden.[48] King hoped that having Charles II in Sweden would ensure the successful launch of Montrose's invasion. The possibility of a marriage between Charles II and Christina was also discussed as a means of drawing the two royal families closer together. Charles II never came to Sweden, however, and nothing came of the proposed match between the two monarchs.[49]

In the meantime, Montrose's preparation for the invasion of Scotland proceeded. While in Gothenburg, Montrose stayed with Johan Macklier, who arranged for the purchase of more weapons and stored the equipment for Montrose's forces in his warehouses. Although Montrose officially held the status of diplomat, he did not try to establish contact with Queen Christina and he conducted his business with the greatest secrecy. Because Christina was not in a position to support Charles II openly, Montrose was willing to gather his forces discreetly in Gothenburg and then leave. In return, Christina turned a blind eye to the royalist activities in Gothenburg and instructed her officials to follow the same practice.[50]

According to the plan for the invasion, the Earl of Kinnoul would lead an advance force of about two hundred men who would capture the Orkney Islands. They would establish a base there for the main contingent of troops that would arrive later under the command of Montrose. In the meantime, Kinnoul planned to expand the number of troops involved in the main assault on Scotland by recruiting and training the islanders.[51] Montrose would then follow with the majority of the army, with James King later bringing reinforcements.

In the autumn of 1649, Kinnoul successfully invaded Orkney and recruited five hundred men for Montrose. Shortly after concluding the invasion Kinnoul died of an illness, and his troops were left leaderless. While this invasion took place, Montrose tried to establish his own invasion force, but the recruitment did not proceed as smoothly or as quickly as he wanted. The aid that various European leaders had promised to Montrose fell short of his expectations. In addition, Montrose lacked sufficient funds to transport to Gothenburg the mercenaries recruited in Germany. Montrose also lost time waiting for James King to bring the troops he had promised but who never arrived. In December 1649, some of the troops sailed to the Orkneys. Montrose was unable to leave Sweden until March 1650, however, because he was waiting for additional troops and instructions from Charles II.[52] In the spring of 1650, Montrose landed in the Orkneys and invaded the Scottish mainland but was defeated at the Battle of Carbisdale on May 7, 1650. Although he escaped from the battlefield, he was caught and executed on May 21, 1650.[53]

Throughout 1649 and 1650, a third individual, William Bellenden, also became involved in keeping both the Stuarts and Queen Christina informed of each other's actions. Bellenden was a Scot who had entered Swedish military service during the Thirty Years' War and served as the colonel of an enlisted regiment.[54] Sometime during the early 1640s he returned to the British Isles to take part in the Civil Wars on the royalist side. His diplomatic career began in the late 1640s, when Charles I sent him to Stockholm as his unofficial representative. While Patrick Ruthven negotiated military aid for the Stuarts, Bellenden helped him finance and collect the equipment. Bellenden remained in Sweden until September 1649, when Queen Christina sent him to the Stuart court in exile to act as her representative.[55]

Throughout this period, Christina and the Council of the Realm maintained the official appearance of neutrality toward the Stuarts. Although they were supplying the Stuarts with military equipment, allowing an invasion of Scotland to be launched from Swedish shores and sending diplomatic representatives to the court of Charles II, the queen and council believed it was in the best interests of the kingdom to preserve the outward appearance of impartiality and to encourage Charles II to come to terms with the Scottish commissioners sent to Breda to negotiate a settlement with him.[56] Despite their efforts to preserve the secrecy of their actions, the royalist movement in Sweden was known to the English Parliament partly because of the efforts of another former Swedish officer, Christopher Potley. Potley was an Englishman who had enlisted in the Swedish army in 1612 and had risen to the rank of colonel. Sometime in the late 1630s or early 1640s, he returned to England and fought for Parliament in the first Civil War.[57] Potley's attachment to Sweden did not end during this period, however. In the 1640s he returned to Sweden, where in 1647 he entered Swedish diplomatic service as an envoy to England. Upon his arrival in England, he assumed the post of envoy held by another former officer in Swedish service, Hugh Monat. Throughout 1647 and 1648, Potley wrote to Anders Gyldenklou, secretary of the Council of the Realm during Christina's reign, regarding political affairs in England.[58] In 1649, after the execution of Charles I, the English Council of State sent Potley to Sweden to gather intelligence on the Swedish crown's attitude toward Parliament and the Stuart cause. While in Stockholm, Potley met with Queen Christina, who questioned him about Parliament's attitude toward her. According to Potley's account of the meeting, he informed Christina that Parliament knew of the arms she had supplied to Charles II's forces and that he had heard some members of Parliament state that "your Ma.tie was a wise and virtuous Princesse, And they did hope you would not looke into their affaires in England no more, then they did looke into the affaries of Sweden."[59] In this same account, Christina charged Potley with being a representative of Parliament, which he denied, probably to preserve his ability to spy on the affairs of the court. Potley remained in Sweden until 1651. During his stay, his reports included lists of suspected royalists at the Swedish court and an account of the Marquis of Montrose's attempts to launch an invasion of Scotland from Gothenburg.[60]

After Montrose's defeat in 1650, the Swedish crown continued to allow individuals within its realm to raise support for the Stuart cause. These attempts were far less successful than those under the direction of Patrick Ruthven and James King, however, because they lacked the direct support of the Stuart court. Instead, they were organized by a private individual, Alexander, Lord of Forbes, who engaged in personal diplomacy to aid the exiled king.

Alexander, Lord of Forbes, was a Scottish nobleman who led the Forbes clan. He entered Swedish service in 1630 as the commander of a regiment he had recruited in the Scottish Highlands. He remained in Swedish service for five years until his regiment was decimated at the Battle of Nördlingen in 1634.[61] In 1636, he received a diplomatic commission from Charles I to travel to Denmark and Sweden to develop better trade contacts with these kingdoms. Forbes did not take an active role in the Civil Wars of the 1640s, although he turned out to be a strong supporter of Charles I. In 1641, he commanded troops involved in suppressing the rebellion in Ireland. The campaign drained Forbes's personal finances, however, and he spent much of 1643 in Scotland trying to recover his lost funds. Between 1644 and 1645, he traveled on the continent, first in Holland and later in Sweden. In 1646, he returned to the British Isles, where he was imprisoned until 1648 for unpaid debts incurred as a result of the Irish campaigns. Forbes left England permanently in 1649 because the execution of Charles I greatly upset him.[62]

Forbes then settled in Sweden and took over the role of pressing the Swedish queen to support the Scottish king. His attempts to encourage Queen Christina to extend aid to the Stuart cause had already begun in 1645 during his visit to the Swedish court. During these early meetings with the queen and the chancellor, Axel Oxenstierna, Forbes tried to persuade Christina to send Oxenstierna to England to serve as a mediator between Charles I and Parliament. The queen and the Council of the Realm did not give serious consideration to this request because Forbes lacked a commission from Charles I to make such a demand. Forbes tried to justify his actions by stating that it was his duty as a subject to do all that was possible to preserve the welfare of his king.[63]

In 1649, Forbes returned to Sweden and again began to press the queen to support the Stuart cause. As a result of these requests, Christina gave Forbes a commission in 1652 to raise all of the sunken ships in Swedish waters. Forbes planned to take the cannons off the vessels to supply Charles II with guns for his artillery and his navy.[64] Interestingly, one of the ships that Forbes planned to raise was the *Vasa*. Built as part of Gustavus Adolphus's expansion of the royal navy in the 1620s, the *Vasa* was one of the largest warships of its day. The king had planned for the ship to be the showpiece of the reformed navy to illustrate the power and might of the Swedish crown. The ship was poorly designed, however, and sank in Stockholm harbor on its maiden voyage in 1628.[65] The queen probably was happy to have someone raise the ship because its mast, which was visible from Stockholm castle as it protruded from the water, was a constant embarrassment for the Swedish crown. The project, however, was never carried out. In 1654 Queen Christina abdicated, and her cousin, Charles X Gustavus, took over the Swedish throne. With the accession of the new king, the crown lost interest in the project and Forbes's pension from his previous military service, which had financed the project, was cut off. In addition, Forbes became very ill and began to suffer from deafness, which hampered his efforts to carry out the commission.[66]

In the early 1650s, Forbes and his brother William, who was a colonel in Swedish service, also received permission from Queen Christina to try to raise money among Scottish merchants and soldiers in Sweden to purchase arms for Charles II. At the same time, the queen gave the brothers permission to recruit Scottish soldiers in Swedish service to fight for Charles II. They succeeded in raising some money and soldiers for the cause, but once Cromwell soundly defeated the Scottish army at Worcester in 1651, support for and interest in launching another invasion force from Sweden evaporated.[67]

The royalist activities in Sweden ground to a halt in 1654 with the abdication of Queen Christina. Whereas the queen had been interested in providing secret help to the Stuarts, the new king, Charles X Gustavus, was more concerned about receiving aid from the English Commonwealth to thwart the growing economic influence of the Dutch in the Baltic region. As a result, all official support for royalist activities in Sweden dried up. The career of William Bellenden, who had returned to Sweden during the 1650s as Charles II's resident ambassador in Stockholm, in particular reflects these changes. During the last years of Queen Christina's reign, Bellenden had enjoyed great favor with the queen. In order to provide financial support for the ambassador, Christina gave Bellenden land donations in the Älvsborg county area and allowed him to hold the positions of "furst Lun:t of hir Gaird and as Gentilman of the Chamber."[68] After her abdication in 1654, however, he lost these positions. In a letter to Charles II's secretary, Edward Nicholas, Bellenden described Charles X Gustavus's attitude toward Charles II in the following manner: "I can assure he wantis no intentionall kindnes for him [Charles II] and his interests."[69]

Ruthven, King, Bellenden, and Forbes illustrate the potential influence that former military officers of the Swedish crown could have in terms of swaying Swedish foreign policy. All of them successfully persuaded Queen Christina to help Charles II reclaim his crown. Ruthven and King probably had the most success in achieving their goals because they enjoyed the status of official diplomats and their schemes enjoyed the support of Charles II. In contrast, Forbes's attempts were perhaps hampered because he came to Sweden as a concerned subject without an official position. In addition, his projects coincided with Cromwell's victory over the Scots in the 1650s, which ended any hope of a Stuart government in Scotland.

In contrast, Christopher Potley's activities in Sweden reveal the means by which the loyalty and trust that the Swedish rulers placed upon certain foreign officers could be used against them. Because Potley had faithfully served in the army and had served as an informant for the Swedish crown in England, Christina had no reason to believe that he would betray the secrets of the crown. It was because of this trust, however, and because of Potley's close connections with members of the court that he was able to live in Sweden and successfully spy upon the activities of the royalists.

Potley was not the only individual to use his military connections in Sweden to establish himself as an informant for a foreign government. Another individual who engaged in such activities was James Jefferyes, who used his father's and his brother's status as army officers to set himself up as an unofficial diplomat who could report back to the English monarch regarding Swedish royal actions. Jefferyes's case is particularly important because it illustrates not only the circumstances enabling individuals to become spies but also the possible consequences of these activities.

James Jefferyes emigrated from the British Isles to Sweden sometime during the second half of the seventeenth century and became an officer in the pay of Charles XI. In 1690 he left Sweden and entered the service of William III of England. He became governor of Cork in 1698 and rose to the rank of brigadier general in charge of all of Queen Anne's forces in 1704.[70]

While in Sweden, Jefferyes married a Swedish noblewoman by whom he had two sons, Gustav and James. When the family left Sweden for Ireland, it is unknown if Gustav accompanied them. He was in Swedish service, however, serving as a volunteer in the army at the outbreak of the Great Northern War. He died in 1700 during the Battle of Narva.[71] In contrast, James, who was only ten or eleven years old when his parents left Sweden, grew up in Ireland. His parents' move, however, did not sever his connection to Sweden. In 1702, James became the private secretary of John Robinson, who was the resident English ambassador in Stockholm. James's father was a friend of Robinson, and he acquired the position as secretary for his son in 1701, after James had received his bachelor of arts degree from Dublin University.[72]

James Jefferyes served as Robinson's secretary between 1702 and 1707. In 1707, his career changed when he entered the Swedish army as a volunteer. This status was a cover for his real mission, which was to be a secret diplomatic agent for the English monarch and to send regular reports on the progress of Charles XII's invasion of Russia.[73] The English crown had wanted to send Robinson as an official representative to accompany the army, but Charles XII would not allow diplomats to follow the army. The king allowed Jefferyes to act as a secret agent because of his father's previous service in the Swedish military. The king kept the young man's status a secret, however, because he did not want to have to allow other diplomats to accompany the army.[74]

While the secret nature of Jefferyes's commission granted him full access to the workings of the Swedish army and allowed him to provide the English ruler with eyewitness accounts of the Swedish campaigns, his status within the army had unforeseen consequences. Jefferyes held the rank of captain and fought alongside Swedish soldiers during Charles XII's invasion of Russia. As part of the Swedish army, Jefferyes participated in the Battle of Poltava in 1709 and, as was the case with the majority of the Swedish soldiers, was captured and imprisoned by the Russians when the Swedish army was defeated there. At the time of his capture, Jefferyes's secret diplomatic status caused him great problems. He described the situation as follows:

> From the time we came into this country, I much fear that but few of my letters have had the good fortune to come into Y:r Hon:rs hands, sinse many of them laid windbound at the Svedish chancery before owr late unfortunate battle, and I found as many here sinse my arrivall that had been intercepted. 'Twill not be my fault if Y:r Hon:r be not oftner acquainted for the future of what passes here, for I am allmost in the same condition as th' other prisonners, uncertain whether they will send me to Mosco, or suffer me to go with their army to Poland; they alledge for this their hard

using of me, that I have been engag'd in the Svedish service, and all the arguments I can use, the letters they have
intercepted, some I have receiv'd from Y:r Hon:r which I
have shew'd them, and the testimony of the whole Svedish
army canot perswade them to the contrary.[75]

Because of his unofficial diplomatic position, the Russian commanders
sent Jefferyes to Moscow as a prisoner of war and kept him in captiv-
ity until the English ambassador at the court of Peter the Great could
persuade the Russians that Jefferyes was a representative of the English crown and not a Swedish soldier.[76] In the end, his service with the
Swedish army launched an official diplomatic career for Jefferyes. After
his release from a Russian prison, Jefferyes returned to England. Because
of his extensive knowledge of the Swedish army and his family's long-
term connections with Sweden, Queen Anne commissioned Jefferyes to
serve as the English minister to Charles XII's court in exile in Turkey.[77]

The diplomatic activities that these officers engaged in as representatives of the English rulers to the Swedish court reveal the value of personal connections to the success of diplomatic endeavors and the influence that particular officers had with the Swedish monarchs and the
Council of the Realm. Often English rulers chose these men to represent
their interests at the Swedish court because of their personal connections with the Swedish nobility and rulers. Their status as former officers in the Swedish military and their friendships with many members
of the nobility helped them to gain audiences with the Swedish monarchs and the Council of the Realm in a timely fashion. Their connections
thus quickly granted them access to the Swedish policy makers. Additionally, as was seen in the cases of Ruthven, King, and Forbes, former
officers could possess enough influence with the crown and council to
encourage the Swedish administration to engage secretly in diplomatic
overtures that were not necessarily in the best political interests of the
Swedish realm.

Informal Diplomatic Contacts

Besides serving in official and semiofficial diplomatic positions, military officers from the British Isles also served the Swedish and English
crowns in more informal settings. Most often acts of informal diplo-

macy came about as a result of the contacts that the officers maintained both with their friends and families in the British Isles and, for those who had returned to their homelands, with their colleagues and friends in Sweden. These connections helped to maintain diplomatic channels between Sweden and the British Isles and to keep both governments informed of each other's policies. The officers also helped to facilitate the official diplomatic efforts of both crowns by providing aid to British diplomats visiting Sweden and by arranging assistance for Swedish diplomats in the British Isles.

Although it was probably not their intent, one of the officers' most useful acts of informal diplomacy was establishing a network of correspondence between the British Isles and Sweden that allowed current political information to flow between the kingdoms. In the course of keeping in touch with their families, friends, and colleagues, some officers would comment upon the current political issues of the day and their attitudes toward them. By doing this, the officers were informing members of a foreign government of the policies and actions of their rulers. Although these letters offered only the opinions of their authors and may not have reflected the political reality of the time accurately, they help to reveal the political issues that seemed of contemporary importance.

An example of the type of information that these casual letters contained can be seen in the correspondence that Col. Hugo Hamilton maintained with the Swedish Marshal of the Realm, Carl Gustaf Wrangel, between 1666 and 1671. Hamilton, who had recently left Swedish service to return to his family lands in Ireland, wrote a series of letters to Wrangel, with whom he had served in the Swedish army during the Thirty Years' War. Hamilton's letters primarily addressed such issues as horses that he was sending to the Swedish king and presents that he was sending to Wrangel and his family as an illustration of his friendship and willingness to be of service to Wrangel and the Swedish crown. The letters also, however, address political matters such as the possibility of recruiting troops in the British Isles for Swedish service and a potential alliance between Sweden and England. Hamilton gave his opinion that the English nobility were inclined to make an alliance with Sweden and that he hoped that an alliance between Sweden and France would not be concluded. He also stated that while in London he had tried to persuade other members of the English nobility that it was not in Sweden's interest to become an ally of France.[78] Although Hamilton was not serving the Swedish crown in an official capacity, he kept a high-ranking official of the Swedish government informed about English policies regarding foreign alliances and prevailing opinions among the English nobility about these diplomatic negotiations.

Former military officers also continued to be of service to the Swedish crown by providing aid to Swedish diplomats in England and by accompanying English diplomats to Sweden. While in England, some Swedish diplomats used the family connections of British officers to ease their way into the society of the British Isles and to accomplish the goals that had been set for them. Having aid from individuals who knew the local scene was particularly important when the recruitment of mercenaries in the British Isles was being organized. Usually, a recruiting agent from the British Isles was hired, and this agent would then hire colonels from the recruitment areas. The colonels would then be directly in charge of the hiring of soldiers. Occasionally, former officers of the Swedish crown who were in the British Isles helped to arrange the recruitment. Doing so was a means of showing their loyalty to the Swedish crown.[79] Sometimes Swedish officers were chosen as recruiting agents. When this situation arose, officers from the British Isles would offer to have family members escort the Swedish agents to ease their travels through various regions of the British Isles and to help them establish contacts with individuals who could help speed the recruitment process.[80]

Besides providing aid to Swedish diplomats in the British Isles, occasionally English rulers called upon the officers to accompany English diplomats to Sweden. In addition, officers from the British Isles who were still in Swedish service frequently offered to help English diplomats visiting the Swedish court to accomplish the goals of their mission. One of the better known examples of this phenomenon is the aid that Bulstrode Whitelocke received during his visit to the court of Queen Christina between 1653 and 1654. Whitelocke wrote a very detailed account of his embassy to Sweden in which he discussed not only the diplomatic business he was engaged in but also the individuals with whom he had contact in Sweden.[81] His work gives the reader insight into the assistance that both former and current British officers in Swedish service provided to his ambassadorial mission.

Before leaving for his ambassadorial post in Sweden, one of Whitelocke's most important goals was to pick the individuals who would accompany him. One of the leading members of his retinue was Col. Christopher Potley, who had returned to England in 1651 after spending time spying on royalist activities at the court of Queen Christina. Whitelocke wanted Potley to travel with him because of his familiarity with the Swedish court, his acquaintance with the queen and the Swedish nobility, and his ability to speak German fluently. Whitelocke also was well acquainted with Potley because they were kinsmen.[82]

Throughout Whitelocke's stay in Sweden, Potley accompanied him and at times acted as an interpreter. Potley also acted as an intermediary for Swedes who wished to lodge complaints with the English ambassador. For example, while Whitelocke was staying in Gothenburg, one of his captains regularly visited ships that were coming into the harbor. A vice admiral from the Swedish navy approached Potley and asked him to talk to Whitelocke about this matter. The vice admiral had received numerous complaints and wanted Whitelocke to prevent the captain from spying on the Swedish ships.[83]

While in Sweden, Whitelocke also received help from officers from the British Isles who were still in Swedish service. The aid that these officers offered to Whitelocke took many forms. Some served in an official capacity, such as Lt. Col. Frans Sinclair, a Scot in the Swedish army who served as the interpreter for the governor of Gothenburg during Whitelocke's stay there, and Vice Admiral Clerck, a Scot serving in the Swedish navy who commanded the Swedish ship that brought Whitelocke and his entourage from Stockholm to Lübeck.[84] Other officers offered Whitelocke informal aid. These were men with whom Whitelocke became acquainted socially during his stay in Sweden. They included individuals such as Colonel Nerne, who guided Whitelocke through the fortifications of Gothenburg and showed him the sights of the town, and George Fleetwood, who arranged for the shipment of Whitelocke's possessions to England.[85]

These practices of writing letters to colleagues and providing aid to diplomats may not seem to be central to the running of foreign affairs. But while diplomatic relations would not be based upon such actions, the letters served to keep the channels of communications open between the kingdoms and helped the process of diplomacy to run more smoothly.

Conclusion

Throughout the late sixteenth century and the entire seventeenth century, Sweden and England enjoyed close diplomatic ties. This diplomatic relationship was fostered in part through agreements to allow the Swedish crown to recruit mercenaries in the British Isles. This practice in turn helped to strengthen the connections between the two kingdoms as officers from the British Isles helped to form ties between the two kingdoms on both official and unofficial levels. Some officers held official diplomatic positions and thus used their ties at both courts to further the policy goals of the kingdom they represented. Diplomatic ties were also developed informally through the officers' attempts to maintain social and professional contacts in both kingdoms. These officers created an informal diplomatic network that allowed information to flow between the two monarchies. Such activities helped to keep the Swedish and English rulers apprised of the policies and workings of both governments, which contributed to sustaining the close diplomatic relationship these realms enjoyed throughout the seventeenth century.

CONCLUSION

In June 1679, William Leslie wrote to Charles XI of Sweden regarding his failed attempts to recruit a regiment in the British Isles for Swedish service. The king had commissioned Leslie to recruit soldiers for the crown's military campaigns during its war against Brandenburg and Denmark, which began in 1674 and ended in 1679. Leslie was unsuccessful in his attempt, however, because the Swedish crown did not provide enough funds for him to use while recruiting. In his letter, Leslie stated that he had written to the crown many times to ask permission to abandon his commission but had not received an answer. He finally had written to Maj. Gen. Hans Wachtmeister, whom he hoped would intercede with the crown on his behalf, so that he could be released from the very expensive burden of maintaining himself in London without any means of financial support.[1]

Leslie's efforts to organize a regiment for Swedish service constitute the last known attempt of the Swedish crown to recruit mercenaries in the British Isles during the seventeenth century. Coming more than twenty years after the last large-scale attempt to hire British soldiers, Leslie's commission was doomed to fail because of changing economic and political circumstances in Sweden. By the late 1670s, the expense of maintaining a far-flung empire with a small population and few resources was taking its toll on the Swedish crown. The crown no longer possessed the money to hire regiments of foreign mercenaries. In the 1680s, Charles XI resolved the economic problems of the kingdom through a process of reclaiming crown land that had been alienated to the nobility. The king used the land to finance a reformed military and to pay the salaries of civil servants.[2] With the revamped military system, the need to hire so many foreign mercenaries ceased to exist, and the crown never reinstituted the extensive recruitment of soldiers in the British Isles.

The year 1680 also marked the establishment of an absolute monarchy in Sweden. With the creation of this new political system, Charles XI and his administration took a greater interest in military affairs. During this period, the process of domestic recruitment was standardized, officers became more accountable to the crown through the regular submission of annual reviews, and the king regularly inspected the kingdom's troops and fortifications.[3] Such changes were part of a broader royal policy of granting the crown greater control over different aspects of the kingdom's bureaucracy. Similar changes were occurring in other contemporary European kingdoms. In regard to the military, the Swedish crown created policies similar to those instituted in France and Brandenburg–Prussia, at the end of the century, which increasingly made the recruitment and funding of troops the responsibility of the state rather than private, entrepreneurial enterprises.[4] Although commanders throughout Europe continued to employ mercenaries during the eighteenth century, the establishment of standing armies and the increasing control that rulers exerted over the process of recruiting, supplying, and training troops led to a continuing decline in reliance upon mercenary forces.[5] Thus, the Swedish monarchy's attempt to increase its control over the kingdom's military forces after 1680 was part of a wider European trend toward the development of national armies.

Although the hiring of British mercenaries ended, individuals from the British Isles continued to enter Swedish service. These men sought new lives in Sweden for reasons similar to those of their counterparts earlier in the century. Some followed relatives who had settled in Sweden, while others immigrated for better economic opportunities. Toward the end of the seventeenth century, however, the flow of military immigrants began to dry up until it ceased completely in the early eighteenth century. The last known individual from the British Isles to enter Swedish service was Thomas Chapman, who became an officer in the Swedish navy in 1715. By the end of the Great Northern War (1700–1721), Sweden had lost most of its overseas provinces, and the Swedish government focused on a less expansive foreign policy during much of the eighteenth century. As a result, the military needs of the state could be met with domestic recruitment.

The end of Sweden's era as an imperial power brought the migration of mercenaries from the British Isles to Sweden to a close. As an immigrant group, the British officers did not have a long-term impact upon Swedish society or Swedish culture. Because of strict laws that forbade the practice of foreign religions within the Swedish kingdom, the officers did not found uniquely British institutions such as churches that could have served as focal points for preserving British culture or disseminating British culture to the local community. Additionally, when the British officers settled in Sweden, they held lands scattered throughout the Swedish empire. The lack of concentrated British settlements within the Swedish realm also reduced the spread of British traditions and ideas into Swedish society. Nonetheless, the experiences of the British officers in Sweden provide significant insights into the connections between state centralization, warfare, and migration in northern Europe during the early modern period.

First, the state-building process in Sweden encouraged the migration of foreigners into the kingdom and created many opportunities for these immigrants to rise to the highest levels of Swedish society. The experiences of the officers from the British Isles reveal the social mobility that foreigners could enjoy in seventeenth-century Sweden. Officers who were skilled military leaders rose through the ranks of the army and navy to reach the highest levels of command within the military. Often these same individuals received noble titles and lands as rewards for their loyal service to the Swedish crown. Their prominent positions within Swedish society also led some of the military immigrants into important political careers as members of the Swedish parliament and as diplomatic representatives of the Swedish crown.

This work has suggested, however, that these opportunities for advancement within Swedish society were a unique feature of the Swedish state-building process. While other northern European rulers employed foreigners to sustain the expansion of their states, military officers in these regions did not enjoy the same opportunities for social mobility that others found in Sweden. In kingdoms such as Denmark and Russia, foreign soldiers could enjoy prestigious military careers, but the laws of these realms, which regulated interactions between foreigners and native-born subjects, in most cases barred immigrants from finding wealth and social acceptance beyond the confines of the military. In both kingdoms, tradition generally excluded immigrants from receiving noble status and all the privileges that came with such a position.

In the case of the Danish kingdom, the king could confer noble status on deserving men, but such a decision had to receive the approval of the Council of the Realm. As the Danish nobility held a monopoly over membership of the council and used the council to further their political interests at the expense of the crown, the councillors usually refused to grant noble status to foreigners.[6] Additionally, the Danish crown's wealth acquired through the levying of the Sound Dues meant that the monarchs did not have to resort to the alienation of crown land to finance the kingdom's state-building process, as was the case in Sweden. This factor, in combination with restrictions upon the sale of noble property, left few possibilities for immigrants to become landowners in Denmark.[7]

In comparison, Russian rulers not only excluded foreigners from the ranks of the nobility but also restricted their interaction with the realm's native-born subjects. Beginning in the mid–seventeenth century, the Russian crown required foreigners to live in specific areas of the kingdom's cities, forbade foreigners to wear Russian clothes, and barred foreigners from hiring Russian workers. These policies seemed to stem from a desire, particularly on the part of the Russian religious leadership, to prevent immigrants from introducing foreign ideas, beliefs, customs, or practices, which church leaders feared could corrupt native-born Russians.[8]

Thus, the migration of skilled men and their families to seventeenth-century Sweden was part of a larger migration pattern that took place in northern Europe. As these kingdoms lacked large numbers of highly educated men, merchants who possessed economic connections across Europe, or soldiers trained in the latest military tactics, rulers throughout the Baltic region sponsored the immigration of skilled foreigners to aid in the growth of their kingdoms' bureaucracies, economies, and militaries. The Swedish case stands out from the other contemporary examples, however, as foreigners who settled in this kingdom could become members of the Swedish aristocracy and acquire vast amounts of wealth and property.

Second, while the seventeenth-century expansion of the Swedish state offered foreign officers many opportunities for social, economic, and professional advancement, the ability of individual officers to enjoy these opportunities depended upon many factors. Among first-generation immigrants, numerous possibilities existed for professional and economic success due to the constant state of warfare in the Baltic during the first half of the seventeenth century and the subsequent state-building process. In comparison, members of subsequent generations had fewer options available to them to gain professional status and wealth through military service as a consequence of the decreasing level of warfare between the Swedish kingdom and its neighbors during the second half of the seventeenth century. Second-, third-, and fourth-generation descendants thus increasingly had to build upon the status and wealth inherited from their ancestors instead of acquiring property, positions, and honors for themselves. Their closer social ties to the wider Swedish community, however, made it easier for these men to achieve these goals. Although officers born in the British Isles had many opportunities to interact with Swedes through their military and parliamentary service, many appear to have been assimilated into the social life of the Swedish kingdom only on a superficial level. As a consequence of the officers' foreign birth, allegiance to non-Lutheran religions, and unconfirmed social status, many Swedish families probably were reluctant to make formal connections with these individuals through alliances such as marriages. The officers' sons, however, frequently married into Swedish noble families and enjoyed greater social acceptance among the Swedish nobility due to their native birth and higher social status. As a result, the British officers' descendants were quickly assimilated into Swedish society and lost their "immigrant" ways.

During the eighteenth century, a few descendants of the military immigrants continued to maintain contact with the British Isles, but these ties usually were motivated by economic interests and not by feelings of personal attachment to their ancestral homeland. The Sinclairs, in particular, illustrate the type of lingering contacts that the families maintained. In the 1790s, individuals from this family sought to stake a claim to the title of the Earl of Caithness after they had received reports that a man from a more remote branch of the family had taken over the title. They were unsuccessful in this attempt to claim the title mostly because no members of the family had visited the British Isles or maintained ties with family who remained behind when their ancestors immigrated in the early 1600s.[9] Thus, the Swedish branch of the family did not reestablish contact with their relatives in Scotland until a valuable economic opportunity presented itself. As the case of the Sinclair family suggests, the immigrants' descendants continued to live in Sweden and to enjoy the prestigious positions their ancestors had created, but as the eighteenth century progressed, their emotional and familial ties to the British Isles gradually disappeared.

Finally, similar to immigrants in other kingdoms throughout Europe, British officers in Sweden attempted to maintain contact with their comrades from their homelands and with their friends and family overseas. These contacts helped to create a community among the officers within Sweden, which in turn became significant as it served to perpetuate the military connections between Sweden and the British Isles. As soldiers from the British Isles advanced through the ranks of the Swedish military, they often would encourage their relatives to enter Swedish service. Occasionally, British officers offered low-ranking officer commissions in their regiments to their relatives who remained in the British Isles or helped their relatives gain positions in other units within the Swedish military. The Swedish crown also used these officers as recruiting agents who would return to the British Isles to enlist more men for the military.

The stable nature of this community and its attempts to perpetuate the military might of the Swedish crown challenge traditional assumptions regarding the transitory nature of mercenary forces in early modern European armies. While there is merit in characterizing some mercenaries as untrustworthy, transient, and disloyal, the careers of these British officers suggest that given the right incentives and rewards, foreign soldiers could become loyal, trustworthy leaders of native military forces and could make long-term commitments to serve the interests of their employers.

NOTES

Abbreviations

BL	British Library, London
KA	Krigsarkivet, Stockholm
KB	Kungliga Biblioteket, Stockholm
LUB	Lund Universitetsbibliotek
PRO	Public Record Office, London
RA	Riksarkivet, Stockholm
UUB	Uppsala Universitetsbibliotek

Preface

1. Elgenstierna, *Den introducerade svenska adelns ättartavlor.*

2. Ramsay, *Frälsesläkter i Finland;* Schlegel and Klingspor, *Den med sköldebref förlänade.*

3. The main archival source for information on familial relationships is the Biographica collection located at Riksarkivet, which contains diverse papers from many different Swedish families. Information from printed sources came from Wieselgren, ed., *De la Gardieska arkivet,* and Almquist, *Frälsegodsen i Sverige,* part 1, *Stockholms och Uppsala län,* and part 4, *Småland.* Family histories used include H. A. Hamilton, *Svenska ätterna Hamiltons;* Paul, ed., *The Scots Peerage,* vols. 3 and 4; *Svenskt biografiskt lexikon,* vols. 8 and 11; Tayler and Tayler, eds., *The House of Forbes;* Ruthven, *Letters and Papers of Patrick Ruthven;* and *The Melvilles, Earls of Melville.*

4. Because of the lack of comprehensive genealogies, it is impossible to find and include every nonnoble British military family that immigrated to Sweden during the seventeenth century. I have, however, been able to positively identify enough nonnoble families to provide a representation of the general experiences of the nonnoble immigrants.

5. Upton, *Charles XI and Swedish Absolutism,* ix–x.

6. Upton, *Charles XI and Swedish Absolutism*, ix–x.

Introduction

1. According to Geoffrey Parker and Lesley M. Smith, the categorization of the seventeenth century as a period of profound crisis has been accepted by historians throughout the twentieth century. Two of the earliest historians to discuss this phenomenon were Paul Hazard and Roger B. Merriman, who in the 1930s debated the connections between the major political upheavals of the period. The discussion broadened in the 1950s with Eric Hobsbawm's work, which examined the economic decline of the seventeenth century, thus adding economic change as an additional factor to the crisis debate. Hobsbawm's work inspired numerous articles published in the 1960s and the 1970s that sought to distinguish the underlying causes of the crisis and to pinpoint the exact nature of the problems plaguing society in the seventeenth century. For more information on the historiography of the seventeenth-century crisis, see Parker and Smith, introduction to *The General Crisis of the Seventeenth Century*, 1–7.

2. Although the exact causes of the development of European absolutism are still a source of historical debate, many scholars see centralized absolutist states as a consequence of the upheaval and chaos of the seventeenth century. For an overview of these debates see Tilly, "Reflections on the History of European State-Making," 3–45.

3. Porter, *War and the Rise of the State*, 63–69.

4. Villstrand, "Statsmakt och migration," 10.

5. Sweden proper had a small population of roughly one million, with the duchy of Finland having a population of only two hundred thousand. See McEvedy and Jones, *Atlas of World Population History*, 53.

6. Berg and Lagercrantz, *Scots in Sweden*, 13.

7. Works in this ancestral history category include Douglas, *Robert Douglas*; Sörensson, *Generalfälttygmästaren Hugo Hamilton*, vol. 1; Uddgren, *Karolinen Hugo Johan Hamilton*, vol. 2; Terry, *The Life and Campaigns of Alexander Leslie*; and Granberg, "Skotten James Keith," 19–28.

8. See Donner, *A Brief Sketch of the Scottish Families in Finland and*

Sweden; Fischer, *The Scots in Germany;* Fischer, *The Scots in Sweden;* Sinclair, "The Scottish Officers of Charles XII," 178–92; and Berg and Lagercrantz, *Scots in Sweden.*

9. For works that cover the late sixteenth century and the first half of the seventeenth century, see Steuart, "Scottish Officers in Sweden," 191–96; Berg, "Skottar i Sverige," 115–24; and Åberg, "Scottish Soldiers in the Swedish Armies."

10. Works that address the participation of mercenaries from the British Isles in the Thirty Years' War include J. Mackay, *An Old Scots Brigade;* Åberg, "Scots in the Army of Gustavus Adolphus," 226–30; and Grimble, "The Royal Payment of Mackay's Regiment," 23–38.

11. Dow, "Ruthven's Army in Sweden and Estonia."

12. Recent studies addressing similar questions include Henry, *The Irish Military Community in Spanish Flanders,* and Cross, *By the Banks of the Neva.*

1. British Mercenaries

1. Roberts, *The Swedish Imperial Experience,* 3.
2. Roberts, *The Swedish Imperial Experience,* 124–25.
3. McEvedy and Jones, *Atlas of World Population History,* 53.
4. Andrew Keith, Personregister, Militieräkenskaper, KA.
5. Dow, "Ruthven's Army in Sweden and Estonia," 3. See also *The Register of the Privy Council of Scotland,* 2:235.
6. Dow, "Ruthven's Army in Sweden and Estonia," 12.
7. Dow, "Ruthven's Army in Sweden and Estonia," 31–37.
8. Dow, "Ruthven's Army in Sweden and Estonia," 40–41.
9. Berg and Lagercrantz, *Scots in Sweden,* 16–17.
10. Dow, "Ruthven's Army in Sweden and Estonia," 74.
11. Dow, "Ruthven's Army in Sweden and Estonia," 76.
12. Roberts, *The Early Vasas,* 399.
13. Roberts, *The Early Vasas,* 353.
14. Roberts, *The Early Vasas,* 369–93.
15. Oakley, *War and Peace in the Baltic,* 40.
16. Platonov, *The Time of Trouble,* 108–11.
17. Whyte, "Poverty or Prosperity?" 20.
18. Whyte, "Population Mobility in Early Modern Scotland," 56.
19. Whyte, "Population Mobility in Early Modern Scotland," 54.

20. Whyte, "Population Mobility in Early Modern Scotland," 55.

21. Henry, *The Irish Military Community in Spanish Flanders*, 28–29.

22. Charles IX to James Spens, Örebro, April 1606, and Charles IX to James Spens, Stockholm, January 3, 1609, "The Diplomatic Correspondence of Sir James Spens," ed. and intro. by Archibald Duncan, E:397:d, Manuscript Collections, UUB (hereafter cited as Spens Diplomatic Correspondence). See also Berg and Lagercrantz, *Scots in Sweden*, 26.

23. James Spens to the Earl of Salisbury, Stockholm, September 30, 1610, Spens Diplomatic Correspondence.

24. Andrew Greep to Salisbury, July 28, 1609, vol. 1, no. 156, S.P. 95, PRO.

25. James Spens to the Earl of Salisbury, Stockholm, November 8, 1610, Spens Diplomatic Correspondence; Sir William Stewart to the Earl of Salisbury, April 4, 1610, vol. 1, no. 162, S.P. 95, PRO.

26. Palme, *Sverige och Danmark*, 534–41.

27. Tandrup, *Mod triumf eller tragedie*, 1:63.

28. Sir Robert Anstruther to James Spens, Ösby, July 18, 1612, Spens Diplomatic Correspondence; "Draft from the King's Secretary to Sir Robert Anstruther, August 9, 1612," in Michell, *History of the Scottish Expedition to Norway*, 135–36.

29. Michell, *History of the Scottish Expedition to Norway*, 42, 48.

30. "The First Official Report to the Danish Chancellor respecting the Scottish Expedition from the Norwegian Stadtholder Envold Kruse and Others," in Michell, *History of the Scottish Expedition to Norway*, 180–83.

31. Gustavus Adolphus to James Spens, Stockholm, December 17, 1614, and James Spens to Gustavus Adolphus, London, September 13, 1615, both in Spens Diplomatic Correspondence.

32. Adams, "Europe and the Palatine War," 63–64.

33. Lockhart, *Denmark in the Thirty Years' War*, 110–11.

34. Adams, "Europe and the Palatine War," 69–70.

35. Roberts, *Gustavus Adolphus and the Rise of Sweden*, 60.

36. Lockhart, *Denmark in the Thirty Years' War*, 114.

37. Lockhart, *Denmark in the Thirty Years' War*, 118.

38. Lockhart, *Denmark in the Thirty Years' War*, 125–26.

39. Heiberg, *Christian 4*, 285–95. See also Lockhart, *Denmark in the Thirty Years' War*, 131–54.

40. The exact reason as to why Gustavus Adolphus decided to enter the Thirty Years' War in 1630 is still an issue of historical debate. As Erik Ringmar has written, the historical arguments surrounding this issue can be broken into three general categories. The first one focuses upon religion as the motivating factor and views Gustavus Adolphus as the savior of the Protestant religion. The second argument stresses the political and military interests of the Swedish crown as the prime motivation. According to these historians, the Swedish king entered the war to guard against a possible invasion of Sweden and to secure the Swedish crown's political influence in the Baltic region. The third set of theories emphasizes the economic interests of the Swedish realm and the king's need to preserve the growing economic influence of the Swedish kingdom in the region. See Ringmar, *Identity, Interest, and Action,* 19–24.

41. Parker, "The Soldiers in the Thirty Years' War," 305.

42. Fallon, "Scottish Mercenaries in the Service of Denmark and Sweden," 249, 276.

43. Monro, *Monro: His Expedition with the Worthy Scots Regiment (Called Mac-Keys Regiment),* part I, 85.

44. Åberg, "Scottish Soldiers in the Swedish Armies," 94.

45. Åberg, "Scottish Soldiers in the Swedish Armies," 95. For further information on Hamilton's regiment see Royal Commission on Historical Manuscripts, *The Manuscripts of the Duke of Hamilton,* 11th Report, appendix, part VI, and Steckzén, "James, 1:ste hertig av Hamilton," 63–121.

46. For more detailed information regarding the specific campaigns in which British soldiers were involved, see Åberg, "Scots in the Army of Gustavus Adolphus," 226–30, and Fallon, "Scottish Mercenaries in the Service of Denmark and Sweden."

47. *Calendar of State Papers, Domestic Series of the Reign of Charles I, 1638–1639,* 409.

48. Åberg, "Scots in the Army of Gustavus Adolphus," 230. In Riksregistratur, August 12, 1639, RA, there is a list of thirty Scottish officers who were given permission to leave Swedish service during the summer of 1639.

49. Roberts, ed., *Swedish Diplomats at Cromwell's Court,* 35–36.

50. Instruction för General Maijoren Edel och Wälb: George Fletwod

fryheere till Jälunda. Hwareffter han sigh utih den honom omförtrodde Commission till Her Protecteuren af Engellandh, hafwer att
rätta och förhålla, vol. 532, Anglica, Diplomatica, RA.

51. "Peter Julius Coyet to Charles X Gustavus, London, May 18, 1655,"
in Roberts, ed., *Swedish Diplomats at Cromwell's Court*, 68–71.

52. "Coyet to Charles X Gustavus," in Roberts, ed., *Swedish Diplomats
at Cromwell's Court*, 68–71.

53. Firth, ed., *Scotland and the Protectorate*, xxxi–xxxiii.

54. "General Monck to the Protector, Campe at Duffree in Aberfoyle,
August 17, 1654," in Firth, ed., *Scotland and the Protectorate*, 154–55.

55. Individuals who concluded such treaties with General Monck in-
cluded "the Earl of Atholl, the Earl of Glencairne, the Laird of
Lugton, Lord Kenmure, the Marquis of Montrose, and the Earl of
Selkirk" (Firth, ed., *Scotland and the Protectorate*, xxxi–xxxiii).

56. Alexander Leslie was a Scot who entered Swedish service in 1608
and progressed through the ranks of the Swedish army until he
achieved the rank of field marshal. He left Sweden in 1638 to return
to Scotland to aid the Scottish Covenanters in their fight against
the English king. Leslie became the commanding officer of the
Covenanters. For further information on Leslie's life and campaigns see *The Melvilles, Earls of Melville* and Terry, *The Life and
Campaigns of Alexander Leslie*.

57. Charles II to Alexander Leslie, Collen, August 12, 1655, vol. 4156,
Additional Manuscripts, BL.

58. "Christer Bonde to Charles X Gustavus, London, September 28,
1655," in Roberts, ed., *Swedish Diplomats at Cromwell's Court*, 167–
68; Cranstone to Peter Julius Coyet, London, November 1655, vol.
4, no. 94, Coyetska samlingen, RA; Leven's Security for Cranstone's
Recruitment, 1655, vol. 3, no. 106, Coyetska samlingen, RA.

59. Roberts, ed., footnote comment in *Swedish Diplomats at Cromwell's
Court*, 221; Charles X Gustavus to Secretary Gambrotius, April 5,
1657, Riksregistratur, RA.

60. Commission for Ludvig Leslie, November 30, 1657, and Charles X
Gustavus to Fleetwood, Odense, February 28, 1658, both in Riksregistratur, RA.

61. Capp, *Cromwell's Navy*, 108.

62. Capp, *Cromwell's Navy*, 108; commission for Admiral Ascue and his crew, September 10, 1658, Riksregistratur, RA.

63. William Leslie to Charles XI, London, June 14, 1679, vol. L14, Leslie, Biographica, RA.

64. Nilsson, "Imperial Sweden," 20.

65. Upton, "The Riksdag of 1680," 288–89.

66. Upton, "The Riksdag of 1680," 284.

67. Upton, *Charles XI and Swedish Absolutism*, 34–41. One reason why the adoption of a *reduktion* was possible in 1680 was a split within the House of the Nobility between the lower nobility, who derived their income from salaries earned through state service, and the titled nobility, who enjoyed the bulk of the royal land donations. For a discussion of the declining political position of the higher nobility and their relationship to Charles XI, see Sjödell, *Kungamakt och högaristokrati*, 227–82.

68. Upton, *Charles XI and Swedish Absolutism*, 71–75.

69. Svanberg and Tydén, *Tusen år av invandring*, 104.

70. *Register of the Privy Council of Scotland*, series 2, 1:542.

71. Charles I to the Earl of Northampton, June 19, 1631, vol. 4, no. 85, S.P. 95, PRO.

72. Gustavus Adolphus to James Spens, Nyköping, November 16, 1611, Spens Diplomatic Correspondence.

73. James Spens to Gustavus Adolphus, London, December 5, 1615, Spens Diplomatic Correspondence.

74. "Memoir given by Sir Thomas Roe to the Prince of Orange, December 27, 1628," in Gardiner, ed., "Letters Relating to the Mission of Sir Thomas Roe," 2.

2. Motivations for Migration

1. Whyte, "Migration in Early-Modern Scotland and England," 92.

2. Hohenberg and Lees, *The Making of Urban Europe*, 93–94.

3. Canny, "The Marginal Kingdom," 40–42.

4. Canny, "English Migration into and across the Atlantic," 62.

5. Smout, Landsman, and Devine, "Scottish Emigration in the Seventeenth and Eighteenth Centuries," 78.

6. Armitage, "Making the Empire British," 42.

7. Dodgshon, *From Chiefs to Landlords*, 102–7.

8. Macinnes, *Clanship, Commerce, and the House of Stuart*, 56–59.

9. Macinnes, *Clanship, Commerce, and the House of Stuart*, 59, 65.

10. Cullen, "The Irish Diaspora of the Seventeenth and Eighteenth Centuries," 126. For a reassessment of the Irish migratory activities in the Atlantic world see Ohlmeyer, "Seventeenth-Century Ireland," 458–60.

11. Ohlmeyer, "Seventeenth-Century Ireland," 458.

12. Cullen, "The Irish Diaspora of the Seventeenth and Eighteenth Centuries," 121–23.

13. For more information on Irish mercenaries in Spanish service, see Stradling, *The Spanish Monarchy and Irish Mercenaries*.

14. "Peter Julius Coyet to Charles X Gustavus, London, June 1, 1655," in Roberts, ed., *Swedish Diplomats at Cromwell's Court*, 74–75.

15. Henry, *The Irish Military Community in Spanish Flanders*, 107.

16. McGurk, "Wild Geese: The Irish in European Armies," 38.

17. For more information on the Irish military immigrants see Henry and Stradling, *The Spanish Monarchy and Irish Mercenaries*.

18. Canny, "English Migration into and across the Atlantic," 41.

19. Fissel, *The Bishops' Wars*, 251. See also Schwoerer, *"No Standing Armies!"* 20.

20. Lenman, "The Highland Aristocracy and North America," 174–77.

21. Richards, "Scotland and the Uses of the Atlantic Empire," 70–71.

22. Lenman, "The Highland Aristocracy and North America," 178.

23. Landsman, "Nation, Migration, and Province in the First British Empire," 465–66.

24. Smout, Landsman, and Devine, "Scottish Emigration in the Seventeenth and Eighteenth Centuries," 80–82. See also Bieganska, "A Note on the Scots in Poland," 157–65.

25. For information on Scottish merchant communities in the Baltic, see Grage, "Scottish Merchants in Gothenburg," 112–42; Dow, "Scottish Trade with Sweden, 1512–80," 64–79; Dow, "Scottish Trade with Sweden, 1580–1622," 124–50; Dow, "Skotter in Sixteenth-Century Scania," 34–51; Riis, *Should Auld Acquaintance Be Forgot*; Berg and Lagercrantz, *Scots in Sweden*; Fischer, *The Scots in Sweden*; Fischer, *The Scots in Eastern and Western Prussia*; and Fischer, *The Scots in Germany*.

26. Smout, Landsman, and Devine, "Scottish Emigration in the Seventeenth and Eighteenth Centuries," 82–84.

27. Parker, *The Military Revolution*, 46–51.

28. Parker, *The Thirty Years' War*, 124–25, 134–36.

29. Kenyon and Ohlmeyer, "The Background to the Civil Wars in the Stuart Kingdoms," 4. See also Nolan, "The Militarization of the Elizabethan State," 396.

30. Furgol, *A Regimental History of the Covenanting Armies*, 1–2.

31. Cannon, "The British Nobility, 1660–1800," 54.

32. Thirsk, "Younger Sons in the Seventeenth Century," 367.

33. H. A. Hamilton, *Svenska ätterna Hamiltons*, 4–5.

34. Elgenstierna, *Den introducerade svenska adelns ättartavlor*, 3:453–54, 457–58.

35. Elgenstierna, *Den introducerade svenska adelns ättartavlor*, 3:453.

36. Elgenstierna, *Den introducerade svenska adelns ättartavlor*, 3:457–58.

37. H. A. Hamilton, *Svenska ätterna Hamiltons*, 5.

38. *The Melvilles, Earls of Melville*, 1:387.

39. *The Melvilles, Earls of Melville*, 1:389.

40. *The Melvilles, Earls of Melville*, 1:391–93.

41. *The Melvilles, Earls of Melville*, 1:404–6.

42. Willson, *King James VI and I*, 126–27, 130.

43. Charles IX to James Spens, Örebro, April 1606, and Charles IX to James Spens, Stockholm, January 3, 1609, both in Spens Diplomatic Correspondence.

44. *Dictionary of National Biography*, s.v. "Patrick Ruthven, Earl of Forth and Brentford."

45. *Dictionary of National Biography*, s.v. "Patrick Ruthven, Earl of Forth and Brentford." See also Instructions for Patrick Ruthven, July 31, 1637, vol. 4, no. 234, S.P. 95, PRO.

46. Instructions for Patrick Ruthven, July 31, 1637.

47. Paul, ed., *The Scots Peerage*, 2:596.

48. Paul, ed., *The Scots Peerage*, 2:596. For more information on the Scottish defeat at Worcester and the fate of the Scottish prisoners, see Grainger, *Cromwell against the Scots*, 128–48.

49. Paul, ed., *The Scots Peerage*, 2:596.

50. "Christer Bonde to Charles X Gustavus, London, September 28, 1655," in Roberts, ed., *Swedish Diplomats at Cromwell's Court*, 167–

68; Cranstone to Peter Julius Coyet, London, November, 1655, vol. 4, no. 94, and Leven's Security for Cranstone's Recruitment, 1655, vol. 3, no. 106, both in Coyetska samlingen, RA.

51. Paul, ed., *The Scots Peerage*, 2:596.

52. Upton, "The Swedish Nobility, 1600–1772," 18–19.

53. For a discussion of noble privileges in Denmark and the political relationship between the nobility and the Danish king, see Lockhart, *Denmark in the Thirty Years' War*, 39–50.

54. Roberts, "On Aristocratic Constitutionalism in Swedish History," 22–25.

55. "Gustav Adolf's Accession Charter, 31 December 1611," in Roberts, ed., *Sweden as a Great Power, 1611–1697*, 8.

56. "The Form of Government," in Roberts, ed., *Sweden as a Great Power, 1611–1697*, 19–20, 27.

57. Asker, "Aristocracy and Autocracy in Seventeenth-Century Sweden," 92.

58. "The Addition to the Form of Government, 1634," in Roberts, ed., *Sweden as a Great Power, 1611–1697*, 52, 53.

59. Using Elgenstierna's genealogies, I have established that the following British mercenaries were ennobled as a reward for their military service: Alexander Andersson, William Barclay, James Bennett, Johan Burdon, Richard Clerck the younger, Owen Coxe, Robert Douglas, Johannes Douglies, George Fleetwood, Robert Gairdner, Herbert Gladsten, Hugo Hamilton of Deserf, Ludvig Hamilton of Deserf, Malkolm Hamilton of Hageby, Hugo Hamilton of Hageby, Alexander Irving, Jakob King, Henrik King, Patrick Kinninmond, Thomas Kinninmond, Erik Andersson Kirby, Johan Lowrie, Patrick Ogilwie, Johan Orcharton, William Philp, Henrik Primrose, Anders Sinclair, David Sinclair, Frans Sinclair, Tomas Thomson, James Spens, Simon Stewart, Johan Urqvard, Magnus Gabriel Willemsens, and Samuel Zeedtz.

60. Cavallie, *De höga officerarna*, 48.

61. Upton, "The Swedish Nobility, 1600–1772," 18.

62. These men were Field Marshal Robert Douglas, Maj. Gen. George Fleetwood, Col. Hugo Hamilton, Gen. Hugo Hamilton, Col. Ludvig Hamilton, Maj. Gen. Malkolm Hamilton, and Gen. James

Spens. See Elgenstierna, *Den introducerade svenska adelns ättartavlor*, 2:716, 3:453, 457–58, 7:428–29.

63. Wernstedt, "Om främmande adels naturalisation och introduktion på svenska Riddarhuset," 126.

64. Wernstedt, "Om främmande adels naturalisation och introduktion på svenska Riddarhuset," 131–34.

65. Elgenstierna, *Den introducerade svenska adelns ättartavlor*, 7:273.

66. Dackman, "Sinclairs i Sverige," 4–5.

67. For a discussion of the period when the Sinclair family ruled the Orkney Isles, see Crawford, "William Sinclair, Earl of Orkney, and His Family," 232–53.

68. Dackman, "Sinclairs i Sverige," 4–5.

69. *Sveriges ridderskaps och adels riksdags-protokoll*, 5:369.

70. Dackman, "Sinclairs i Sverige," 5.

3. Military Careers

1. James Spens to Gustavus Adolphus, London, April 15, 1629, Spens Diplomatic Correspondence.

2. James Spens to Axel Oxenstierna, London, April 26, 1624, Spens Diplomatic Correspondence.

3. "Gustavus Adolphus' Contract with Donald, Lord of Reay, Marienburg, June 17, 1629," in J. Mackay, *An Old Scots Brigade*, 228–31. See also Gustavus Adolphus—for the Regiment to be Raised by Colonel Arthur Aston, August 19, 1631, vol. 3, no. 105, S.P. 95, PRO.

4. Riis, *Should Auld Acquaintance Be Forgot*, 1:96–97.

5. Elgenstierna, *Den introducerade svenska adelns ättartavlor*, 2:47.

6. Dodgshon, " 'Pretense of Blude' and 'Place of Thair Duelling,' " 173–76. For a more in-depth discussion of the nature of Highland clans see Dodgshon, *From Chiefs to Landlords*, 31–50.

7. Dodgshon, " 'Pretense of Blude,' " 189.

8. "Memorial of Alexander Forbes, 11th Lord Forbes, presented to Charles II. Westminster, August, 1661," in *The House of Forbes*, 185.

9. "Memorial of Alexander Forbes, 11th Lord Forbes, presented to Charles II," 186; "Memoriale af överste Wilhelm Forbes," in Wieselgren, ed., *De la Gardieska arkivet*, 60.

10. "Memoriale af överste Wilhelm Forbes," 64–65.

11. Macinnes, *Clanship, Commerce, and the House of Stuart*, 8–14.

12. Åberg, "Scots in the Army of Gustavus Adolphus," 227–28.

13. Brockington, introduction to *Monro: His Expedition with the Worthy Scots Regiment*, xxx.

14. Brockington, glossary of persons in *Monro: His Expedition with the Worthy Scots Regiment*, 389, 390; Riis, *Should Auld Acquaintance Be Forgot*, 1:126; and Stevenson, *Scottish Covenanters and Irish Confederates*, 80.

15. Åberg, "Scottish Soldiers in the Swedish Armies," 95.

16. Receipt for James Lumdain's regiment, June 7, 1631, Viggo Keys samlingen, KA.

17. M. Wroughton to [unknown recipient], Wollgast, August 17, 1631, vol. 3, no. 103, S.P. 95, PRO.

18. Oxenstierna to Queen Christina, in Alexander Gordon, Biografiska anteckninger från 1600 talet, huvudarkivet FVa: 47, Per Sondén, Riksarkivets ämbetsarkiv-1966, RA.

19. Åberg, "Scottish Soldiers in the Swedish Armies," 97.

20. For the period prior to 1620, the main sources for following the careers of military officers are the *militieräkenskaper* (military receipts). This collection contains monthly receipts for the payment of individual regiments. Usually, the documents consist only of a statement regarding how much payment an individual commander and his regiment received. Occasionally, however, the receipt includes a list of every member of the regiment.

For the period after 1620, more diverse sources are available. The *rullor* (military rolls) are lists of individuals in a regiment submitted monthly as a record of who needed to be paid. This source is particularly valuable because it lists not only a regiment's officers but also every rank-and-file soldier in a regiment in any given month. Most often the *rullor* list only the names of individual soldiers, lacking any further personal information. Complementing the *rullor* is the *personregister* (index of persons), an index of the officers found in the *rullor*. This collection lists all of the officers in alphabetical order and gives a chronological account of the ranks individual officers held and the regiments in which they served. For the late seventeenth century, the *meritförteckningar* (catalogs of merit) provide additional information on the careers of both army and naval officers. Used for determining promotions and keeping the officers accountable to their superiors, these annual reviews contain accounts of officers' activities during a given year. While *meritförteckningar* exist for the entire seventeenth century, they are more plentiful for the later period because, after the establishment of absolutism in 1680, the king took a more direct interest in military affairs and began to require that officers submit *meritförteckningar* on a regular basis. All of these sources are held by Krigsarkivet in Stockholm.

21. The Names of Each Ship in the Fleet under the comand of Generall Lord Montague Bound From Saabi Bay For the Sound the 27th March 1659, no. 1247, Harlian Manuscripts, BL.

22. Instructions for Edw. Lord Montagu, Commander in Chief of the fleet, vol. 5A, no. 97, S.P. 95, PRO.

23. No foreign officers were found in the Swedish navy until 1615, before which there was no permanent naval officer corps. Instead, crews were recruited for individual campaigns. In 1615, Gustavus Adolphus, as part of his broader program to reform the military, established for the navy a permanent officer corps that had a set system of ranks. At the same time, he also created a government budget to support the institution. See E. Spens, "Sjövapnets bemanning under stormaktstiden fram till 1679," 331.

24. These officers included William Netherwood, who served as a captain of a Swedish warship; Simon Stewart, an admiral in the 1630s who helped transport Swedish troops to the Holy Roman Empire during the Thirty Years' War; Hans Foratt, who was the captain of Gustavus Adolphus's ship *Merkurius;* Alexander Foratt, who commanded the ship *Solan,* which took part in a blockade of Danzig in 1627; Johan Clerck and Richard Clerck, who were both admirals; Owen Coxe, who was a vice admiral with a fleet that cruised the Sound in 1659; and Thomas Chapman, who served as captain of a warship that was part of the Gothenburg Squadron in 1715.

25. Roberts, *Gustavus Adolphus: A History of Sweden,* 2:211. See also Sörensson, "Adelns rusttjänst och adelsfanans organisation 1521–1680," 214–23.

26. Roberts, *Gustavus Adolphus: A History of Sweden,* 223.

27. Parker, *The Military Revolution,* 17–18.

28. Asker, *Officerarna och det svenska samhället,* 106–8, 109–11.

29. Asker, *Officerarna och det svenska samhället*, 107.

30. George Fleetwood, Personregister, rullor-1700, KA.

31. Elgenstierna, *Den introducerade svenska adelns ättartavlor*, 2:716; Shirren, *The Chronicles of Fleetwood House*, 47–48, 53–56.

32. George Fleetwood, "Letter from George Fleetwood to his Father Giving an Account of the Battle of Lutzen," 4, 11.

33. Shirren, *The Chronicles of Fleetwood House*, 47.

34. "Anzolo Correr, Venetian Ambassador in England to the Doge and Senate, April 24, 1637," in *Calendar of State Papers and Manuscripts, Relating to English Affairs, Existing in the Archives and Collections of Venice*, 24:189–90.

35. Elgenstierna, *Den introducerade svenska adelns ättartavlor*, 2:716.

36. Egerton, introduction to "Letter from George Fleetwood to his Father," 3.

37. Jones, *The Diplomatic Relations between Cromwell and Charles X Gustavus of Sweden*, 22.

38. See material in Jacob Spens the younger, in A. Hammarskjöld, Anteckningar om skottar i svensk tjänst, RA.

39. Margareta Foratt to Axel Oxenstierna, April 2, 1650, Bref till Rikskansleren Axel Oxenstierna, vol. E619, Oxenstierna samlingen, RA.

40. See Jacob Spens the younger, in A. Hammarskjöld, Anteckningar om skottar i svensk tjänst, RA.

41. G. W. Fleetwood, "Kring 300-årsminnet av ett bröllop vid hovet på Nyköpings slott," 78.

42. Letters from George Fleetwood to Carl Gustaf Wrangel, vol. E8359, Skokloster samlingen, RA.

43. Asker, *Officerarna och det svenska samhället*, 110.

44. Eskil Thomson, Samuel Thomson, Jakob Thomson, Patrick Thomson, and Alexander Thomson, Personregister, rullor-1700, KA.

45. Cavallie, *De höga officerarna*, 28, 48.

46. Böhme, "Officersrekryteringen vid tre landskapsregementen, 1626–1682," 240.

47. Berg and Lagercrantz, *Scots in Sweden*, 47–48.

48. Elgenstierna, *Den introducerade svenska adelns ättartavlor*, 2:284, 2:717, 3:454, 458, 5:278.

49. Nilsson, "1634 års regeringsform," 9–15.

50. Steckzén, *Krigskollegii historia*, 1:53–54.

51. Wendt, *Amiralitetskollegiets historia*, 1:29–31.
52. Elgenstierna, *Den introducerade svenska adelns ättartavlor*, 2:20–21, 716, 4:629–30.
53. Anteckningar, Clerck, Meritförteckningar (Flottan), KA.

4. Immigrant Military Society

1. Hufton, *The Prospect before Her*, 1:102–4.
2. James Spens to Gustavus Adolphus, April 27, 1627, Spens Diplomatic Correspondence.
3. Hacker, "Women and Military Institutions in Early Modern Europe," 653.
4. Monro, *Monro: His Expedition with the Worthy Scots Regiment (Called Mac-Keys Regiment)*, part 2, 6.
5. Monro, *Monro: His Expedition with the Worthy Scots Regiment (Called Mac-Keys Regiment)*, part 2, 25, 161.
6. Roberts, *Gustavus Adolphus: A History of Sweden*, 2:240–42.
7. Watts, *The Swedish Discipline, Religious, Civile, and Military*, 55.
8. Elgenstierna, *Den introducerade svenska adelns ättartavlor*, 4:126, 8:581.
9. Elgenstierna, *Den introducerade svenska adelns ättartavlor*, 5:142; Maclean, *The Macleans of Sweden*, 26.
10. Maclean, *The Macleans of Sweden*, 7–10.
11. Marshall, *Virgins and Viragos*, 71.
12. Hufton, *The Prospect before Her*, 1:63–64.
13. Dackman, "Sinclairs i Sverige," 16.
14. Elgenstierna, *Den introducerade svenska adelns ättartavlor*, 7:273.
15. Elgenstierna, *Den introducerade svenska adelns ättartavlor*, 3:457–58.
16. Dackman, "Sinclairs i Sverige," 11–12.
17. Dackman, "Sinclairs i Sverige," 10.
18. Elgenstierna, *Den introducerade svenska adelns ättartavlor*, 2:328.
19. Elgenstierna, *Den introducerade svenska adelns ättartavlor*, 1:535–36, 7:272–73.
20. Elgenstierna, *Den introducerade svenska adelns ättartavlor*, 3:453.
21. Elgenstierna, *Den introducerade svenska adelns ättartavlor*, 7:429.
22. Genealogical Notes, Hamilton Family, vol. 213:201; Brita Hamilton's Marriage Contract, vol. 213:239; Genealogical Notes, Nef Family, vol. 227:11, 15, all in Palmsköldska samlingen, UUB.

23. Elgenstierna, *Den introducerade svenska adelns ättartavlor,* 7:319.

24. See letter to Col. Johan Skytte the younger from A. Forbes, March 1635, and the pamphlet "The Words of Command Practised in the Regiment of S. Johan Skytte, Baron of Diedorst, knight and gentleman of his Maiesti of Great Britain his privie chamber," vol. E5412, Depositio Skytteana, RA.

25. Elgenstierna, *Den introducerade svenska adelns ättartavlor,* 3:458; Sörensson, *Generalfälttygmästaren Hugo Hamilton,* 112.

26. Elgenstierna, *Den introducerade svenska adelns ättartavlor,* 3:452–58, 7:272–75, 428–29.

27. Henry, *The Irish Military Community in Spanish Flanders,* 84.

28. Scott and Storrs, "Introduction: The Consolidation of Noble Power in Europe," 1:18.

29. Letter from M. Drummond to his brother, London, October 18 [year not given], vol. D23b, Drummond, Biographica, RA.

30. In his study of the marriage patterns of the Swedish aristocracy during the seventeenth century, Kurt Ågren argues that the majority of Swedish aristocratic families intermarried extensively as a means of preserving their control over the most important government positions, in particular the Council of the Realm. See Ågren, "Rise and Decline of an Aristocracy," 55–80.

31. Svanberg and Tydén, *Tusen år av invandring,* 130–32.

32. The bishops and priests' statement on the practitioners of foreign religions, January 19, 1641, vol. 108:639–44, Palmsköldska samlingen, UUB. See also Roberts, "The Swedish Church," 144.

33. Douhan, "Vallonerna i Sverige," 75. See also Pehrsson, *De till Sverige inflyttade vallonernas religiösa förhålland.*

34. Bishops and priests' statement, vol. 108:741–43, Palmsköldska samlingen, UUB. Such a document was signed by an Irish officer in Swedish service, James Jefferyes, before his marriage to Catharina Drakenhielm in 1693. See James Jefferyes's Marriage Contract, vol. 139, Acta Ecclesiastica, RA.

35. For an in-depth discussion of the elements involved in finding a suitable spouse see Cressy, *Birth, Marriage, and Death,* 252–63.

36. Elgenstierna, *Den introducerade svenska adelns ättartavlor,* 2:716–17.

37. Elgenstierna, *Den introducerade svenska adelns ättartavlor,* 2:717, 725–26.

38. Fullerton and Williams, *Scandinavia: An Introductory Geography,*
    198–207.
39. Fullerton and Williams, *Scandinavia: An Introductory Geography,*
    185–89.
40. In 1645, with the signing of the Treaty of Brömsebro, the Swedes began to erode Danish control of the provinces on the eastern side of the Sound. In 1645, Sweden gained control of the Danish province of Halland for thirty years, which expanded Sweden's access to the North Sea. The Swedes increased their control of this region after successfully invading Denmark in 1657. A peace treaty was signed between the Swedes and the Danes in 1658. This treaty, known as the Treaty of Roskilde, gave Sweden permanent control of the Danish provinces of Skåne, Blekinge, and Halland, which are located in present-day southern Sweden. This treaty extended Sweden to its modern borders. After another Swedish invasion of Denmark in 1658, the Swedish acquisition of these provinces was finalized in the Treaty of Copenhagen, signed by Denmark and Sweden in 1660. For further details see Oakley, *War and Peace in the Baltic,* 76–92.
41. Fullerton and Williams, *Scandinavia: An Introductory Geography,*
    185–86.
42. Nilsson, *På väg mot militärstaten,* 47–48, 65–66.
43. Nilsson, *På väg mot militärstaten,* 61, 122–24.
44. Nilsson, *På väg mot militärstaten,* 94. For more details on the distribution of forfeited estates during Charles IX's reign see T. Berg, "De sarskilda fögderierna för förbrutna gods under Karl IX:s och Gustav II Adolfs regeringar," 118–225.
45. Brännman, *Frälseköpen under Gustav II Adolfs regering,* 5, 13. See also Nilsson, "Från förläning till donation," 426.
46. Heckscher, *An Economic History of Sweden,* 117–20; Brännman, *Frälseköpen under Gustav II Adolfs regering,* 18–19.
47. Magnus Eriksson's Land Law was the first law code to apply to the entire Swedish kingdom. Established in 1350 during the reign of Magnus Eriksson (1319–63), this law code specified the rights and duties of the Swedish kings. For further information see Ingvar Andersson, *A History of Sweden,* trans. Carolyn Hannay (New York: Praeger, 1956), 50.
48. Roberts, ed., *Sweden as a Great Power, 1611–1697,* 93.

49. "Resolution of the Diet of Norrköping, 1604," in Roberts, ed., *Sweden as a Great Power, 1611–1697*, 93.

50. "The Form of Government, 1634," in Roberts, ed., *Sweden as a Great Power, 1611–1697*, 27.

51. "Minutes of the Council of the Realm, 1 June 1638," in Roberts, ed., *Sweden as a Great Power, 1611–1697*, 96–98.

52. Upton, "The Swedish Nobility, 1600–1772," 19, 21.

53. Roberts, "Queen Christina and the General Crisis," 114.

54. Upton, "The Swedish Nobility, 1600–1772," 12, 21–22.

55. Roberts, "Queen Christina and the General Crisis," 115–17.

56. Roberts, ed., *Sweden as a Great Power, 1611–1697*, 110–11.

57. Ågren, "The reduction," 240–41.

58. Rystad, "The Estates of the Realm, the Monarchy, and Empire," 80.

59. Rystad, "The Estates of the Realm, the Monarchy, and Empire," 80; Roberts, ed., *Sweden as a Great Power, 1611–1697*, 121.

60. Ågren, "The reduction," 243–46.

61. Nilsson, *På väg mot militärstaten*, 53.

62. Almquist, *Frälsegodsen i Sverige*, part 4, *Småland*, 1:64.

63. Almquist, *Frälsegodsen i Sverige*, part 1, *Stockholms och Uppsala län*, 86–87.

64. Almquist, *Frälsegodsen i Sverige*, part 4, *Småland*, 1:64.

65. Elgenstierna, *Den introducerade svenska adelns ättartavlor*, 2:283–84; Almquist, *Frälsegodsen i Sverige*, part 4, *Småland*, 2:1033.

66. Almquist, *Frälsegodsen i Sverige*, part 4, *Småland*, 2:1030, 1049–50.

67. *Dictionary of Scandinavian History*, s.v. "Oxenstierna, Axel."

68. Bohman, ed., *Svenska män och kvinnor*, 1:432–35.

69. Elgenstierna, *Den introducerade svenska adelns ättartavlor*, 8:331.

70. Brännman, *Frälseköpen under Gustav II Adolfs regering*, 144–45.

71. Thomas Muschamp, Personregister, rullor-1700, KA.

72. Gustavus Adolphus to Thomas Muschamp, September 27, 1627, M18, Muschamp, Biographica, RA. See also Almquist, *Frälsegodsen i Sverige*, part 4, *Småland*, 4:736.

73. Gustavus Adolphus to Elin Lindsay, May 1, 1630, M18, Muschamp, Biographica, RA.

74. Margareta Muschamp to Charles XI, July 11, 1682, M18, Muschamp, Biographica, RA; Almquist, *Frälsegodsen i Sverige*, part 4, *Småland*,

4:1513; and Elgenstierna, *Den introducerade svenska adelns ättar-tavlor*, 1:625.

75. Almquist, *Frälsegodsen i Sverige*, part 4, *Småland*, 2:628.

76. Catherine Guthrie to Queen Christina [no date], vol. L16, Lichton, Biographica, RA.

77. See Kiernan, "Foreign Mercenaries and Absolute Monarchy," 121; Roberts, "The Military Revolution," 200; and Hale, *War and Society in Renaissance Europe*, 69–73.

78. A similar practice existed in England during the middle decades of the seventeenth century. In contrast to the Swedish case, widows in England were given stipends. This practice was short lived, however, as Parliament granted compensation only to women whose husbands had supported the parliamentary cause during the Civil War. After the Restoration, the crown discontinued this system of support. For further details see Hudson, "Negotiating for Blood Money," 146–48.

79. An example of such a transaction can be seen in the morning gift letter that described the money Field Marshal Robert Douglas gave to his wife, Hedvig Mörner, on the day after their wedding (Mor-gongafvebref, November 27, 1645, Släktarkiven—Douglas, De la Gardieska samlingen, LUB).

80. L. Carlsson, *"Jag giver dig min dotter,"* 209–13.

81. Brita Hamilton's Marriage Contract, vol. 213:239, Palmsköldska samlingen, UUB; G. Hamilton, *A History of the House of Hamilton*, 1016.

82. Hugo Hamilton to Charles XI, vol. H5, Hamilton, Biographica, RA.

83. "Resolution of the Diet of Norrköping, 1604," in Roberts, ed., *Sweden as a Great Power, 1611–1697*, 93.

84. Letter from Johan Lichton to [unknown recipient], vol. L16, Lichton, Biographica, RA.

85. Ågren, "The reduction," 244.

86. In 1633, the crown donated an estate in Uppland to the Scottish naval officer Hans Clerck. The estate reverted back to the crown in 1644 because Clerck had died without direct male heirs who could inherit the property. In 1647, Clerck's daughter Elisabet bought her father's property from the crown (Almquist, *Frälsegodsen i Sverige*, part 1, *Stockholms och Uppsala län*, 810).

87. Kongl. Mayt. Resolution öfver Felt Marskalkens Gref Douglases Insuneradhe Supplication efter Kongl. Mayt. befalning giord af Gustaf Bergh, May 12, 1658, Riksregistratur, RA.

88. Almquist, *Frälsegodsen i Sverige*, part 4, *Småland*, 1:232, 270, 2:1043. See also Douglas, *Robert Douglas*, 152.

89. Rystad, "The Estates of the Realm, the Monarchy, and Empire," 65–66, 97.

90. Wernstedt, "Om främmande adels naturalisation och introduktion på svenska Riddarhuset," 126.

91. Wernstedt, "Om främmande adels naturalisation och introduktion på svenska Riddarhuset," 86.

92. *Sveriges ridderskaps och adels riksdags-protokoll.*

93. Rystad, "The Estates of the Realm, the Monarchy, and Empire," 69.

94. Ahnlund, *Sveriges Riksdag*, 3:166–67.

95. Rystad, "The Estates of the Realm, the Monarchy, and Empire," 88.

96. Ahnlund, *Sveriges Riksdag*, 3:493.

97. Elgenstierna, *Den introducerade svenska adelns ättartavlor.*

98. *Sveriges ridderskaps och adels riksdags-protokoll*, 1:138.

99. *Sveriges ridderskaps och adels riksdags-protokoll*, 2:20.

100. *Sveriges ridderskaps och adels riksdags-protokoll*, 2:266–67.

101. Scott and Storrs, "Introduction: The Consolidation of Noble Power in Europe," 1:18.

102. Elgenstierna, *Den introducerade svenska adelns ättartavlor*, 7:782–83, 787, 793; Wernstedt, "Om främmande adels naturalisation och introduktion på svenska Riddarhuset," 124.

103. David and Hans Stuart's Memorial to the House of the Nobility, Stockholm, November 10, 1652, vol. s92a, Stuart, Biographica, RA. See also *Sveriges ridderskaps och adels riksdags-protokoll*, 5:47.

104. Queen Christina's dispensation for Johan Anders Stuart, Stockholm, February 17, 1652, vol. 243:523, Palmsköldska samlingen, UUB.

105. David and Hans Stuart's Memorial to the House of the Nobility, Stockholm, November 10, 1652, vol. s92a, Stuart, Biographica, RA.

106. *Sveriges ridderskaps och adels riksdags-protokoll*, 5:47.

107. *Sveriges ridderskaps och adels riksdags-protokoll*, 5:59; Charles XI's confirmation of Johan Anders Stuart and Brita Stuart's Noble Status, July 27, 1675, vol. 243:520–21, Palmsköldska samlingen, UUB.

108. Stuart, Sköldebrevsamlingen, RA. The sources do not reveal that the House of the Nobility ever directly answered the regent's question.

109. Elgenstierna, *Den introducerade svenska adelns ättartavlor,* 7:784.

110. *Sveriges ridderskaps och adels riksdags-protokoll,* 4:161; Elgenstierna, *Den introducerade svenska adelns ättartavlor,* 2:356–57.

111. *Sveriges ridderskaps och adels riksdags-protokoll,* 4:162.

112. *Sveriges ridderskaps och adels riksdags-protokoll,* 4:163–64.

113. See Jespersen, "Social Change and Military Revolution in Early Modern Europe"; and Roberts, "The Military Revolution," 210–11.

114. *Sveriges ridderskaps och adels riksdag-protokoll,* 4:103–8.

115. *Sveriges ridderskaps och adels riksdag-protokoll,* 4:38, 74, 161–64.

116. Elgenstierna, *Den introducerade svenska adelns ättartavlor,* 1:357.

117. *Sveriges ridderskaps och adels riksdag-protokoll,* 13:11, 61.

118. *Sveriges ridderskaps och adels riksdag-protokoll,* 13:17, 31, 33.

119. Elgenstierna, *Den introducerade svenska adelns ättartavlor,* 6:140–41.

120. Förteckning över Robert Lichtons arkiv, 15, RA.

5. Migrants and Diplomacy

1. Mattingly, *Renaissance Diplomacy,* 10.

2. Roosen, *The Age of Louis XIV,* 64, 65.

3. Andrew Keith, Militieräkenskaper, Personregister, KA.

4. Berg and Lagercrantz, *Scots in Sweden,* 19.

5. Instructions for the Swedish Ambassadors Count Erik Brahe and Anders Keith, Knight of Forsholm, to Queen Elizabeth of England, June 22, 1583, vol. 531, Anglica, Diplomatica, RA.

6. Berg and Lagercrantz, *Scots in Sweden,* 20.

7. Tunberg et al., *Histoire de l'administration des affaires étrangères de Suède,* 81–82.

8. Archibald Duncan, introduction, iii, Spens Diplomatic Correspondence.

9. Charles IX to James Spens, Örebro, April 1606, Spens Diplomatic Correspondence.

10. Duncan, introduction, iii–iv, Spens Diplomatic Correspondence.

11. Charles IX to James Spens, Örebro, January 24, 1611, Spens Diplomatic Correspondence.

12. Duncan, introduction, ix–xv, Spens Diplomatic Correspondence.

13. Duncan, introduction, xv, xxvii, Spens Diplomatic Correspondence.

14. Gustavus Adolphus to James Spens, Gripsholm, September 23, 1623, Spens Diplomatic Correspondence.

15. Duncan, introduction, xxxii–xli, Spens Diplomatic Correspondence.

16. Duncan, introduction, lvii–lxi, Spens Diplomatic Correspondence. See also Berg and Lagercrantz, Scots in Sweden, 28–29.

17. Svanberg and Tydén, Tusen år av invandring, 71–76.

18. Revera, "The Making of a Civilized Nation," 104.

19. Niléhn, "Sweden and Swedish Students Abroad," 112.

20. Eriksson, "Science and Learning in the Baroque Era," 69–70.

21. Roberts, ed., Swedish Diplomats at Cromwell's Court, 3, 8, 10.

22. Roberts, ed., Swedish Diplomats at Cromwell's Court, 6.

23. Jones, The Diplomatic Relations between Cromwell and Charles X Gustavus of Sweden, 22.

24. Instruction för General Maijoren Edel och Wälb: Georg Fletwod fryherre till Hwareffter han Sigh utih den honom omförtrodde Commission till Jälunda Her Protecteuren af Engellandh, hafwer att rätta och förhålla, Datum Stockholm den A.0 1655, vol. 532, Anglica, Diplomatica, RA.

25. Calendar of State Papers and Manuscripts, Relating to English Affairs, Existing in the Archives and Collections of Venice, 24:189–90.

26. George Fleetwood to Charles X Gustavus, Gravisend, August 26, 1656, George Fleetwood brev till Kungl. Maj:t 1655–1657, vol. 22, Anglica, Diplomatica, RA. See also Elgenstierna, Den introducerade svenska adelns ättartavlor, 2:716.

27. The regency government of Charles XI to George Fleetwood, June 2, 1660, Riksregistratur, RA.

28. Instructions for our right trustie and wellbeloved S:r Patrick Ruthven knight Lord lieutenant general of the Swedish forces in Germanie, vol. 4, no. 234, S.P. 95, PRO.

29. Calendar of State Papers, Domestic Series of the Reign of Charles I, 409.

30. Till Rickz och Cammar Rådh att låta dee Skotshe Officerere bekomma till affsteedh Twå Månaders Solld, August 8, 1639, Riksregistratur, RA.

31. Hutton, *Charles the Second*, 13–14, 35.

32. Macray, introduction to Ruthven, *Letters and Papers of Patrick Ruthven*, xv.

33. *Dictionary of National Biography*, s.v. "Patrick Ruthven," 17:512–13; Ruthven, *Letters and Papers of Patrick Ruthven*, 17, 28, 34–37.

34. "Instructions for our right trusty and right welbeloved cousin Patrick, Earle of Brainceford, imployed by us into Sweden. Dated the 29th day of January, 1649," in Ruthven, *Letters and Papers of Patrick Ruthven*, 97–99.

35. "Sir Robert Long to the Earl of Brentford, February 25, 1649," in Ruthven, *Letters and Papers of Patrick Ruthven*, 99–100.

36. Kullberg, Bergh, and Sondén, eds., *Svenska riksrådets protokoll*, 13:16–17.

37. Lorents, *Efter Brömsebrofreden*, 93–100.

38. Maclean, "Montrose's Preparations for the Invasion of Scotland," 8.

39. Maclean, "Montrose's Preparations for the Invasion of Scotland," 8; Kullberg, Bergh, and Sondén, eds., *Svenska riksrådets protokoll*, 13:40–41.

40. Kullberg, Bergh, and Sondén, eds., *Svenska riksrådets protokoll*, 13:43. In the Egerton Manuscripts Collection located in the British Library is a document listing the military equipment provided by Christina to Charles II. The amounts listed are different from what is stated in the minutes of the meeting of the Council of the Realm, which are cited in this chapter. According to the document in the British Library, Christina supplied 6,000 muskets, 5,000 pikes, 8,000 bandoliers, 4,000 footmen swords, 150 halberts and partizans, 1,800 pairs of pistols, 600 horsemen swords, 2,000 sets of horsemen's armor, 50 drums, 12 cannons, 5 lasts of powder, 8 lasts of match, 1,200 cannonballs, and proportional amounts of ammunition for the muskets and pistols. The document gives no indication of who wrote it or from where it came. See Egerton Manuscripts, vol. 2542, BL.

41. "The Earl of Brentford to J. Mackliere, St. Germaine, August 30, 1649," in Ruthven, *Letters and Papers of Patrick Ruthven*, 110. See also Instrucions for our Trusty & welbeloved Robert Meade Esqr.

by Us employed to Our deare Sister the Queene of Sweaden, Jersey, November 11/21, 1649, Egerton Manuscripts, vol. 2542, BL.

42. Maclean, "Montrose's Preparations for the Invasion of Scotland," 11.

43. James King, Riksarkivets ämbetsarkiv-1966, huvudarkivet FVA:47, ed. Per Sondén, Biografiska anteckninger från 1600 talet, RA.

44. Fissel, *The Bishops' Wars*, 172–73.

45. Berg and Lagercrantz, *Scots in Sweden*, 39; *Dictionary of National Biography*, s.v. "James King," 11:135.

46. Maclean, "Montrose's Preparations for the Invasion of Scotland," 12. Charles II made James King's appointment official on March 19, 1650. See "Warrant to Sir Edward Nicholas, March 19, 1650," in *Letters and Papers Illustrating the Relations between Charles the Second and Scotland*, 38.

47. Almquist, *Frälsegodsen i Sverige*, part 4, *Småland*, 1:270. See also Douglas, *Robert Douglas*, 152.

48. "Captain Meade to Secretary Nicholas, Stockholm, May 11, 1650," in *Letters and Papers Illustrating the Relations between Charles the Second and Scotland*, 100–101.

49. Steckzén, "En höglandshjälte," 154.

50. Maclean, "Montrose's Preparations for the Invasion of Scotland," 17.

51. Williams, *Montrose: Cavalier in Mourning*, 334.

52. Williams, *Montrose: Cavalier in Mourning*, 335, 340–41.

53. Maclean, "Montrose's Preparations for the Invasion of Scotland," 27. For a more recent account of events in Scotland surrounding Montrose's invasion see Furgol, "The Civil Wars in Scotland," 61–65.

54. William Bellenden, Personregister, rullor-1700, KA.

55. Maclean, "Montrose's Preparations for the Invasion of Scotland," 8–12.

56. Queen of Sweden to Charles II, 1649, vol. 5A, no. 32, S.P. 95, PRO; Charles II to Christina, July 8, 1649, vol. 1, Scotica, Diplomatica, RA.

57. Ansökningar och merit förteckningar arméen, M1134, Militaria, RA; Spalding, *Contemporaries of Bulstrode Whitelocke*, 272.

58. Christopher Potley to Gyldenklou, London, September 10, 1647,

vol. 514, Anglica, Diplomatica, RA. See also Tunberg et al., *Histoire de l'administration des affaires étrangères de Suède*, 86.

59. Col. Potley to [?] from Sweden, December 1650, vol. 5A, no. 36, S.P. 95, PRO.

60. Col. Potley to [?] from Sweden, December 1650; Spalding, *Contemporaries of Bulstrode Whitelocke*, 272.

61. Tayler and Tayler, eds., *The House of Forbes*, 178.

62. Tayler and Tayler, eds., *The House of Forbes*, 179–84.

63. "Memorial of Alexander Forbes, 11th Lord Forbes, presented to King Charles II, Westminster, August 26, 1661," in Tayler and Tayler, eds., *The House of Forbes*, 185–87.

64. "Memorial of Alexander Forbes," 185–87. See also Charles XI's commission to Alexander Forbes to take up sunken ships and their goods in Swedish waters, August 27, 1663, vol. F15, Forbes, Biographica, RA.

65. Landström, *The Royal Warship Vasa*, 144–53.

66. "Memorial of Alexander Forbes," 185–87. See also the documents about the controversy over financing the raising of the ships and the Council of the Realm's decision to revoke Forbes's privilege to continue the project in 1663 (vol. F15, Forbes, Biographica, RA).

67. "Memorial of Alexander Forbes," 185–87. For more information surrounding the defeat of Charles II and the Scottish army in 1651 see Grainger, *Cromwell against the Scots*, 128–46.

68. William Bellenden to Edward Nicholas, Stockholm, June 24, 1654, no. 170, Egerton Manuscripts, vol. 2534, BL. For a discussion of Bellenden's land donations see Dackman, "Sinclairs i Sverige," 13.

69. William Bellenden to Edward Nicholas, Stockholm, June 24, 1654.

70. Hatton, introduction to "Captain James Jefferyes' Letters to the Secretary of State, Whitehall, from the Swedish Army, 1707–1709," 8–9.

71. Hatton, ed., introduction to "Captain James Jefferyes' Letters," 9; Sparre, *Kungl. Västmanlands regementes historia*, vol. 4, *Biografiska anteckningar om officerare och vederlikar*, 85.

72. Hatton, ed., introduction to "Captain James Jefferyes' Letters," 9–10.

73. Hatton, *Charles XII of Sweden*, 233.

74. Hatton, ed., introduction to "Captain James Jefferyes' Letters," 15–17.

75. "James Jefferyes to the Secretary of State, Poltava, July 13, 1709," in Hatton, ed., "Captain James Jefferyes' Letters," 75–78.

76. "James Jefferyes to the Secretary of State, Moscow, August 3, 1709," in Hatton, ed., "Captain James Jefferyes' Letters," 78–81.

77. Hatton, ed., introduction to "Captain James Jefferyes' Letters," 25.

78. Hugo Hamilton to Carl Gustaf Wrangel, 1666–1671, vol. E8368, Skrivelser till Carl Gustaf Wrangel, Skokloster samlingen, RA.

79. "Peter Julius Coyet to Charles X Gustavus, London, March 30, 1655," in Roberts, ed., *Swedish Diplomats at Cromwell's Court*, 53–54.

80. A. Forbes to Col. Johan Skytte the Younger, March 1635, vol. E5412, Depositio Skytteana, RA.

81. Whitelocke, *A Journal of the Swedish Embassy*.

82. Whitelocke, *A Journal of the Swedish Embassy*. There were also two other men with Swedish connections in Whitelocke's retinue. They were Christopher Potley's son Andrew and Thomas Vavassour, whose father, William Vavassour, was an officer in the Swedish army who began his career in the 1630s and retired in 1648. He reentered Swedish service as the colonel of a regiment he had recruited in Scotland in 1656. See list of the retinue that accompanied Whitelocke to Sweden, vol. 532, Anglica, Diplomatica, RA, and William Vavassour, Militära chefer i svenska arméen 1620 talet-1840 samts deras i riksarkivet förvarade skrivelser, RA.

83. Whitelocke, *A Journal of the Swedish Embassy*, 1:146, 2:336.

84. Whitelocke, *A Journal of the Swedish Embassy*, 1:138, 2:321–33.

85. Whitelocke, *A Journal of the Swedish Embassy*, 1:147, 2:304.

Conclusion

1. William Leslie to Charles XI, London, June 14, 1679, vol. L14, Leslie, Biographica, RA.

2. Nilsson, "Imperial Sweden," 30.

3. Dahlgren, "Karl XI," 129.

4. Duffy, *The Military Experience in the Age of Reason*, 14–15.

5. Duffy, *The Military Experience in the Age of Reason*, 32–34.

6. Lockhart, *Denmark in the Thirty Years' War*, 34. For further information on the political power of the Danish nobility during the

seventeenth century see Jespersen, "The Rise and Fall of the Danish Nobility," 41–70.

7. Riis, *Should Auld Acquaintance Be Forgot*, 1:79.

8. Phipps, "Britons in Seventeenth-Century Russia," 387–403. For a discussion of the difficulties Scottish officers experienced in adjusting to life in Russia, see Dukes, "Problems Concerning the Departure of Scottish Soldiers," 143–56.

9. Count Sinclair to John Mitchell, Stockholm, January 1834, vol. H.S.5., Genealogiska samlingen, KB.

BIBLIOGRAPHY

Manuscript Sources

British Library (London)
    Additional Manuscripts
    Egerton Manuscripts
    Harlian Manuscripts
Krigsarkivet (Stockholm)
    Meritförteckningar (Flottan)
    Militieräkenskaper
    Personregister, rullor-1700
    Rullor 1620–1723
    Viggo Keys samlingen
Kungliga Biblioteket (Stockholm)
    Autografsamlingen
        Hans Clerck
        Hugo Hamilton af Hageby
        Frederik Henrik af Chapmans autobiografi
    Genealogiska samlingen
        Sinclair
    Rålambska samlingen
        Douglas
Lund Universitetsbibliotek
    De la Gardieska samlingen
        Biographica minora
            Kurtzer Verlauff seiner Hoch-Gräfflichen Excellence
            Herren General Douglas geführten Lebens, So viel
            man Sich besinnen kan
        Släktarkiven
            Douglas
            Forbes

Public Record Office (London)
    State Papers, Foreign, Denmark (S.P. 75)
    State Papers, Foreign, Sweden (S.P. 95)
Riksarkivet (Stockholm)
    Acta Ecclesiastica
        Främmande trosbekännare: katoliker och reformerta
    Biographica
    Coyetska samlingen
    De la Gardieska samlingen
        Skrivelser till Magnus Gabriel de la Gardie
    Depositio Skytteana
    Diplomatica
        Anglica
        Scotica
    Enskilda samlingar: Arkivfragment: Brevskrivare
        Hamilton af Hageby, Charlotte Catharina senare g.m. Carl
            Magnus Lilliehöök af Fårdala
        Spens, Jakob, frih. slutl. överste (d. 1665)
    Eriksbergsarkivet
        Autografsamlingen
    Hammarskjöld, A. Anteckningar om skottar i svensk tjänst
    Kopiesamling I, vol. 98. Hammarskjöld biografiska registratur
        utdrag rörande engelska och skotske officerare
    Lichtons samlingen
    Militaria
        Ansökningar och meritförteckningar arméen
        Axel Oxenstiernas Brefväxling
    Oxenstierna samlingen
        Bref till Rikskansleren Axel Oxenstierna
    Riksarkivets ämbetsarkiv-1966, huvudarkivet FVa: 47, Per Son-
        dén. Biografiska anteckninger från 1600 talet
    Riksregistratur
    Skokloster Samlingen
        Skrivelser till Carl Gustaf Wrangel
    Sköldebrevsamlingen
    Skrivelser till konungen
        Kristinas tid (1633–54) II. Strödde Skrivelser

Sondén, Per. *Militära chefer i svenska arméen 1620 talet -1840 samts deras i riksarkivet förvarade skrivelser*
Stegeborgsamlingen
Generalguvernörens i Västergötland m.m. arkiv
Skrivelser till Gen. Guvernören Hert. Adolf Johan
Skrivelser till Carl Gustaf
Uppsala Universitetsbibliotek
"The Diplomatic Correspondence of Sir James Spens of Wormiston." Edited and with an introduction by Archibald Duncan. Box E:379:d, Manuscript Collections.
Hamiltonska arkivet
Palmsköldska samlingen

Printed Primary Sources

Almquist. Joh. Ax. *Frälsegodsen i Sverige under Storhetstiden med särskild hänsyn till proveniens och säteribildning.* 4 parts. 9 vols. Stockholm: Norstedts Tryckeri, 1931–76.

Calendar of State Papers, Domestic Series of the Reign of Charles I, 1638–1639, Preserved in Her Majesty's Public Record Office. Vol. 13, edited by John Bruce and William Douglas Hamilton. London: Her Majesty's Stationery Office, 1871. Reprint, Nendeln, Liechtenstein: Kraus Reprint, 1967.

Calendar of State Papers and Manuscripts, Relating to English Affairs, Existing in the Archives and Collections of Venice, and in Other Libraries of Northern Italy. Edited by Allen B. Hinds. Vol. 24, 1636–1639. London: His Majesty's Stationery Office, 1923.

"Ceremonial of the Funeral of Field-Marshall Robert Douglas, Stockholm, June 1662." Pp. 327–32 in vol. 2 of *The Spottiswoode Miscellany: A Collection of Original Papers and Tracts, Illustrative Chiefly of the Civil and Ecclesiastical History of Scotland,* edited by James Maidment. Edinburgh: Alex. Laurie, 1845.

Cockburn, Robert, and Harry A. Cockburn. *The Records of the Cockburn Family.* London: T. N. Foulis, 1913.

The Declaration and Message, Sent from the Queen of Bohemia, Lord Graven, Lord Goring, And divers other English Gentlemen, resident at the Hague in Holland, on Friday last, Novemb. 5. 1652: To Charles the Second. . . . London: G. Horton, 1652.

Egerton, Philip de Malpas Grey, ed. "Letter from George Fleetwood to his Father Giving an Account of the Battle of Lutzen and the Death of Gustavus Adolphus." *The Camden Miscellany* 1, no. 39 (1847): 3–12.

Elgenstierna, Gustaf. *Den introducerade svenska adelns ättartavlor med tillägg och rättelser.* 9 vols. Stockholm: P. A. Nordstedt & Söner, 1925–36.

Firth, C. H., ed. *Scotland and the Protectorate: Letters and Papers Relating to the Military Government of Scotland from January 1654 to June 1659.* Edinburgh: Scottish Historical Society, 1899.

Fowler, J. *The History of the Troubles of Suethland and Poland: . . . With a Continuation of those Troubles untill the Truce. . . . As also, a Particular Narration of the Daily Passages at the Last and Great Treaty of Pacification between those two Kingdomes. . . . Concluding with a Breife Commemoration of the Life and Death of Sir George Duglas Knight. . . .* London: Thomas Roycroft, 1656.

Fraser, William, ed. *The Douglas Book.* 4 vols. Edinburgh, 1885.

Gardiner, Samuel Rawson, ed. "Letters Relating to the Mission of Sir Thomas Roe to Gustavus Adolphus, 1629–30." *The Camden Miscellany,* vol. 7 (1875).

Hatton, Rahnhild, ed. "Captain James Jefferyes' Letters to the Secretary of State, Whitehall, from the Swedish Army, 1707–1709." *Historisk magasin,* vol. 1. *Historisk handlingar* 35, no. 1 (1953).

Kullberg, N. A., Severin Bergh, and Per Sondén, eds. *Svenska riksrådets protokoll.* Vol. 13 in *Handlingar rörande sveriges historia,* 3d ser. Stockholm: P. A. Norstedt & Söner, 1880–1959.

A Letter Sent from the Queen of Sweden to the King of France Touching the Affairs of that Kingdome, and the King of Scots with her Majesties desire and gracious promise thereupon. London: G. Horton, 1652.

Letters and Papers Illustrating the Relations between Charles the Second and Scotland in 1650. Edited by Samuel Rawson Gardiner. Vol 17. Scottish Historical Society, 1894.

"List of the Scottish Officers under Gustavus Adolphus, King of Sweden." Pp. 383–84 in vol. 2 of *The Spottiswoode Miscellany: A Collection of Original Papers and Tracts, Illustrative Chiefly of the Civil and Ecclesiastical History of Scotland,* edited by James Maidment. Edinburgh: Alex. Laurie, 1845.

The Melvilles, Earls of Melville, and the Leslies, Earls of Leven. Edited by William Fraser. 3 vols. Edinburgh, 1890.

Monro, Robert. *Monro: His Expedition with the Worthy Scots Regiment (Called Mac-Keys Regiment) Levied in August 1626 by Sir Donald Mac-Key Lord Rhees, Colonell for His Majesties Service of Denmark.* . . . London: William Jones, 1637.

Paul, James Balfour, ed. *The Scots Peerage, founded on Wood's ed. of sir R. Douglas's Peerage* of Scotland. Vols. 2, 3, and 4. Edinburgh: David Douglas, 1905–7.

Ramsay, Jully. *Frälsesläkter i Finland intill stora ofreden.* Helsinki: Förlagsaktiebolaget Söderström, 1909.

The Register of the Privy Council of Scotland. Edited by John Hill Burton. Series 1, vols. 2–8, and series 2, vol 1. Edinburgh: H. M. General Register House, 1878.

Rikskansleren Axel Oxenstierna skrifter och brefvexling: Bref från Herman Wrangel, med flera generaler. Vol 9. Stockholm: P. A. Norstedt & Söner, 1898.

Roberts, Michael, ed. *Sweden as a Great Power, 1611–1697: Government, Society, Foreign Policy.* London: Edward Arnold, 1968.

————. *Swedish Diplomats at Cromwell's Court, 1655–1656: The Missions of Peter Julius Coyet and Christer Bonde.* London: Royal Historical Society, 1988.

Robinson, John. *An Account of Sueden: Together with an Extract of the History of that Kingdom.* 2d ed. London, 1711.

Royal Commission on Historical Manuscripts. *The Manuscripts of the Duke of Hamilton.* 11th Report. Appendix, part VI. London: Eyre and Spottiswoode, 1887.

Ruthven, Patrick. *Ruthven Correspondence: Letters and Papers of Patrick Ruthven, Earl of Forth and Brentford and of His Family:* A.D.1615–A.D. 1662: *With an Appendix of Papers Relating to Sir John Urry.* Edited by W. D. Macray. London: J. B. Nichols and Sons, 1868.

Schlegel, Bernhard, and Carl Arvid Klingspor. *Den med sköldebref förlänade men ej på riddarhuset introducerade svenska adelns ättartaflor.* Stockholm: P. A. Norstedt & Söner, 1875.

Sveriges ridderskaps och adels riksdags-protokoll. Edited by S. Bergh and B. Taube. 31 vols. Stockholm: P. A. Norstedt & Söner, 1871–1906.

Tayler, Alistair Norwich, and Henrietta Tayler, eds. *The House of Forbes.*

Aberdeen, Scotland: Third Spalding Club/Aberdeen University Press, 1937.

Watts, William. *The Swedish Discipline, Religious, Civile, and Military.* . . . London: Nath: Butter and Nich: Bourne, 1632.

Whitelocke, Bulstrode. *A Journal of the Swedish Embassy in the Years 1653 and 1654.* Edited by Henry Reeve. 2 vols. London: Longman, Brown, Green, and Longmans, 1855.

Wieselgren, P., ed. *De la Gardieska arkivet eller handlingar ur Grefl. De la Gardieska biblioteket på Löberöd.* Lund, Sweden: Lundberska Boktryckeriet, 1837.

Secondary Works

Åberg, Alf. "Scots in the Army of Gustavus Adolphus." *Anglo-Swedish Review* (April 1957): 226–30.

————. "Scottish Soldiers in the Swedish Armies in the Sixteenth and Seventeenth Centuries." Pp. 90–99 in *Scotland and Scandinavia, 800–1800,* edited by Grant G. Simpson. Edinburgh: John Donald, 1990.

————. "The Swedish Army from Lützen to Narva." Pp. 265–87 in *Sweden's Age of Greatness, 1632–1718,* edited by Michael Roberts. London: Macmillan, 1973.

Adams, Simon. "Europe and the Palatine War." Pp. 61–70 in *The Thirty Years' War,* edited by Geoffrey Parker. London: Routledge & Kegan, 1984.

Ågren, Kurt. "Breadwinners and Dependents: An Economic Crisis in the Swedish Aristocracy during the 1600s?" Pp. 9–27 in *Aristocrats, Farmers, Proletarians: Essays in Swedish Demographic History,* by Kurt Ågren et al. Stockholm: Esselte Studium, 1973.

————. "The reduction." Pp. 237–64 in *Sweden's Age of Greatness, 1632–1718,* edited by Michael Roberts. London: Macmillan, 1973.

————. "Rise and Decline of an Aristocracy: The Swedish Social and Political Elite in the 17th Century." *Scandinavian Journal of History* 1 (1976): 55–80.

Ahnlund, Nils. *Sveriges Riksdag.* Vol. 3, *Ståndsriksdagens utdaning 1592–1672,* edited by Nils Edén. Stockholm: Victor Petterson, 1933.

Anderson, R. C. "Ayscue and Cox in Sweden." *Mariner's Mirror* 47, no. 3 (August 1961): 298–300.

————. "English Officers in Sweden." *Mariner's Mirror* 12, no. 4, (October 1926): 458.

Armitage, David. "Making the Empire British: Scotland in the Atlantic World, 1542–1717." *Past and Present* (May 1997): 34–63.

Asker, Björn. "Aristocracy and Autocracy in Seventeenth-Century Sweden: The Decline of the Aristocracy within the Civil Administration before 1680." *Scandinavian Journal of History* 15, no. 2 (1990): 89–95.

————. *Officerarna och det svenska samhället, 1650–1700.* Stockholm: Almqvist & Wiksell International, 1983.

Aylmer, Gerald E. "English Perceptions of Scandinavia in the Seventeenth Century." Pp. 181–93 in *Europe and Scandinavia: Aspects of the Process of Integration in the Seventeenth Century,* edited by Göran Rystad. Lund, Sweden: Wallin & Dalholm, 1983.

Behre, Göran. "Gothenburg in Stuart War Strategy, 1649–1760." Pp. 107–17 in *Scotland and Scandinavia, 800–1800,* edited by Grant G. Simpson. Edinburgh: John Donald, 1990.

Berg, Jonas. "Skottar i Sverige." *Fataburen: Nordiska museets och Skansens årsbok* (1981): 115–24.

Berg, Jonas, and Bo Lagercrantz. *Scots in Sweden.* Stockholm: Nordiska Museet, 1962.

Berg, Tor. "De särskilda fögderierna för förbrutna gods under Karl IX:s och Gustav II Adolfs regeringar." *Meddelanden från svenska riksarkivet* (1929): 118–225.

————. *Johan Skytte: Hans ungdom och verksamhet under Karl IX:s regering.* Stockholm: Albert Bonnier, 1920.

Bieganska, Anna. "A Note on the Scots in Poland, 1550–1800." Pp. 157–65 in *Scotland and Europe, 1200–1850,* edited by T. C. Smout. Edinburgh: John Donald, 1986.

Bohman, Nils, ed. *Svenska män och kvinnor: Biografisk uppslagsbok.* Vol. 1. Stockholm: Albert Bonnier, 1942.

Böhme, Klaus-Richard. "Officersrekryteringen vid tre landskapsregementen, 1626–1682." Pp. 215–52 in *Bördor, bönder, börd i 1600-talets Sverige,* edited by Margareta Revera and Rolf Torstendahl. Motala, Sweden: Borgströms, 1979.

Bonner, Elizabeth A. "Continuing the 'Auld Alliance' in the Sixteenth Century: Scots in France and French in Scotland." Pp. 31–46 in

The Scottish Soldier Abroad, 1247–1967, edited by Grant G. Simpson. Edinburgh: John Donald, 1992.

Brännman, Erik. Frälseköpen under Gustav II Adolfs regering. Lund, Sweden: Gleerup, 1950.

Brockington, William S. Introduction to Monro: His Expedition with the Worthy Scots Regiment Called Mac-Keys, by Robert Monro. Westport CT: Praeger, 1999.

Cannon, John. "The British Nobility, 1660–1800." Pp. 53–81 in The European Nobilities in the Seventeenth and Eighteenth Centuries, edited by H. M. Scott. Vol. 1, Western Europe. London: Longman, 1995.

Canny, Nicholas. "English Migration into and across the Atlantic during the Seventeenth and Eighteenth Centuries." Pp. 1–9 in Europeans on the Move: Studies on European Migration, 1500–1800, edited by Nicholas Canny. Oxford: Clarendon Press, 1994.

————. "The Marginal Kingdom: Ireland as a Problem in the First British Empire." Pp. 35–66 in Strangers within the Realm: Cultural Margins of the First British Empire, edited by Bernard Bailyn and Philip D. Morgan. Chapel Hill: University of North Carolina Press, 1991.

Capp, Bernard. Cromwell's Navy: The Fleet and the English Revolution 1648–1660. Oxford: Clarendon Press, 1989.

Carlsson, Lizzie. "Jag giver dig min dotter": Trolovning och äktenskap i den svenska kvinnans äldre historia. Vol. 18 of Rättshistoriskt Bibliotek. Stockholm: A. B. Nordiksa, 1965.

Carlsson, Sten. "Tyska invandrare i Sverige." in Fataburen: Nordiska museets och Skansens årsbok (1981): 9–31.

Cavallie, James. De höga officerarna: Studier i den svenska militära hierarkien under 1600-talets senare del. Lund, Sweden: Bloms Boktryckeri, 1981.

Crawford, Barbara E. "William Sinclair, Earl of Orkney, and His Family: A Study in the Politics of Survival." Pp. 232–53 in Essays on the Nobility of Medieval Scotland, edited by K. J. Stringer. Edinburgh: John Donald, 1985.

Cressy, David. Birth, Marriage, and Death: Ritual, Religion, and the Life-Cycle in Tudor and Stuart England. Oxford: Oxford University Press, 1997.

Cross, Anthony. By the Banks of the Neva: Chapters from the Lives and

Careers of the British in Eighteenth-Century Russia. Cambridge: Cambridge University Press, 1997.

Cullen, L. M. "The Irish Diaspora of the Seventeenth and Eighteenth Centuries." Pp. 113–52 in *Europeans on the Move: Studies on European Migration, 1500–1800*, edited by Nicholas Canny. Oxford: Clarendon Press, 1994.

————. "Scotland and Ireland, 1600–1800: Their Role in the Evolution of British Society." Pp. 226–44 in *Scottish Society, 1500–1800*, edited by R. A. Houston and I. D. Whyte. Cambridge: Cambridge University Press, 1989.

Dackman, Håkan. "Sinclairs i Sverige." *Släkt och hävd: Tidskrift utgiven av Genealogiska Föreningen Riksförening för Släktforskning*, no. 1–2 (1978): 3–33.

Dahlgren, Stellan. "Karl XI." In *Kungar och krigare: Tre essäer om Karl X Gustaf, Karl XI och Karl XII*, by Anders Floren, Stellan Dahlgren, and Jan Lindegren. Stockholm: Atlantis, 1992.

The Dictionary of National Biography. Edited by Leslie Stephen and Sidney Lee. Vols. 11, 17. London: Oxford University Press, 1917–22.

Dictionary of Scandinavian History. Edited by Byron Nordstrom. Westport CT: Greenwood Press, 1986.

Dodgshon, R. A. *From Chiefs to Landlords: Social and Economic Change in Western Highlands and Islands, c.1493–1820.* Edinburgh: Edinburgh University Press, 1998.

————. " 'Pretense of Blude' and 'Place of Thair Duelling': The Nature of Highland Clans, 1500–1745." Pp. 169–98 in *Scottish Society, 1500–1800*, edited by R. A. Houston and I. D. Whyte. Cambridge: Cambridge University Press, 1989.

Donaldson, Gordon. *Scotland: James V to James VII.* Edinburgh: Oliver & Boyd, 1965.

————. *The Scots Overseas.* London: Robert Hale, 1966.

Donner, Otto. *A Brief Sketch of the Scottish Families in Finland and Sweden.* Helsinki: Finnish Literary Society's Press, 1884.

Douglas, Archibald. *Robert Douglas: En krigargestalt från vår storhetstid.* Stockholm: Albert Bonnier, 1957.

Douhan, Bernt. "Vallonerna i Sverige." *Fataburen: Nordiska museets och Skansens årsbok* (1981): 66–90.

Dow, James. "Ruthven's Army in Sweden and Estonia." *Kungliga vitter-*

hets historie och antikvitets akademien. Historiskt arkivet 13 (1965): 1–102.

———. "Skotter in Sixteenth-Century Scania." *Scottish Historical Review* 154 (1965): 34–51.

———. "Scottish Trade with Sweden, 1512–80." *Scottish Historical Review* 48 (1969): 64–79.

———. "Scottish Trade with Sweden, 1580–1622." *Scottish Historical Review* 48 (1969): 124–50.

Duffy, Christopher. *The Military Experience in the Age of Reason, 1715–1789.* New York: Scribner, 1987.

Dukes, Paul. "The First Scottish Soldiers in Russia." Pp. 47–54 in *The Scottish Soldier Abroad, 1247–1967,* edited by Grant G. Simpson. Edinburgh: John Donald, 1992.

———. "The Leslie Family in the Swedish Period (1630–5) of the Thirty Years' War." *European Studies Review* 12 (1982): 401–24.

———. "Problems Concerning the Departure of Scottish Soldiers from Seventeenth-Century Muscovy." Pp. 143–56 in *Scotland and Europe, 1200–1850,* edited by T. C. Smout. Edinburgh: John Donald, 1986.

Durkan, John. "The French Connection in the Sixteenth and Early Seventeenth Centuries." Pp. 19–44 in *Scotland and Europe, 1200–1850,* edited by T. C. Smout. Edinburgh: John Donald, 1986.

Ellenius, Allan. "Visual Culture in Seventeenth-Century Sweden: Images of Power and Knowledge." Pp. 41–68 in *The Age of New Sweden,* edited by Arne Losman, Agneta Lundstrom, and Margareta Revera. Stockholm: Livrustkammaren, 1988.

Elmroth, Ingvar. *För Kung och Fosterland: Studier i den svenska adelns demografi och offentliga funktioner, 1600–1900.* Lund, Sweden: Gleerup, 1981.

Englund, Peter. "Om klienter och deras patroner." Pp. 86–97 in *Makt och vardag: Hur man styrde, levde och tänkte under svensk stormaktstid,* edited by Stellan Dahlgren and Anders Floren. Stockholm: Atlantis, 1993.

Enloe, Cynthia H. *Ethnic Soldiers: State Security in Divided Societies.* Athens: University of Georgia Press, 1980.

Eriksson, Gunnar. "Science and Learning in the Baroque Era." Pp. 69–84 in *The Age of New Sweden,* edited by Arne Losman, Agneta Lundstrom, and Margareta Revera. Stockholm: Livrustkammaren, 1988.

Fallon, James A. "Scottish Mercenaries in the Service of Denmark and Sweden, 1626–1632." Ph.D. dissertation, University of Glasgow, 1972.

Fedosov, Dmitry G. "The First Russian Bruces." Pp. 55–66 in *The Scottish Soldier Abroad, 1247–1967*, edited by Grant G. Simpson. Edinburgh: John Donald, 1992.

Fischer, Th. A. *The Scots in Eastern and Western Prussia*. Edinburgh: Otto Schulze, 1903.

————. *The Scots in Germany: Being a Contribution Towards the History of the Scot Abroad*. Edinburgh: Otto Schulze, 1902.

————. *The Scots in Sweden: Being a Contribution Towards the History of the Scot Abroad*. Edinburgh: Otto Schulze, 1907.

Fissel, Mark Charles. *The Bishops' Wars: Charles I's Campaigns against Scotland, 1638–1649*. Cambridge: Cambridge University Press, 1994.

Fleetwood, G. W. "Kring 300-årsminnet av ett bröllop vid hovet på Nyköpings slott." *Sörmlandsbygden* (1941): 77–84.

Flinn, Michael, et al. *Scottish Population History: From the Seventeenth Century to the 1930s*. Cambridge: Cambridge University Press, 1977.

Fullerton, Brian, and Alan F. Williams. *Scandinavia: An Introductory Geography*. New York: Praeger, 1972.

Furgol, Edward M. "The Civil Wars in Scotland." Pp. 41–72 in *The Civil Wars: A Military History of England, Scotland, and Ireland, 1638–1660*, edited by John Kenyon and Jane Ohlmeyer. Oxford: Oxford University Press, 1998.

————. *A Regimental History of the Covenanting Armies, 1639–1651*. Edinburgh: John Donald, 1990.

————. "Scotland Turned Sweden: The Scottish Covenanters and the Military Revolution, 1638–1651." Pp. 134–54 in *The Scottish National Covenant in the British Context, 1638–1651*, edited by J. S. Morrill. Edinburgh: Edinburgh University Press, 1990.

Garstein, Oskar. *Rome and the Counter-Reformation in Scandinavia: Until the Establishment of the S. Congregatio de Propaganda Fide in 1622*. 2 vols. Oslo: Universitetsförlaget, 1980.

Grage, Elsa-Britta. "Scottish Merchants in Gothenburg, 1621–1850." Pp. 112–42 in *Scotland and Europe, 1200–1850*, edited by T. C. Smout. Edinburgh: John Donald, 1986.

Grainger, John D. *Cromwell against the Scots: The Last Anglo-Scottish War, 1650–1652*. East Linton, Scotland: Tuckwell Press, 1997.

Granberg, Eva. "Skotten James Keith, major i svensk tjänst hans anknytning till Älghult och något om hans ättlingar." *Älghultskrönika* 29 (1972): 19–28.

Grimble, Ian. *Chief of Mackay*. London: Routledge & Kegan Paul, 1965.

———. "The Royal Payment of Mackay's Regiment." *Scottish Gaelic Studies* 11 (1961): 23–38.

Hacker, Barton C. "Women and Military Institutions in Early Modern Europe: A Reconnaissance." *Signs* 6, no. 4 (1981): 643–71.

Hale, J. R. *War and Society in Renaissance Europe, 1450–1620*. Baltimore: John Hopkins University Press, 1986.

Hamilton, Everard. *Hamilton Memoirs: Being Historical and Genealogical Notices of a Branch of That Family Which Settled in Ireland in the Reign of King James I*. Dundalk, Ireland, 1920.

Hamilton, George. *A History of the House of Hamilton*. Edinburgh: J. Skinner, 1932.

Hamilton, Henning Adolf. *Svenska ätterna Hamiltons engelska härstamning*. Hamiltonska Släktforeningen, 1934.

Hatton, Ragnhild. *Charles XII of Sweden*. London: Weidenfeld and Nicolson, 1968.

Heckscher, Eli F. *An Economic History of Sweden*. Translated by Göran Ohlin. Cambridge MA: Harvard University Press, 1954.

Heiberg, Steffen. *Christian 4: Monarken, mennesket, og myten*. Copenhagen: Gyldendalske Boghandel, 1988.

Heimer, August. *De diplomatiska förbindelserna mellan Sverige och England, 1633–1654*. Lund, Sweden: Gleerupska Universitets-Bokhandeln, 1893.

Henry, Gráinne. *The Irish Military Community in Spanish Flanders, 1586–1621*. Dublin: Irish Academic Press, 1992.

Hohenberg, Paul M., and Lynn Hollen Lees. *The Making of Urban Europe, 1000–1950*. Cambridge MA: Harvard University Press, 1985.

Houston, R. A. "Women in the Economy and Society of Scotland, 1500–1800." Pp. 37–58 in *Scottish Society, 1500–1800*, edited by R. A.

Houston and I. D. Whyte. Cambridge: Cambridge University Press, 1989.

Hudson, Geoffrey L. "Negotiating for Blood Money: War Widows and the Courts in Seventeenth-Century England." Pp. 146–69 in *Women, Crime, and the Courts in Early Modern England*, edited by Jennifer Kermode and Garthine Walker. Chapel Hill: University of North Carolina Press, 1994.

Hufton, Olwen. *The Prospect before Her: A History of Women in Western Europe*. Vol. 1, *1500–1800*. New York: Knopf, 1996.

Hutton, Ronald. *Charles the Second, King of England, Scotland, and Ireland*. Oxford: Clarendon Press, 1989.

Jespersen, Knud J. V. "The Rise and Fall of the Danish Nobility, 1600–1800." Pp. 41–70 in *The European Nobilities in the Seventeenth and Eighteenth Centuries*, edited by H. M. Scott. Vol. 2, *Northern, Central, and Eastern Europe*. London: Longman, 1995.

————. "Social Change and Military Revolution in Early Modern Europe: Some Danish Evidence." *Historical Journal* 26, no. 1 (1983): 1–14.

Jones, Guernsey. *The Diplomatic Relations between Cromwell and Charles X Gustavus of Sweden*. Lincoln NE: State Journal Company Printers, 1897.

Kenyon, John, and Jane Ohlmeyer. "The Background to the Civil Wars in the Stuart Kingdoms." Pp. 3–40 in *The Civil Wars: A Military History of England, Scotland, and Ireland, 1638–1660*, edited by John Kenyon and Jane Ohlmeyer. Oxford: Oxford University Press, 1998.

Kiernan, V. G. "Foreign Mercenaries and Absolute Monarchy." Pp. 117–40 in *Crisis in Europe, 1560–1660: Essays from Past and Present*, edited by Trevor Aston. London: Routledge & Kegan Paul, 1966.

Klieforth, Alexander Leslie. *Grip Fast: The Leslies in History*. Chichester, England: Phillimore, 1993.

Kuylenstierna, Oswald. *Karl XII:s drabanter*. Stockholm: A. B. Nordiska, 1910.

Landsman, Ned C. "Nation, Migration, and Province in the First British Empire: Scotland and the Americas, 1600–1800." *American Historical Review* 104, no. 2 (April 1999): 463–75.

Landström, Björn. *The Royal Warship* Vasa. Stockholm: Stenström Interpublishing, 1980.

Lenman, Bruce. "The Highland Aristocracy and North America, 1603–1784." Pp. 172–85 in *The Seventeenth Century in the Highlands.* Inverness, Scotland: Inverness Field Club, 1986.

Lewenhaupt, Adam. *Karl XII:s officerare: Biografiska anteckningar.* Stockholm: P. A. Norstedt & Söner, 1920.

Lockhart, Paul. *Denmark in the Thirty Years' War, 1618–1648: King Christian IV and the Decline of the Oldenburg State.* Selinsgrove PA: Susquehanna University Press, 1996.

Lorents, Yngve. *Efter Brömsebrofreden: Svenska och danska förbindelser med Frankrike och Holland, 1645–1649.* Uppsala, Sweden: Almqvist & Wiksells Boktryckeri, 1916.

Macinnes, Allan I. *Clanship, Commerce, and the House of Stuart, 1603–1788.* East Linton, Scotland: Tuckwell Press, 1996.

Mackay, Angus. *The Book of Mackay.* Edinburgh: Norman Macleod, 1906.

Mackay, John. *An Old Scots Brigade: Being the History of Mackay's Regiment Now Incorporated with the Royal Scots.* Edinburgh: William Blackwood and Sons, 1885.

Maclean, James N. M. *The Macleans of Sweden.* Edinburgh: Ampersand, 1971.

———. "Montrose's Preparations for the Invasion of Scotland, and Royalist Missions to Sweden, 1649–1651." Pp. 7–31 in *Studies in Diplomatic History: Essays in Memory of David Bayne Horn,* edited by Ragnhild Hatton and M. S. Anderson. London: Longman, 1970.

Marshall, Rosalind K. *Virgins and Viragos: A History of Women in Scotland from 1080 to 1980.* Chicago: Academy Chicago, 1983.

Mattingly, Garrett. *Renaissance Diplomacy.* Baltimore: Penguin Books, 1955.

McEvedy, Colin, and Richard Jones. *Atlas of World Population History.* New York: Penguin Books, 1978.

McGurk, John. "Wild Geese: The Irish in European Armies, Sixteenth to Eighteenth Centuries." Pp. 36–62 in *Patterns of Migration,* edited by Patrick O'Sullivan. Vol. 1 of *The Irish World Wide: History, Heritage, Identity.* New York: St. Martin's Press, 1992.

Michell, Thomas. *History of the Scottish Expedition to Norway in 1612.* London: T. Nelson & Sons, 1886.

Mitchison, Rosalind. *Lordship to Patronage: Scotland, 1603–1745.* London: Edward Arnold, 1983.

Moch, Leslie Page. *Moving Europeans: Migration in Western Europe since 1650.* Bloomington: Indiana University Press, 1992.

Montgomery, David. "Bidrag till släkten Montgomerys historia." *Personhistorisk tidskrift* (1913): 81–112.

————. "Några bidrag till belysning af frågan om ätten Montgomerys n:r 1960, B. härstamning." *Personhistorisk tidskrift* (1910): 160–63.

Niléhn, Lars. "Sweden and Swedish Students Abroad: The Seventeenth Century and Its Background." Pp. 97–117 in *Europe and Scandinavia: Aspects of the Process of Integration in the Seventeenth Century,* edited by Göran Rystad. Lund, Sweden: Wallin & Dalholm, 1983.

Nilsson, Sven A. "Från förläning till donation: Godspolitik och statshushållning under Gustav II Adolf." *Historisk tidskrift* 4 (1968).

————. "Imperial Sweden: Nation Building, War, and Social Change." Pp. 7–40 in *The Age of New Sweden,* edited by Arne Losman, Agneta Lundstrom, and Margareta Revera. Stockholm: Livrustkammaren, 1988.

————. *På väg mot militärstaten: Krigsbefälets etablering i den äldre Vasatidens Sverige.* Uppsala, Sweden: Historiska institutionen, 1989.

————. "1634 års regeringsform." Pp. 7–20 in *1634 års regeringsform 350 år. 1734 års lag 250 år: Jubileumssammankomst i Riksarkivet den 30 november 1984.* Stockholm: Allmänna Förlaget, 1985.

Nolan, John S. "The Militarization of the Elizabethan State." *Journal of Military History* 58, no. 3 (July 1994): 391–420.

Oakley, Stewart. *War and Peace in the Baltic, 1560–1790.* London: Routledge, 1992.

Ohlmeyer, Jane. "Seventeenth-Century Ireland and the New British and Atlantic Histories." *American Historical Review* 104, no. 2 (April 1999): 446–62.

Palme, Sven Ulric. *Sverige och Danmark, 1596–1611.* Uppsala, Sweden: Almqvist & Wiksells, 1942.

Parker, Geoffrey. *The Military Revolution: Military Innovation and the*

Rise of the West, 1500–1800. Cambridge: Cambridge University Press, 1988.

———. "The Soldiers of the Thirty Years' War." Pp. 303–17 in *Krieg und Politik, 1618–1648: Europäische Probleme und Perspektiven,* edited by Konrad Repgen. Munich: R. Oldenbourg, 1988.

———. *The Thirty Years' War.* London: Routledge & Kegan Paul, 1984.

Parker, Geoffrey, and Lesley M. Smith. Introduction to *The General Crisis of the Seventeenth Century,* edited by Geoffrey Parker and Lesley M. Smith. 2d ed. London: Routledge, 1997.

Pehrsson, Per. *De till Sverige inflyttade vallonernas religiösa förhålland: En studie öfver svenskt församlingslif och religionslagstiftning på 1600-talet.* Uppsala, Sweden: Wretmans Boktryckeri, 1905.

Phipps, Geraldine Marie. "Britons in Seventeenth-Century Russia: A Study in the Origins of Modernization." Ph.D. dissertation, University of Pennsylvania, 1971.

Platonov, S. F. *The Time of Trouble: A Historical Study of the Internal Crises and Social Struggle in Sixteenth- and Seventeenth-Century Muscovy.* Translated by John T. Alexander. Lawrence: University Press of Kansas, 1970.

Porter, Bruce D. *War and the Rise of the State: The Military Foundations of Modern Politics.* New York: Free Press, 1994.

Revera, Margareta. "Hur bönders hemman blev säterier: Ett användningsområde för frälsegodsen under storhetstiden." Pp. 73–114 in *Bördor, bönder, börd i 1600-talets Sverige,* edited by Margareta Revera and Rolf Torstendahl. Motala, Sweden: Borgströms, 1979.

———. "The Making of a Civilized Nation: Nation-Building, Aristocratic Culture, and Social Change." Pp. 103–31 in *The Age of New Sweden,* edited by Arne Losman, Agneta Lundstrom, and Margareta Revera. Stockholm: Livrustkammaren, 1988.

Richards, Eric. "Scotland and the Uses of the Atlantic Empire." Pp. 67–114 in *Strangers within the Realm: Cultural Margins of the First British Empire,* ed. Bernard Bailyn and Philip D. Morgan. Chapel Hill: University of North Carolina Press, 1991.

Riis, Thomas. *Should Auld Acquaintance Be Forgot . . . : Scottish-Danish Relations c. 1450–1707.* 2 vols. Odense, Denmark: Odense University Press, 1988.

Ringmar, Erik. *Identity, Interest, and Action: A Cultural Explanation of*

Sweden's Intervention in the Thirty Years' War. Cambridge: Cambridge University Press, 1996.

Roberts, Michael. "Cromwell and the Baltic." Pp. 138–94 in *Essays in Swedish History*, edited by Michael Roberts. Minneapolis: University of Minnesota Press, 1967.

————. *The Early Vasas: A History of Sweden, 1523–1611*. Cambridge: Cambridge University Press, 1968.

————. "Gustav Adolf and the Art of War." Pp. 56–81 in *Essays in Swedish History*, edited by Michael Roberts. Minneapolis: University of Minnesota Press, 1967.

————. *Gustavus Adolphus: A History of Sweden, 1611–1632*. 2 vols. London: Longmans, Green, 1953.

————. *Gustavus Adolphus and the Rise of Sweden*. London: English Universities Press, 1973.

————. "The Military Revolution, 1560–1660." Pp. 195–225 in *Essays in Swedish History*, edited by Michael Roberts. Minneapolis: University of Minnesota Press, 1967.

————. "On Aristocratic Constitutionalism in Swedish History, 1520–1720." Pp. 14–55 in *Essays in Swedish History*, edited by Michael Roberts. Minneapolis: University of Minnesota Press, 1967.

————. "The Political Objectives of Gustav Adolf in Germany, 1630–32." Pp. 82–110 in *Essays in Swedish History*, edited by Michael Roberts. Minneapolis: University of Minnesota Press, 1967.

————. "Queen Christina and the General Crisis of the Seventeenth Century." Pp. 111–37 in *Essays in Swedish History*, edited by Michael Roberts. Minneapolis: University of Minnesota Press, 1967.

————. "The Swedish Church." Pp. 132–73 in *Sweden's Age of Greatness, 1632–1718*, edited by Michael Roberts. London: Macmillan, 1973.

————. *The Swedish Imperial Experience, 1560–1718*. Cambridge: Cambridge University Press, 1979.

Roosen, William James. *The Age of Louis XIV: The Rise of Modern Diplomacy*. Cambridge MA: Schenkman Publishing, 1976.

Rudfors, Aron. *De diplomatiska förbindelserna mellan Sverige och England, 1624-maj 1630*. Uppsala, Sweden: Almqvist & Wiksells, 1890.

Rystad, Göran. "The Estates of the Realm, the Monarchy, and Empire, 1611–1718." Pp. 61–108 in *The Riksdag: A History of the Swedish*

Parliament, edited by Michael F. Metcalf. New York: St. Martin's Press, 1987.

──────. "The King, the Nobility, and the Growth of Bureaucracy in Seventeenth Century Sweden." Pp. 59–70 in *Europe and Scandinavia: Aspects of the Process of Integration in the Seventeenth Century*, edited by Göran Rystad. Lund, Sweden: Wallin & Dalholm, 1983.

Saint-Clair, Roland William. *The Saint-Clairs of the Isles: A History of the Sea-Kings of Orkney and Their Scottish Successors of the Sirname of Sinclair*. Auckland, New Zealand: H. Brett, 1898.

Scander, Ralph. "Holländarnas Göteborg." *Fataburen: Nordiska museets och Skansens årsbok* (1981): 91–114.

Schwoerer, Lois G. *"No Standing Armies!" The Antiarmy Ideology in Seventeenth-Century England*. Baltimore: Johns Hopkins University Press, 1974.

Scott, H. M., and Christopher Storrs. "Introduction: The Consolidation of Noble Power in Europe, c. 1600–1800." Pp. 1–52 in *The European Nobilities in the Seventeenth and Eighteenth Centuries*, edited by H. M. Scott. Vol. 1, *Western Europe*. London: Longman, 1995.

Sheldon, Peter. *Tal om Sheldonska ätten i Sverige*. Uppsala, Sweden: L. M. Höjer, 1755.

Shirren, Adam John. *The Chronicles of Fleetwood House*. London: Barnes Printers, 1951.

Sinclair, George A. "Scotsmen Serving the Swede." *Scottish Historical Review* 9 (1912): 37–51.

──────. "The Scottish Officers of Charles XII." *Scottish Historical Review* 21 (1924): 178–92.

Sjödell, Ulf. *Kungamakt och högaristokrati: En studie i Sveriges inre historia under Karl XI*. Lund, Sweden: Gleerup, 1966.

Smout, T. C., N. C. Landsman, and T. M. Devine. "Scottish Emigration in the Seventeenth and Eighteenth Centuries." Pp. 76–112 in *Europeans on the Move: Studies on European Migration, 1500–1800*, edited by Nicholas Canny. Oxford: Clarendon Press, 1994.

Sörensson, Per. "Adelns rusttjänst och adelsfanans organisation 1521–1680." Part 3, "Rusttjänsten enligt Gustav II Adolfs privilegier. Adelsfanans organisation genomföres (1611–1680)." *Historisk tidskrift* 44, no. 7 (1924): 214–23.

―――. *Generalfälttygmästaren Hugo Hamilton: En karolinsk krigare och landshöfding.* Stockholm: P. A. Norstedt & Söner, 1915.

Spalding, Ruth. *Contemporaries of Bulstrode Whitelocke, 1605–1675: Biographies, Illustrated by Letters and Other Documents.* New York: Oxford University Press, 1990.

Sparre, Sixton. *Kungl. Västmanlands regementes historia.* Vol. 4, *Biografiska anteckningar om officerare och vederlikar, 1623–1779.* Stockholm: Aktiebolaget, 1930.

Spens, E. "Sjövapnets bemanning under stormaktstiden fram till 1679." Pp. 331–54 in *Svenska flottans historia: Örlogsflottan i ord och bild från dess grundläggning under Gustav Vasa fram till våra dagar,* edited by S. Artur Svensson. Malmö, Sweden: A. B. Allhem, 1942.

Stadin, Kekke. "Stormaktskvinnor." Pp. 177–96 in *Makt och vardag: Hur man styrde, levde och tänkte under svensk stormaktstid,* edited by Stellan Dahlgren and Anders Floren. Stockholm, 1993.

Steckzén, Birger. "En höglandshjälte." Pp. 122–70 in *Svenskt och brittiskt: Sex essayer av Birger Steckzén.* Stockholm: Almqvist & Wiksell/Gebers, 1959.

―――. "James, 1:ste hertig av Hamilton." Pp. 63–121 in *Svenskt och brittiskt: Sex essayer av Birger Steckzén.* Stockholm: Almqvist & Wiksell/Gebers, 1959.

―――. *Krigskollegii Historia.* Vol. 1, *1630–1697.* Stockholm: Kurt Lindberg, 1930.

Steuart, A. Francis. "Scottish Officers in Sweden." *Scottish Historical Review* 1 (1904): 191–96.

Stevenson, David. *Scottish Covenanters and Irish Confederates: Scottish-Irish Relations in the Mid-Seventeenth Century.* Belfast: Ulster Historical Foundation, 1981.

Stone, Lawrence. *The Crisis of the Aristocracy, 1558–1641.* Abridged ed. London: Oxford University Press, 1967.

Stradling, R. A. *The Spanish Monarchy and Irish Mercenaries: The Wild Geese in Spain, 1618–68.* Dublin: Irish Academic Press, 1994.

Svanberg, Ingvar, and Mattias Tydén. *Tusen år av invandring: En svensk kulturhistoria.* Stockholm: Gidlunds Bokförlag, 1992.

Svenskt biografiskt lexicon. Edited by Bengt Hildebrand. Vols. 8 and 11. Stockholm: Albert Bonnier, 1929, 1945.

Tandrup, Leo. *Mod triumf eller tragedie: En politisk-diplomatisk studie over forløbet af den dansk-svenske magtkamp fra Kalmarkrigen til Kejserkrigen.* . . . Vol. 1, *Scenen og de agerende: Tiden fra 1612 til 1621.* 2 vols. Århus, Denmark: Universitetsforlaget i Århus, 1979.

Terry, Charles Sanford. *The Life and Campaigns of Alexander Leslie, First Earl of Leven.* London: Longmans, Green, 1899.

Thirsk, Joan. "Younger Sons in the Seventeenth Century." *History* 54, no. 182 (October 1969): 358–77.

Tilly, Charles. "Reflections on the History of European State-Making." Pp. 3–45 in *The Formation of National States in Western Europe,* edited by Charles Tilly. Princeton: Princeton University Press, 1975.

Tunberg, Sven, et al. *Histoire de l'administration des affaires étrangères de Suède.* Uppsala, Sweden: Imprimerie Almqvist & Wiksell, 1940.

Uddgren, H. E. *Karolinen Hugo Johan Hamilton: En lefnadsteckning.* Vol. 2, *Skrifter utgifna af Hamiltonska släktföreningen.* Stockholm: P. A. Norstedt & Söner, 1916.

Upton, A. F. *Charles XI and Swedish Absolutism.* Cambridge: Cambridge University Press, 1998.

——. "The Riksdag of 1680 and the Establishment of Royal Absolutism in Sweden." *English Historical Review* no. 403 (April 1987): 281–308.

——. "The Swedish Nobility, 1600–1772." Pp. 11–42 in *The European Nobilities in the Seventeenth and Eighteenth Centuries,* ed. H. M. Scott. Vol. 2, *Northern, Central, and Eastern Europe.* London: Longman, 1995.

Villstrand, Nils Erik. "Statsmakt och migration under svensk stormaktstid." *Historisk tidskrift för Finland* 74, no. 1 (1989): 1–29.

Wendt, Einar. *Amiralitetskollegiets historia.* Vol. 1, *1634–1695.* Stockholm: Lindberg, 1950.

——. "Flottans överstyrelse och lokala förvaltningar under stormaktstiden till enväldet." Pp. 311–30 in *Svenska flottans historia: Örlogsflottan i ord och bild från dess grundläggning under Gustav Vasa fram till våra dagar,* edited by S. Artur Svensson. Malmö, Sweden: A. B. Allhem, 1942.

Wernstedt, Folke. "Om främmande adels naturalisation och introduktion på svenska Riddarhuset under storhetstiden." *Personhistorisk tidskrift* 38 (1937): 122–64.

Whyte, I. D. "Migration in Early-Modern Scotland and England: A Comparative Perspective." In *Migrants, Emigrants, and Immigrants: A Social History of Migration,* edited by Colin G. Pooley and Ian D. Whyte. London: Routledge, 1991.

———. "Population Mobility in Early Modern Scotland." Pp. 169–98 in *Scottish Society, 1500–1800,* edited by R. A. Houston and I. D. Whyte. Cambridge: Cambridge University Press, 1989.

———. "Poverty or Prosperity? Rural Society in Lowland Scotland in the Late Sixteenth and Early Seventeenth Centuries." *Scottish Economic and Social History* 18 (1998): 19–32.

Williams, Ronald. *Montrose: Cavalier in Mourning.* London: Barrie & Jenkins, 1975.

Willson, David Harris. *King James VI and I.* New York: Oxford University Press, 1967.

INDEX